∽ PRAISE

When I first heard of Karen... ing women who were abortion vulnerable, it was like a flash of truth revealed. What I did not know was Karen's arduous journey of faith by fire and agony to receive, obey, promote, and mentor others tirelessly in that revelatory truth and at any cost. In *Only if God Says So!*, the full story is disclosed to the glory of God and beckons us all to courageously follow the path we believe He is laying before us despite the cost, but *only if God says so!*

—Jim Pinto, life, marriage, and family activist
Co-Host, At Home with Jim and Joy, Eternal Word
Television Network

When God says so, we are set free to repent and give testimony of forgiveness and healing. Readers rejoice in the goodness and grace of God.

—Evangelist Alveda C. King

It is an honor to give an endorsement for Karen Mercer, who I have known for forty years. She taught my wife and me much of what we know about sidewalk counseling. As a pastor, I know we had to go where the babies were dying, and like Karen, we knew God had called us to be missionaries to the unborn. I had the privilege of praying for her in that capacity to go to Atlanta, Georgia, in 1989. Thousands of babies are alive because of this gentle warrior who impacted and influenced so many of us. Her book is truth with the fist of God. My prayer is it will pierce the hearts of many who will read it. Karen is one of the most dedicated sidewalk counselors I've ever known. Reading her book flooded my mind with so many memories.

—Dr. Al Howard

In this book, Karen Black Mercer has a remarkable story to tell. But be forewarned. This story is not just an account of one woman's journey; rather, it is a convicting call for all of us to embark on the pathway of justice, mercy, and humility before God.

—George Grant
Author, Grand Illusions
Pastor, Parish Presbyterian Church

Karen, a pioneer in the pro-life battle, has been a tireless advocate for women and unborn children, having begun the fight to prevent abortion on demand in the late sixties. She labored through the political arena, crisis pregnancy centers, post-abortion counseling, Operation Rescue, and the founding of Women 4 Women, a long-term ministry to women that chose to give their children life. It was, however, her compassionate, woman-centered sidewalk counseling method that won her the title of the Billy Graham of Sidewalk Counseling. It is with refreshing honesty and humor she shares her journey in life, consistently giving glory to the Lord for working courage and perseverance into a once timid and easily frightened woman. I have always called Karen my hero. I promise you will be saying the same long before you reach the close of this captivating and challenging story.

—Joseph M. Scheidler
Author of *Closed: 99 Ways to Stop Abortion*
Founder of Prolife Action League

A memoir of pain and glory, poignant and inspiring. One essence of this book places it among the most captivating reads you will have. Karen, the author, tells this portion of her life's story with raw honesty. Those who appreciate literary works have great respect for one who writes such a memoir because it takes a brave soul to tell the gut-wrenching truth about her own life as well as the lives of those with whom she has interacted. To know what the author does is one thing; to know what the author was thinking when it was done is another.

For the generation alive when this book is published, it will stir a lot of memories of experiences. You will be reminded of where you were at the time, what you were doing, and what you saw or heard via mass media or friends. When folks heard what happened on the West Coast, they were shocked. Many who heard what happened on the East Coast were moved off the sidelines and into the fray.

For the generations who read this book when the author is dust, this will be an actual historical account with strong spiritual ramifications. Best of all, there is high probability that some reading this book are alive because they were yet-to-be-born, and Karen had a role in ensuring that they were.

—Dr. Johnny M. Hunter, DD
Fayetteville, NC

Only If God Says So!

A MEMOIR

Only If God Says So!

FINDING COURAGE TO PROTECT LIFE
IN A PRO-CHOICE WORLD

KAREN BLACK MERCER

© 2022 by Karen Black Mercer. All rights reserved.

Published by Redemption Press, PO Box 427, Enumclaw, WA 98022.
Toll-Free (844) 2REDEEM (273-3336)

Redemption Press is honored to present this title in partnership with the author. The views expressed or implied in this work are those of the author. Redemption Press provides our imprint seal representing design excellence, creative content, and high-quality production.

The author has tried to recreate events, locales, and conversations from memories of them. In order to maintain their anonymity, in some instances the names of individuals, some identifying characteristics, and some details may have been changed, such as physical properties, occupations, and places of residence.

Noncommercial interests may reproduce portions of this book without the express written permission of the author, provided the text does not exceed five hundred words. When reproducing text from this book, include the following credit line: "*Only if God Says So!* by Karen Black Mercer. Used by permission."

Commercial interests: No part of this publication may be reproduced in any form, stored in a retrieval system, or transmitted in any form by any means—electronic, photocopy, recording, or otherwise—without prior written permission of the publisher/author, except as provided by United States of America copyright law.

Scripture taken from the New King James Version®. Copyright © 1982 by Thomas Nelson. Used by permission. All rights reserved.

Scripture quotations marked (ESV) are taken from The Holy Bible, English Standard Version® (ESV®), copyright © 2001 by Crossway, a publishing ministry of Good News Publishers. Used by permission. All rights reserved.

Scripture quotations marked (NIV) are from the Holy Bible, New International Version®, NIV®. Copyright © 1973, 1978, 1984, 2011 by Biblica, Inc.™ Used by permission of Zondervan. All rights reserved worldwide. www.zondervan.com The "NIV" and "New International Version" are trademarks registered in the United States Patent and Trademark Office by Biblica, Inc.™

Scripture quotations marked (TLB) are taken from The Living Bible copyright © 1971. Used by permission of Tyndale House Publishers, Inc., Carol Stream, Illinois 60188. All rights reserved.

Quotes by Jack Hayford are used with verbal permission.

ISBN 13: 978-1-64645-831-8 (Hardback)
978-1-64645-469-3 (Paperback)
978-1-64645-470-9 (ePub)
978-1-64645-471-6 (Mobi)

Library of Congress Catalog Card Number: 2022906208

Dedicated to my children and grandchildren

Jeromy William
Joshua Paul
Victoria Jo
Andrew Michael

Kimberly Kay
Nathan Daniel
Cameron Nicholas
Ella Grace

For the beautiful host families who cared for me during my missionary days in Atlanta, gratitude and appreciation remain embedded in my heart:

Dan and Melissa Duffy
Jack and Lisa Alexander
Bruce and Louise Carper
Ron and Shawnie Merritt
Jon and Sherrie Cleveland

CONTENTS

Foreword 11
Introduction: Called and Commissioned 15

PART ONE

Chapter 1: A Burden Transferred 21
Chapter 2: The Rendezvous 29
Chapter 3: Incarcerated—Me? 41
Chapter 4: Fear Be Gone! 57
Chapter 5: Only If God Says So! 73
Chapter 6: Losing a Grip on My Will 88
Chapter 7: Saying Goodbye 99
Chapter 8: Pretrial Detention Center 111
Chapter 9: Grady Hospital 125
Chapter 10: Forbidden to Pray 137
Chapter 11: Key Road Prison 147
Chapter 12: Blessed Beyond Measure 163
Chapter 13: A Shift in Direction 175

PART TWO

Chapter 14: A New Work 187
Chapter 15: Pressing On 199
Chapter 16: Climbing the Learning Curve 202
Chapter 17: Blessed Assistance 219
Chapter 18: An Interlude of Peace 229
Chapter 19: Miraculous Changes 239

Chapter 20: Lessons Learned 249
Chapter 21: Christians Aren't Perfect. 263
Chapter 22: I Don't Think So! 273
Chapter 23: Death Threats and the Mafia 281
Chapter 24: Heavy Hearts 293
Chapter 25: Open Doors 303
Chapter 26: Farewell, Sweet Momma. 315
Chapter 27: England Bound 327
Chapter 28: Pulling Down Strongholds 333
Epilogue: Released and Renewed 345

FOREWORD

In the late autumn of 1989, returning to Atlanta clearly would not be a quick trip in and out of jail like it was the first time. And the price of rescue there would be high. Many of the leaders in Operation Rescue were in jail or tied up somehow. Just the fact that I was asked to head up the DC Rescues that fall shows how far into the B team Operation Rescue reached.

Karen talks about that event in this book. From DC, we were going to add to Operation Rescue the component of long-term personal sacrifice. Namely, we were seeking people who, on a permanent basis, would trade their freedom to stand with the children scheduled for slaughter, like old school missionaries getting onto a steam ship in 1905 and going off to a wild and foreign land for the rest of their lives. Operation Rescue would be the camp meeting and evangelistic rally in places where we could hold mass events. But those who came to die in Atlanta would be the core of commitment that would grow there, a seed planted to die and from there bear fruit in God's will.

And so that was the theme of the DC Project. That is the theme of the Christian life. Not a crusade, but a seed falling to the ground and dying so that it might bear much fruit—fruit that will last. Karen heard.

Of course, I thought the seed was of one sort: sit-ins, jail, returning to block the door until we died of old age, helping moms, rallying community support for those who changed their minds and needed help, etc. But in God's plan we were peripheral. In a few short years, most of us found a reason to walk away from actual prison time and rescue. But God wanted to do something with Karen that none of us were able to do.

Karen didn't know it, but she was set apart, like Esther, for just this hour to do things as far beyond her vision and abilities as many of the things which lie in our own futures that we are afraid to dream or talk about.

Only if God Says So! is not the reminiscences of a rather remarkable person, but the call of a remarkable God.

And that is why you should not read this book. What you will see in its pages is not some saint who (thank God) we can never be. We can't read the exciting story and say with great relief, "There is no way God expects anything like that of me. I mean, Karen is great, just the sort of person God would use. Me? I've got kids to feed, a job to go to, a life to live, parents to care for in their old age. That is hard enough. I'll pray for the next saint."

If what you are looking for is a good read about miracles and God working in the most unexpected ways . . . yeah, that's in here—serious modern-day, God-at-work stuff. But as you read, you will know in your heart that nothing is embellished or prettied up. Through Karen's words and life, God lays the dynamite of His gospel at the root of every excuse we use to look the other way, to busy ourselves with our own problems which we call our own ministries, our own gifts and calling, and our families and friends. When you read this, you will know. It is time.

If you had interviewed all the girls in Israel to find the best mother for Jesus, you would not have picked the one who responded in terror to Gabriel. Likewise, as you read this book, you will realize that if you had interviewed all sixteen million people in LA, Karen is not the one you would have chosen that day when she responded to God in terror. And that very fact should rip away the camouflaged bunker wall we use to hide from the work God has laid out for us to do because "Surely God has nothing great for me to do."

God doesn't seek saints; He makes them out of people like you and me.

Karen carried the water in the heat of the day and in the freeze of the winter not because she is good at carrying water. She carried it

FOREWORD

because God is good at supplying her every need. This was not God's special call to her. It is His special call to each one of us.

You hear it just like she did, just like we did, and we all do. It speaks to us in every line of Scripture and every event of your day.

As you read her pages, you will see that in no way is she recruiting you to pro-life. She is warning you. The God whose name we take so lightly in our church worship rituals is the God who calls us to take up our crosses, to be a planted seed that dies. Her story is a dire warning.

This book will make it that much harder to pretend you don't hear and see what He is doing that will change your whole life, and through that, change the world. Put it down now while you still have a chance.

Every child rescued will change the world, as you will when you finally listen to the God who is there and who speaks to you.

—Reverend Joseph L. Foreman
Father of eight, husband of one, friend of Karen

❦ INTRODUCTION
Called and Commissioned

I began writing this book on thin toilet paper in a dark corner of jail in 1989. It has been a long time coming, with many starts and stops. As I write this opening chapter, I don't know if it will ever be published or read by anyone other than my family.

If you read this, Daddy, thank you for your lifetime of loving care. Thank you for faithfully taking me to Northeast Baptist Church as a child. I am grateful for the rich spiritual heritage passed on to me by Pastor Prause and his consistent, unwavering commitment to the Word of God. You and Mom made a rich deposit of love and wisdom into my life, and if you pass on your longevity as well, then my story is far from ending.

If you are my sibling, you may experience both laughter and tears while reading this. I hope you are entertained as you journey down memory lane, reflecting on the legacy that we share.

If you are my child or grandchild, I pray this book will cause you to think of your own journey in life. I encourage you to receive the baton that I pass on to you. Run with boldness and courage. May my life experiences be stepping stones to help you along the way.

If you are my brother or sister in Christ and are of full age, I pray my story will encourage you to keep serving Him. Remember to rest *in* Him in ministry, not rest *from* ministry. If you have been faithful to the call on your life, the wealth of wisdom and knowledge that resides inside of you needs sharing. Finish strong!

If you are young or just beginning your walk with the Lord, I encourage you to call on Him wholeheartedly. Strive to be part of His lion-hearted warriors. Choose to believe that God's Word is the most powerful force in the universe, and act accordingly. Nothing will ever stop you!

If you do not yet know Jesus as your very own Lord and Savior, I pray that my story with my failings and His faithfulness will show both my humanity and His Glory. I pray it will cause a stirring in you to search for Him with your whole heart. He will never disappoint you.

If you are pro-choice, you may be offended as you read. Please know that is not my goal. Abortion is death and darkness. Death always begets death. I pray you will change your mind about abortion and will begin living in His life-giving light. Remember, life always begets life.

If you have experienced abortion firsthand or have supported someone in doing so, you may suffer from the weight of that decision. The Lord is ever waiting to hear your heartfelt repentance. He wants to free you from darkness and the pain of regret and transfer you into the light of His love and forgiveness. Call on Him. He is waiting to hear and to love you to wholeness.

For those entrenched in the battle against abortion, don't grow weary in well doing. I know that sometimes you feel like Elijah and wonder if anyone, anywhere, understands. Don't lose hope and don't ever quit! Remember the saints that went before you. When the enemy comes in like a flood, raise His banner higher than ever before! Walk in love and understanding, believing that you are to judge the darkness, not those that walk in it. Remove from yourself all condemnation. Ask the Lord to help you love the sometimes unlovely with the grace and mercy He shows you, and always, always, speak the truth in love.

If you are a pastor shepherding a flock, whether large or small, I am sure you sometimes wonder if any of us are listening to you at all. I assure you we are. Your hours of prayer and preparation are not wasted. I know that the subject of abortion has caused you much unrest. I would be negligent if I did not encourage you to study the subject further and add to it the understanding of how abortion, child aversion, and abortive birth control are inextricably linked. Many couples are desperate for your direction in this.

Finally, perhaps you fall into another group, feeling you have squandered your life away doing wrong, and now it is too late to change. Please believe that no matter how large the accumulated sin and regret, those things, when truly repented of, become building materials He will use to construct a new and glorious life for you. I encourage you to look to the Lord, Who never tires of bringing beauty out of ashes, and Who takes great delight in redeeming all that we lift up to Him. Forget the past and press forward.

May the reading of my life story end with you fully embracing the Lord's never-ending extravagant love for you!

PART ONE

I can do all things through Christ Who strengthens me.
Philippians 4:13

CHAPTER 1

A Burden Transferred

Annoyed by the sound of crying on the one morning I could sleep in, I turned over in bed, determined to catch a few more minutes of rest. I wondered if it was my mother, but dismissed the thought. She didn't cry like that.

Mom's life was filled with grace and quiet peace. No one ever heard a word of despair or hopelessness escape her lips. Now in her late sixties, she was an invalid and completely dependent on Daddy for her care. Multiple sclerosis had ravaged her body for thirty-one years. These last eleven years, the disease had left her paralyzed from the neck down. Not even this setback could interfere with her unshakable trust in the Lord.

When the crying intensified into fretful sobbing, I realized it *was* Mom. Frightened that something terrible had happened to her, I jumped to my feet and ran into her room.

As I reached her bedside, my heart was pounding. "Momma, what's wrong?"

Through choking sobs, she caught her breath and demanded, "Listen!" She nodded her head toward the radio sitting on the dresser and fixed her attention on the early morning local news broadcast. "I need to be there. I need to do my part!"

"What part, Mom? What are you talking about?"

"Turn the radio up, *please*."

The sounds of angry protestors filled the airwaves.

"What's all that noise about?" I asked.

"It's the pro-choice crowd screaming at the rescuers."

"What are 'rescuers'?"

Annoyed at my ignorance, she blurted out, "Operation Rescue. Just listen!"

We focused our attention back on the program. The broadcaster announced that Operation Rescue was holding a demonstration in front of an abortion clinic in Long Beach. Mom squinted toward the radio, looking thoroughly disgusted as she tried to yell a response. Instead, she only managed a loud whisper.

"Operation Rescue doesn't *demonstrate*—they save babies!" Exhausted, her head fell back on the pillow with a thud.

The broadcaster explained that hundreds of people on both sides of the issue had gathered outside a local abortion clinic. As the police arrived, the yelling and chanting grew louder. Once again, Mom was unable to contain her tears.

In between sobs and gasps for air, she whimpered, "I need to be there for the moms and the babies." Despite her physical limitations, her devastation and determination were the catalysts pushing her forward to respond. With her eyes closed and tears streaming down her face, Mom continued to wail. "Why?"

"Why what?"

"Why would the Lord give me such a burden for the babies and their mothers if I couldn't do anything about it?"

"But you have, Momma, you have."

My parents, George and Rita, were involved in the political arena for many years, helping with the effort to prevent the legalization of abortion. Their passion and activism ignited my own involvement in the political arena of pro-life work, crisis pregnancy centers, and post-abortion counseling. After *Roe v. Wade* was passed in 1973, my mother's burden for pregnant women and their unborn children greatly increased. It remained with her on a daily basis.

"You've done so much," I continued. "Remember when you received a reward from Crusade for Life because of all your efforts? And you did all this from your wheelchair!"

"But not anymore. Now I'm in this bed all the time."

"The Lord knows how much you love babies. He knows how much you care about women in need, especially pregnant ones. Don't you think the Lord would say it's time you rested?"

Then came *the look*. The look that says, "Shame on you for thinking that anyone of us has ever done enough!"

"Mom, for whatever reason, the Lord has not healed you. He knows you're paralyzed and can't go out to an abortion clinic."

"But the babies! I need to help the babies!"

Mom choked on these words as she spoke. Holding her helpless body back with one arm while I struggled with the bed controls in my other hand, I prayed, *Lord, please help and don't let her choke*. I placed the bed at the proper angle and lightly laid my hand on her chest.

"Please try to take slow breaths," I pleaded.

Her sobs grew louder. She panted between labored whispers, "The babies . . . the babies . . . I need to go there to do my part . . . for the babies . . . the babies."

"Now, Momma, stop crying!" My pleas fell on deaf ears. Out of desperation, I yelled, "Okay, Mom . . . okay! I'll go down there for you. I'll be your arms and legs, and I'll stand in the gap for you and the babies. Just stop crying!"

Without hesitation, Mom opened her eyes and lifted her head from the pillow. "You will?"

"Yes, Mom. I'll go for you." I would say just about anything to calm her down.

"Oh, honey, thank you so much!" Her face was radiant, as if a ray of sunshine was bursting out of her very soul. "As my daughter, my own flesh and blood, it would be like me being there myself, wouldn't it?"

The realization of what I had promised sank in. *Oh no! She actually expects me to do this. How am I going to get out of this one?* My mind began spinning, desperate for a way out. *Think fast, big mouth!* I stole a sideways glance at Mom but quickly looked away. *Oh gee, look at that face. That radiant face. Just keep your head down. Don't look at her!* If I locked eyes with her, she would somehow capture me, and I would be cooked.

Her voice quavered. "Honey?"

"Yes, Mom?"

"Look at me, honey."

Reluctantly, I lifted my eyes and was greeted by her joy-filled face. New tears streamed down her cheeks. Reaching for a tissue to wipe her eyes, I asked, "Now what are you crying about?"

"Oh, honey, the Lord has heard my prayer and lifted my burden." Her sigh was long and all-encompassing.

Two guesses where that burden landed, I complained. *Gee whiz, Lord!*

"That's great, Mom," I squeaked out. Outwardly, I maintained a compliant facade, but inwardly I battled new fears.

"You know, honey, there is a rally scheduled for this evening here in Orange County. Would you go to it before going to the rescue tomorrow morning?"

"I...uh..." Thinking I could encourage her to give up this absurd idea, I asked, "Who are these crazy people anyway?"

"You mean who are these *rescuers*?"

"Yes, Mom, who are these rescuers?"

"Remember? I asked you to pray for Christians in Atlanta. They had a rescue there, and the rescuers have been held in jail for over forty days."

"Oh yes, I guess I forgot."

With a gentle rebuke, she said, "Honey, now don't forget that Scripture says we are to pray for those in prison as if we are right there with them."

"Yes, but what is it that these rescuers do, anyway?"

"They sit down in front of the door of an abortion clinic, hold hands, pray, and sing hymns. They place their bodies between the baby and the abortionist in an effort to save the child's life. This gives the sidewalk counselors time to talk to the girls going in for the abortions. The counselors want the girls to know that they care about them and will help them have their babies. The problem is that these rescuers are arrested and charged with trespassing."

"So they go to jail?"

"Yes, dear."

"Then *I* will go to jail?"

With a big smile, she said, "Yes, dear."

"But you told me that the police beat the people in Atlanta."

"Yes, dear."

Since when does she call me "dear"? She must be in some trance. That's it! She'll come out of this soon.

"Then I might get beaten too?"

"Yes, dear."

"Momma!"

"We don't want to miss out on this opportunity, honey. Abortion could come to an end because of this. To know that we were a part of that happening would be forever glorious!"

What's this "we" stuff? Oh yeah, I guess since I'm her arms and legs . . .

I turned my attention to her beautiful smile and helpless body. Without a doubt, I knew she would be there in a heartbeat if she were able. I was ashamed of my reluctance and insistence to think about myself before my mother.

"Okay, Mom, I'll go to the rally tonight," I murmured.

Frustrated by my poor sense of direction, I maneuvered my car into its third U-turn and said out loud, "Here we go again." I leaned over the steering wheel, straining to read street signs in the dark. Still in disbelief that I was actually on my way to the Operation Rescue rally, I had neglected to get proper directions to Melodyland Christian Center before I left home. I'd been told it was near Disneyland. How hard could it be? *Daddy always said I could get lost in my own backyard . . . and he's right.*

Pro-life bumper stickers on the car ahead of me came into view. I followed the car into a crowded parking lot, grateful for the parking attendant who motioned me forward to a space. I locked my car and fell into step with those walking to the door, amazed at the number of people who flooded into the building.

At five foot one, I can seldom see anything in a large crowd, so I was glad to find an aisle seat near the front of the large auditorium. The venue was noisy. Everyone was talking about the radio and TV coverage of the rescue that morning, as well as how pleased they were to see so many pastors attend. The assembly exploded with music and applause as the worship team stepped forward. The words of each song settled deep within my heart and soul. I wished Mom were with me, and I now knew that she was not alone in urging me to come. I felt sure the will of God had swept me here.

Many pastors had attended the rescue that morning, and some of them spoke about the heart of God for precious unborn children. They emphasized the plans the Lord had for each little life. Passionate pleas went out to defend these little ones, who could not defend themselves. Videos of ultrasounds showed the horror experienced by these children as they desperately tried to escape the abortionist's instruments.

Given my background in the pro-life movement, I felt sure that I had seen and heard everything about the abortion issue. But I was completely unprepared for the work the Lord was about to do in my life as a woman carried in a small silk-covered table and placed it close to where I was sitting.

Ever so tenderly, she removed the covering to reveal a perfect little baby girl. People gasped. She had been aborted by saline solution during the eighteenth week of pregnancy. I had already seen many pictures of babies aborted at this gestational age and by this method—but never in person, right in front of my eyes. Her tiny body, preserved in formaldehyde, was unusually plump. She had little fat rolls more common with full-term babies. I marveled at her cute nose and beautiful little lips. She looked as if she was sleeping. The perfect red rose lying next to her paled in comparison to her beauty.

A line formed as people slowly filed by to gaze at this sweet little creation. Except for the blackened burned areas of her body, she reminded me of a porcelain doll. I wondered who her mother was. Tears were flowing from everyone, male and female, young and old. Many were loudly sobbing. I heard one woman cry out in anguish, "I did that! I did that to my very own child!" I watched as others cupped both hands over their mouths, smothering words of unbelief. My heart ached as I thought about the parents, siblings, grandparents, and all of our society deprived of these precious lives.

The Holy-Spirit-induced grieving I felt deep in my spirit was unlike anything I had ever experienced before. The Lord terrorized me with a new level of understanding about abortion. "What can be done? What would You have *me* do?" I pleaded.

In that moment, I knew with God-given certainty that I was meant to join the rescue. This was not just an emotional response stirred up by the evening's events. God filled me with great resolve and purpose that I had not known before.

Driving home, I thought, *I'm glad Mom was not there after all. She would never have been able to handle seeing that baby. Besides, she probably didn't need the wake-up call like the rest of us did.*

This life-changing encounter with the Holy Spirit left me physically and emotionally drained. I was a wreck by the time I arrived home. We all gathered in Mom's room, and I tried to tell my family what I had seen and heard. My words could never properly convey what I had experienced, especially with what had taken place in my heart that night.

I explained that I had to be in downtown Los Angeles very early in the morning for the rescue, before sunrise. "You might need to go get my car if I don't come back by the afternoon," I said to Daddy, "in case I get arrested." The words sounded so strange coming from me.

"Oh, okay," Daddy said, his voice filled with concern. But Mom lay there smiling, beaming with pride for her daughter. She had a remarkable way of looking on the bright side of everything.

A sleepless night ensued as fear invaded my thoughts. I lay there, staring at the ceiling, struggling to breathe. *I can't believe you're actually going to do this. You, the never-break-the-rules introvert. You're the world's biggest scaredy-cat! You're afraid of people, afraid of change, afraid of the dark, and unsure of anything new. Are you really going to go to a rescue tomorrow?*

"Oh my gosh, yes . . . I am!"

With that spoken assertion, a wave of fear raced through my mind and down to my stomach. It was useless to think about changing my plans. Seared into my mind forever was the image of that precious baby. That painful image, along with the joy my mother was feeling, would keep me going for now. More than that, however, was the growing conviction that God had somehow transformed my heart and called me. The discomfort I felt as I lay there in bed was nothing compared to what I would feel if I disobeyed and did not go.

"Shut up and go to sleep!" I told myself.

Little did I know how much I would need every ounce of energy available for the events which were about to unfold.

CHAPTER 2

The Rendezvous

I stood in the middle of my bedroom, a little numb and very confused, wondering why that obnoxious alarm clock had jarred me awake at three thirty. As my sleep-induced fog lifted, I recalled events from the previous night. *I remember now. I'm going to a strange place to do something even stranger this morning.* Fear washed over me again. I dropped to my knees alongside my bed. I didn't know how to pray. Not knowing what to expect, I thought that asking for strength, protection, and direction should cover it. Then I slipped into Mom's bedroom and whispered goodbye.

As a painfully shy introvert, I didn't have an adventurous bone in my body. And yet, there I was driving in the dark all by myself, to meet up with hundreds of strangers to take part in a rescue at a clinic in downtown Los Angeles. I kept repeating out loud, "I can't believe you're doing this!" I was sure no one else shared my struggle. *Why am I so easily frightened?* I couldn't stop thinking about the form I'd signed at the rally, agreeing I understood I was to take part in a nonviolent act of civil disobedience. I agreed I would in no way retaliate if mistreated by either the pro-abortion forces or the police. I was told not to bring anything with me, not even my ID. I wondered what problems could arise from these implications.

The parking lot was jammed with cars and people when I arrived—850 people had signed up to rescue, with another thousand supporting us in prayer from locations nearby. Operation Rescue provided a caravan of vehicles to drive us to the clinic. I climbed into the first van with other rescuers at the front of the line. As we pulled away, I looked back in amazement as hundreds of headlights followed us single file on the freeway.

On our way, our leader gave us instructions for the day. Those who felt that they could not remain calm at all times weren't allowed to participate. He advised us to stay together, whether we were in silent prayer or singing hymns. Since we would not resist arrest, we should let our bodies go limp when the police arrested us. We would feel heavier, and they might get angry as they carried us away. Our leader prayed the police would understand that we couldn't just walk away when we believed babies were being murdered behind the closed doors. He prayed for us, naming each piece of spiritual armor from the book of Ephesians. He prayed for our families, for the mothers making their way to the clinic, and for their unborn children.

Stillness overtook us as we sat in the van—an overwhelming, tangible silence. I wondered if anyone else was as scared as me.

The stillness which had occupied the inside of our van continued as we stepped out onto a parking lot near the Family Planning Associates clinic. It was five thirty, just before sunrise. The lot filled quickly and soon hundreds of rescuers spilled out onto the sidewalks and street near the clinic—a large nondescript one-story building on the corner of Westmoreland and Sixth.

It amazed me to see so many people. What a comfort! Some pro-life leaders had suggested that our ranks might swell to as high as four thousand. Others continued to join us as we slowly moved along as one large in-sync entity. Eventually, I couldn't see anything over the heads of those much taller than me.

Suddenly, all movement came to a standstill. I held my breath and looked up at the beautiful lavender sky as dawn made its arrival. A supernatural shift took place in the atmosphere, evidenced by the sweetness of love, peace, and unity shared by the Body of Christ.

Vibrant and tangible, this incredible sensation settled on us like a weighty but comforting blanket of warmth. I had never felt anything like it. Tears filled my eyes. *It's You, Lord. Dear Holy Spirit, it's You!* Someone behind me started sniffling and then, as if on cue, people began to sob.

Just as suddenly, our golden moment turned nightmarish. A rude voice on a bullhorn jarred us with filthy, vicious chanting, increasing in intensity. It struck me that we were about to walk into Satan's camp. As the rescuers in our ranks moved across the wide street toward the clinic, we instinctively reached out to join our hands and reassured each other that the Lord was with us. Midway across the street, my body encountered an invisible force. I instantly realized that I had walked into a horrible, nearly suffocating wall of evil. I felt a dark, heavy presence reluctantly yield to my advancement as I walked through it. I caught my breath and dropped the hands I was holding on both sides of me. I touched the place on my chest where I experienced the horrific sensation.

With eyes wide open, a lady next to me asked, "Did you feel that too?"

I nodded and saw that she also had her hand on her chest.

Our leader looked at us. "Brace yourselves," he said. "It's about to get much worse. God be with you!"

Continuing to the clinic, it seemed as if I were trudging through a murky swamp. The air was thick with a peculiar stench. As I labored to breathe, I sensed I was inhaling something foul. Never had I experienced the presence of evil with such magnitude. A mass of people swarmed all around. The malicious chanting increased, encouraged by someone who beat on drums. The noise was deafening. Some people screamed and yelled profanity at us through bullhorns. In shock, I watched a small group of men urinate on a cardboard cross. Others threw their heads back in coarse, mocking laughter and said Jesus Christ was their gay lover—followed by vile descriptions of acts they wanted to do to the Lord.

I marveled that my legs kept moving forward. Without warning, an unseen force threw me to the ground. I landed on pavement close to the front door. I sat up, wrapped my arms around my head and ears, and dropped my face into my knees. I thought I was going to vomit! Disbelief overwhelmed my spirit at the things I heard.

I cried out, "I'm so sorry, Lord. I am so, so very sorry!" Internally I screamed, *Don't they realize they are talking about the Great I Am?*

I got on my knees to see what was happening in the front of the now-seated crowd of rescuers. I watched godly men, pastors, and priests look down as pro-abortion women pranced in front of them, moving to the beat of the drums in lewd, provocative movements in attempts to shock them with their blatant displays of uninhibited lesbian behavior. The words coming from the mouths of these women were more horrific than those that came from the men. Revealing the condition of their hearts, they spewed out putrid, hateful rhetoric. I watched and listened in amazement as a sense of anguish for them grew in me. I wondered what and who had contributed to the intense animosity they felt.

Eventually, their voices gave way to hoarseness as they continued to scream foul curses over us. The air was charged with wickedness and hatred. From the moment we arrived, they aimed their words and actions at our *Christianity*, not at our pro-life stance. It was proof once again that abortion is a battle of good against evil, not just a political issue or a woman's right. They continued their physical and verbal assault, attacking us in a frenzied fit of rage. On this day, March 25, 1989, I came into a fuller understanding of the unseen forces of evil.

A Satan worshipper paced back and forth to the side of us. He leaned in close, baring his teeth, hissing at us. Poisonous words flew out of his mouth as he screamed how much he hated our God. Large satanic crosses that hung from his neck swayed and clanged together. "And I hate you too!" he screamed.

Close enough to experience his foul breath and spittle, I looked at him in disbelief. *He doesn't even know us. How could he hate us so much?*

I thought of 1 John 3:13, which says, "Do not marvel, my brethren, if the world hates you." He automatically hated us because of Who we loved.

The rest of the pro-choice forces pushed, shoved, kicked, and spit on us. The noise was deafening as they blew whistles in our ears. They screamed through bullhorns, "Keep your rosaries off my ovaries!" Others mocked, "Baa, baa, dumb little Christian freaks." Skinheads threw hot coffee at us. One of them jeered, "Oh, I'm sorry, let me rinse that off." He then proceeded to urinate on us. They viciously kicked our backs. Some even stood on our shoulders and the bent-over backs of rescuers.

"Stand up to protect the women!" one of our men yelled. As we stood and locked arms, the skinheads threw their bodies into us. We were jostled back and forth in response to the constant onslaught. In unison, they forced us to take a few steps forward, backward, or from side to side. At one point, they forced the crowd off the curb, and my feet could not touch the ground. I was held up by the sheer force of their bodies against mine.

Appointed song leaders, stationed at different points, encouraged us to sing. As we lifted up praise songs, the screaming, hissing crowd temporarily hushed like an animal noting an unfamiliar sound. Then quickly, their blasphemous noise increased in intensity. It was as if they were trying to attack the words they could not bear to hear. I had never seen anyone respond to the name of Jesus in such a way. Feeling the power of His name, they threw their heads back, pressed their hands to their ears, and screamed in sheer horror at the sound of His great name. Eventually, they moved away from us, and we could once again sit down.

While I would occasionally try to see what was happening in the front, I became increasingly worried about the activities behind me. Our leaders had instructed us to face the street when we sat down—this meant our backs were to the clinic and to the clinic escorts. All morning long, pro-abortion agitators had systematically pulled rescuers, both male and female, backward through the front door into the clinic to beat them mercilessly. Casting their bloodied prey back out into the crowd, they soon found another rescuer to drag into their midst.

At one point, an agitator said he was getting tired and needed to take a break. He demanded they find someone else to help. "Beating these damn Christians is hard work!" he complained.

I estimated there were only three more rescuers ahead of me to be beaten before it was my turn. I prayed and begged the Lord for help. I yelled out over the noise, "Send the police, Lord! Please, please hurry up and send the police!"

At that very moment, I heard sirens and felt instant relief. The police arrived by the hundreds. They came in squad cars, motorcycles, buses, helicopters, and on horses.

I turned toward the now quiet bullies just feet from me. With false bravado, I pronounced, "So there! Try to beat me up now, you cowards!"

Quickly, the police removed all the pro-abortion advocates, Satan worshippers, lesbians, gays, and skinheads and escorted them across the street behind police barricades.

For the first time in hours, I felt safe.

Free of the oppressors, the rescuers moved to block the door. I shivered as a soft rain soaked through my clothing.

Next to me sat a petite young woman who offered me a coat. She strained to raise her voice over the pulsating sound of the helicopters and police sirens. She shouted, "It's my husband's coat!"

I asked where her husband was, assuming they had become separated.

Pointing across the street behind the barricades, she yelled, "He's over there." She added, "He just ran over and threw his coat to me, but I don't need it." She explained he was not involved in the rescue.

An older woman next to her yelled, "He's standing by my husband and family." Looking at me, they asked in unison, "Where is *your* prayer support?"

"Were we supposed to have someone?" I asked.

"No, but I think almost everyone does," the older woman said. I felt alone and vulnerable.

As the helicopters moved off and the sirens stopped their wailing, quietness settled over the crowd. We spoke in near whispers, introducing ourselves and wondering out loud what was next. Clinic escorts told our group that several women wanted to get into the clinic for their abortions. I figured they were lying. After all, what woman would want to come for an abortion with the press taking their pictures? I got on my knees to look for these abortion-bound women. Instead, all I saw was a solid wall of police officers. There were hundreds of them, fully dressed in riot gear. Approaching us with a bullhorn, the officer in charge said that if we didn't leave, he would arrest us for trespassing.

I heard one pastor respectfully respond, "We're sorry, sir, but we're not able to do that."

The first line of officers plunged into the crowd. Those sitting in the front were quickly flung to the ground and handcuffed with plastic restraints. A unified gasp came from the throng as the police started digging their fingers deep into eye sockets. They pulled on the ears and the bloodied noses of rescuers already in handcuffs. The ever-increasing sounds of people crying out in pain made me sick and shook me up.

With a loud clap of thunder, the sky opened up, and a deluge of rain poured down on us. *Showers of blessings.* Immediately as these words entered my mind, someone behind me called out, "Showers of blessings."

One pastor stood up, thanking and praising the Lord for the rain after a long drought. Another pastor begged the Lord to forgive us for allowing the blood-guiltiness that covered the land because of abortion. "Is this rain a sign that You have lifted the curse, Lord?" he asked.

I believed this was a sign of the Lord showing His approval for what we were doing. *It's like being wrapped in rain and love,* I thought.

Pro-abortion forces yelled for the police to beat us. "Give them what they deserve! Beat them! Beat them!"

The police responded in a frenzy of abuse. Officers mimicked pushing up their sleeves and said, "Hurry up, it's my turn, let me at 'em!"

From across the street, brothers and sisters in Christ called out words of love and encouragement. *How difficult it must be for them to watch their loved ones hurt like this.*

A voice pleaded, "Please don't hurt the women."

Another man shouted in dismay, "How can this be happening? I can't believe it!"

I watched as officers grabbed cameras out of the hands of the prayer supporters across the street, destroying their film.

Those of us left sitting held hands together, prayed, and sang softly. Everyone stayed calm, anticipating their own arrest and whatever else awaited them. Other rescuers lay quietly on the ground. I watched as officers repeatedly shoved their knees into the backs and sides of the rescuers or into their heads. A few officers yelled at rescuers to get up while they were still sitting on their backs. I marveled at how the rescuers remained so still while being horribly mistreated.

Nearby, five body builders sat together. The men lowered their eyes and shook their heads in disbelief at how the officers were acting. As they were being abused, each one said, "God bless you, sir."

This display of self-control amazed me—especially when the police arrested them too. I admired these incredible, godly men for their commitment to nonviolence. I especially admired them for submitting their bodies to harm so that children would be safe. One of these men repeated his plea for the police to stop hurting the women.

An officer responded by slamming a woman on the ground, face-down. "They're no #%&@# different than you are," he said.

He twisted her arms behind her and handcuffed her. He dragged her to the bus by the plastic cuffs, causing them to cut deeply into her wrists. Other officers continued to twist fingers and arms of the rescuers who walked compliantly with them to the bus.

It was impossible to take in the entire scene. My mind refused to accept what my eyes were seeing. I was incredibly confused. I had been raised to believe the police were the *good* guys. They protect women and children. They help you in your time of need. I was taught to respect them, to look up to them, to admire and appreciate them. What they did was made worse because they seemed to be thoroughly enjoying themselves, gleefully using the same mocking laughter the pro-abortion faction used.

One officer asked, "How d'ya little Christians like it now?"

Another said, "This is nothing compared to what we'll do to you if you come back!"

Someone behind me yelled, "Why don't they just bring out the lions and be done with it!"

Another shift in positions left a large opening in front of me. Several horses quickly filled the space. The police encouraged their mounts to stomp on us. Many cried out in pain as their heavy hooves came down on feet and crossed knees. As one equine chewed on my hair, I raised my hand up to protect my head.

The officer told me not to touch the animal because it was government property. If I did, he would charge me with a felony. "Try it again, and you'll see just how much this horse can make you hurt." He threatened.

His hatred was intense. On cue, the stallion yanked his head up with its mouth full of my hair, jerking my head up violently as my bottom lifted off the ground. Pain radiated through my scalp, running into the nerves behind my ears. Just as suddenly, the horse dropped me back to the ground. He then stomped the priest sitting to my left, thoroughly egged on by its rider. Like a playground bully, the officer laughed and mocked in sheer delight.

The horses backed up, filling me with relief. I quickly changed my mind when I realized they were only making room for more officers to reach more people to brutalize. The police forced the horses to charge the crowd again.

Someone yelled, "I'm a doctor, and you just broke an ankle."

An officer sat up in the saddle, looked over the horse's head, and said, "Oh well..."

The police continued their assault for a long time, leaving me saddened and angry. The child within me felt violated. *If you can't trust the police, then who can you trust? Surely there has to be at least one officer with integrity.*

The next moment, an officer pulled a cop off a female rescuer. "Stop it! There is no need to hurt her!" he yelled.

Another officer stood in the middle of the chaos. He shook his head in disbelief, on the verge of tears. The officer in charge ran up to both of them, jerked them by their arms, and removed them from the crowd. The surrounding cops laughed, calling them "sissy little Christian lovers."

Screams of pain and terror continued to come from the strongest of men as the police jabbed and smashed ribs with their nightsticks. I wondered how I was ever going to bear the pain myself when it was my turn. In agony, I lowered my head and covered my face with my hands. I rocked back and forth as I wrestled with my decision. *If there is a woman trying to get in to abort her child, how can I get up and walk away?*

I felt a soft touch on my shoulder, and a gentle masculine voice said, "There's no dishonor in walking, honey."

I turned to look into the kind face of an elderly man. He smiled and nodded to those walking quietly to the buses.

"Many are doing it," he said.

I patted his hand that was still resting reassuringly on my shoulder. "Thank you, but I just don't know." I yelled out loud, "Lord, I need to know what to do!"

At that very moment, a teenage girl appeared in front of me, reached for my hand, and pulled me up. She begged, "Please, please walk with me."

Relief washed over me. "Sure, honey, I'll walk with you," I said. I assured myself that, after all, she was crying, and I needed to help this frightened young girl. I turned to an officer and told him we would walk to the bus. As he handcuffed me, a strange sensation overwhelmed me, and I started to cry.

I climbed the stairs of the bus and saw many officers in the aisle. The woman in front of me yelled, "No! Please, stop!"

I saw the officer shove her into a seat while fondling her breast as she cried.

Another officer yelled from the rear of the bus, "Hey, here's another young one for you!" I looked for his name tag and realized that none of the officers wore any ID.

Someone pushed me into my seat. My wet clothing stuck to the bench so that I couldn't slide over. Another police officer cussed at me. In anger, he pushed my shoulder, causing me to fall and hit my head on the window. With my hands tied behind my back, I couldn't hold on to anything to help myself sit up. I tried pushing my feet on the floor, only to have my wet sneakers slide out from under me.

The touch from a man's hand helped me to sit up. I looked into the face of a very troubled officer, knowing he felt terrible about what was going on. "Thank you, sir," I said.

He nodded and ushered a female rescuer into the seat next to me. He gently used another plastic handcuff to tie my right arm to her left arm. She sobbed. He patted her on the shoulder, telling her it was going to be okay. I was grateful the Lord used that officer to remind me there are kind, professional police officers who can do their jobs and still be gentlemen.

I looked around and saw many bruises, swollen eyes, and bloody noses. Others boarding the bus limped in. Finally, we were all bound together, and the bus began to move. Someone started singing "Bind Us Together, Lord." Our collective weeping was immediately replaced with hysterical laughing.

An officer looked at us and shook his head. "Weirdos!"

As the bus pulled away, I was curious what would happen to me next.

CHAPTER 3

Incarcerated—Me?

Our bus bounced along the road until we reached our new destination—Sybil Brand Institute, a jail for women. I noticed the rows of razor wire on top of the wall as the gate closed behind us. *This looks like a prison camp.*

We shuffled into the building. Stale, foul air assaulted my senses. Several unbathed women contributed to the stench as they sat in the stuffy entryway. As tears ran down their faces, my heart went out to them. Female guards barked orders at us impatiently. They placed plastic ID bracelets on our wrists, stamped with our prisoner number and arresting code. I didn't blame them for being irritable. We were a large group to process.

A guard moved through the line, performing a pat-down search on each woman. She soon stood in front of me and completed her search. "You've got an underwire in your bra! Take off your bra and put on this prison dress," she barked. She pressed a crudely made, scratchy burlap dress into my hands.

"I'm sorry, ma'am, but this is way too big," I said.

"Put it on anyway!"

As I put the dress over my head, my entire body slipped through the opening in the neck. The dress fell to the floor. The guard stifled a grin as she shoved a smaller sized dress at me. It still hung off my shoulders.

"Make it work!" she demanded.

The guards gave us our first bite of food in hours—baloney sandwiches and a cup of warm purple punch. I was genuinely grateful and enthusiastically thanked the Lord. They placed us in a holding cell where the long night dragged on. We sang hymns to pass the time.

Hours later, the guards moved us into a large open housing dormitory which contained multiple bunk beds. "It's taken us hours to double-up the other inmates so we could corral all of you #%&@# women in one place," one guard shouted. Her language infused with profanity, she made sure we knew how she felt about us—we were traitors to the women who had fought hard to legalize abortion on demand. "Pick a #%&@# bunk and stay put!"

I climbed into a top bunk, nearly losing my dress. Still chilled from being wet for hours, I dove under the gray blanket and tried to get warm. From my top-bunk vantage point, I watched as this angry guard slammed the door shut after the last rescuer filed in. She then stepped into a glass-enclosed booth area reserved for the guards. She ranted to her coworkers in a verbal tirade against us. A new guard walked into our dormitory with her arms filled with pillows and blankets. The angry guard in the booth pounded on the glass and yelled obscenities.

The new guard looked at the booth and then at us. She placed the bedding on a bunk. "Don't you ladies worry about her," she whispered. "You didn't hear it from me, but almost everyone in here is real proud of you for what you did today."

I asked the Lord to bless her as she turned and left.

Most of the rescue women were young, and I wondered if they had children waiting for them at home. Some women had already made calls home and had gotten news about the male rescuers. We learned that the police arrested many more men than women, and they had been taken to three different locations in the city.

The women settled into their bunks. A pastor's wife quieted everyone down so she could pray. She then invited us to share where we were from and why we had joined the rescue today. When it was my turn, I spoke about Mom and her paralysis. I explained how I committed to be her arms and legs and how I stood in the gap for her and the babies. A unified "aww" went through the dorm.

When my new roommates learned I hadn't been able to speak with my mom yet—many women were standing in line ahead of me to use the phone—they all insisted I go to the front of the line. I jumped down from my bunk to go make my call. Daddy answered the phone and said they had waited anxiously to hear from me. They were concerned and upset after hearing disturbing reports about police brutality on TV. I assured him I was fine.

"Tell him to hold the phone to your mom's ear," a lady standing next to me said. She instructed the other women to yell together, "We love you, Rita! We're all here to be your arms and legs!"

I burst out in tears, as did my parents. Daddy's voice filled with emotion. "Thank all the ladies, honey. They've really blessed your mom," he said.

A guard interrupted our conversation. "Lights out!"

The phone went dead. I turned to the ladies. "Thank you, thank you again." I added, "And thank You too, Lord."

The lights went out in our dorm but not in the booth. It annoyed me, but no one else seemed to care. Daddy often called me "The Princess" after the children's story, "The Princess and the Pea." My bed and room environment had to be perfect before I could sleep. It was not the hard mattress, scratchy dress, or whispered conversations around me that were keeping me awake, however. No matter how hard I tried, I couldn't shut my brain off.

I lay quietly in the dark as my mind wandered back through the years. I recalled the pain when my husband of fourteen years walked out on our two children and me eleven years earlier. He said he didn't want to be married anymore. My storybook life shattered.

With eyes as cold as ice, he said, "I'm sick and tired of living with a religious fanatic. You never defy me. That church has turned you into a little Suzie Homemaker, making you so sweet you're sickening."

I couldn't believe how easily he left and never came back. My heart broke for my children as they cried themselves to sleep at night.

I became a single mother overnight. Throughout my marriage I had stayed out of the workplace. The only employment option I found now was a part-time housekeeping job that paid three dollars an hour. How do I pay the bills? How do I feed my children? My ex-husband paid the mortgage for a while, but there was not enough money coming in to cover food, utilities, school expenses, and other needs. In the midst of my fear, I failed to look to the Lord. I had never been in such a situation before. I took for granted the fact that the Lord always provided for me. Instead of dwelling on His power and greatness, I held on to my fear, not trusting the Lord. I was faithless.

Soon a tall, dark, and handsome new music minister came to our church. I was the church pianist, so naturally we spent a lot of time together. Our attraction to each other grew. Friends encouraged our relationship. They thought we were the perfect couple. Almost two years after my husband's abandonment, we got engaged. Everyone at church was excited—everyone except the Lord and me. While friends said yes, the Lord said, *No!*

I first heard clearly from the Lord at age nine, when I received salvation. I knew the Lord was against this marriage, but I couldn't see why. This charismatic man led music at church with his gifted voice. He preached at nursing homes. He taught the young boys' club at church. While we were dating, he'd come over to pray with my children and me. He was always making us laugh. I was so vulnerable. Still grieving from the loss of my childhood sweetheart and reeling from the effects of abandonment, my true self was lost. I felt lonely and unattractive. I was indescribably drawn to him as his silken words and ways left me feeling attractive and desirable once again.

He joined forces with fear, my lifelong companion. He had me fully convinced I could not make it on my own, and my children would suffer without him. He assured me he could care for us and ease our financial stress. Seduced by his irresistible charm, flattery and flowery promises, I reasoned my way into disobedience. A tug-of-war between the Holy Spirit and him ensued with such pain and fury that I was at a place of constant nausea and anxiety—but I married him anyway. In my weak and faithless condition, I took my eyes off the Lord. Instead, I chose to put my trust in a mortal man.

I made the wrong choice.

Four days after the wedding, it became abundantly clear that I had stepped into covenant with cruelty and darkness. The realization that I brought my innocent children into this dark place added to my horror. My disobedience to the Lord was my great sin and failure. We don't have to know why the Lord says yes or no to us. We just need to obey!

The economic poverty that I had feared became a reality. His irresponsible financial decisions and poor work ethic quickly led us to lose all we had. Nothing, however, could compare to the emotional poverty the children and I experienced. My husband's abuse was malicious and constant. Each day he would taunt Jeromy, my son. He told him he would grow up to do drugs, get women pregnant, and go to prison. He attacked Jeromy's identity, saying that he was useless, worthless, and would never amount to anything.

I knew I should leave this man, but the church we attended taught that a woman had to stay, no matter what. They said all problems in a marriage must be the woman's fault. I felt horribly trapped as we went to church with smiles pasted on our faces. No one would believe me if I shared what was going on at home.

On that last night of abuse, I knew what my church would say if I left. I also knew that it would be irresponsible of me to keep my children in this nightmare even one more day. I left with them the next morning.

We arrived on my parents' doorstep in tears. We were crushed, broken, abused, and utterly hopeless. As I lay in bed that first night, I thought about the judgment that came to the kingdom of Judah. Locusts descended as a result of their sin: "What the chewing locust left, the swarming locust has eaten. What the swarming locust left, the crawling locust has eaten. And what the crawling locust left, the consuming locust has eaten" (Joel 1:4).

Our lives had been destroyed and consumed as well. We lost our home, our possessions, our health, our hope, and our peace. These were the consequences of my disobedience—it was not God's punishment. That night I fell to my knees in gut-wrenching repentance. When I stood, a supernatural sense of forgiveness and peace engulfed me. The Lord immediately came into the position of Provider and Protector at my invitation. I quickly secured an excellent job and purchased a better car. The children slept well at night again. Peace and safety had returned to our souls.

The gratefulness that I held for the Lord's incredible forgiveness and restoration was immeasurable. I began to change. I lived in the Word of God. I learned about a brand-new Jesus Who was full of mercy and grace. I went from loving the Lord to falling desperately in love with Him. From childhood I had served Him out of a sense of duty and responsibility. Now it was different. I wanted to give Him my whole life. I prayed for a full-time ministry. Every day I began with this prayer, "Here I am, Lord. Use me."

As I settled in to sleep on my bunk, my body relaxed and sank into the mattress. It amazed and saddened me to know that I felt safer in jail than I had in my own home with an abusive husband.

"Thank You, Lord, for rescuing and restoring us," I whispered.

The experiences I had outside the clinic and inside the jail began a new work of transformation in me. In the morning I will rise a new person. How appropriate. Tomorrow is Easter Sunday.

"Wake up! Now, ladies, now! Chow in fifteen minutes."

I startled awake by the slamming of a steel door, accompanied by a woman's loud, stern voice. It was 4:00 a.m. Holding my dress together to keep it from sliding off, I joined the others in line as we walked to the chow hall.

"Keep your shoulder to the wall. Follow the green line. No talking!"

Inside the chow hall, everything was surprisingly neat and clean. The entire room shined from all the stainless steel. A male officer directed us toward a stack of stainless-steel trays. We moved our trays along the stainless-steel shelf. We received our food from inmates behind large stainless-steel counters. We shuffled forward to constant commands. "Stay in line! Move along. No talking!"

An officer directed us to our seats at long stainless-steel tables. Another walked around the tables shouting, "You have five minutes to eat. Five minutes!" Before I could figure out what strange substances were on my tray, he said, "Four minutes, ladies, four minutes!"

I had to hurry. As much as I tried to swallow the food, I just couldn't do it. Time was ticking—fast. Hungry and tired, I became angry at myself for struggling to eat. With one minute to spare, I shoved an apple in one pocket and a piece of white bread in the other.

"Time's up!" the officer bellowed. "Pick it up. Stand in line!"

We deposited our trays and joined a female guard in the hallway. "Shoulder to the wall! Follow the green line. No talking!" she shouted repeatedly as we made our way back to the dormitory.

You don't have to think at all in this place, I thought. *They make every decision for you.*

In the dorm, we were allowed to talk. I overheard one woman say, "I'm still hungry. When he started yelling off the few minutes we had left, I just couldn't swallow!"

I walked over to her, reached into my pockets, and held out my stash. "Apple or bread?" I asked.

Laughing, she reached into her pockets and pulled out her own apple and piece of bread.

A guard informed us they would turn phones on when the dorm was clean. "And I mean clean!" she said.

Looking around, it surprised her to see the beds already made. She raised an eyebrow and walked into the booth. A few women followed her to ask for more cleaning supplies for the toilets and sinks. Promptly, the phones turned on. While some women made their way to the phones, others went to the showers. Most just sat on their bunks together in small groups and prayed.

The pastor's wife once again called for everyone's attention, reminding us it was Easter Sunday. Easter is uniquely special for me—it is also my spiritual birthday. She then led us in praise and worship. As I remembered the Lord's resurrection, I thanked Him for the best sunrise service ever! Assisted by the acoustics of the dormitory, we lifted our voices up in perfect harmony. I glanced over at the glass-enclosed booth. All the officers were standing up, quietly watching and listening to us. They seemed to enjoy what they were hearing. Many were smiling. One raised her hands in worship.

Our new leader shared an Easter message centered on life, our nation, and our collective concerns. She emphasized the strong pro-life storyline found in the Dr. Seuss children's book, *Horton Hears a Who*: "A person's a person, no matter how small" (Random House, 1954). Just like Horton, we too needed to be a voice for tiny unborn children—children that are unseen and unheard in the womb.

She explained what we could expect from this point on. We learned that because they would hold us for several days in jail, we might experience difficulty functioning when we returned home. After a previous arrest, she had trouble making even simple decisions. For example, it was possible we might put sugar in the washing machine and powdered detergent in our coffee.

We filled the rest of the day in fellowship, singing and praising the Lord. I called home again, relieved to hear from Mom and Dad that all was well. My son, Jeromy, and daughter, Kim, asked more questions about jail than I had time to answer. My parents wondered when I'd appear in court—and how all the rescuers would fit into the courtroom.

"Wake up! Chow in fifteen minutes!" So began a new day and three more rounds of marching to incessant commands. "Keep your shoulder to the wall! Follow the line. No talking!"

As evening closed in, they moved us to a large holding cell. Male guards burst into the room with arms filled with shackles. They put us into groups of three and attempted to bind our wrists, waists, and ankles. Hundreds of sets of shackles tangled up, making a horrific noise. We knew this was meant to intimidate us and make us feel like criminals—our dangerous group of pastors' wives, mothers, and elderly ladies. Soon we all broke out into hysterical laughter at the absurd sight.

The guards initially responded with confusion, which quickly turned to anger. Our laughter increased as we watched each shackled group of women attempt to walk in unison.

One woman shouted, "Make like a potato race and get in sync! On the count of three, move your left foot first!" She continued, "That's it, left, right, left, right." Her instructions worked like a charm as we clumsily made our way to the back door.

Stumbling out into the dark, I took a deep breath and coughed. My lungs burned as fresh air mixed with the stale, smoky air that had permeated the inside of the jail. The darkness in the alley felt heavy and oppressive. I looked up at the razor wire on the top of the tall wall. As our footsteps and clanging chains echoed off the wall and into the darkness, a strange sensation came over me. I felt discouraged and frightened. I sensed others were feeling it too, as they had fallen silent. I wondered what time it was and where they were taking us. We turned the corner to the side of the jail, where rows of buses were waiting for us.

As the guards walked us down between the buses, our discouragement and fear lifted by the soothing, masculine voices singing to us. Although we could not see them, our rescue men could see us from inside their buses. They sang in slow harmonies, "Hold on, hold on, keep your eyes on the prize; hold on." Tears stung my eyes thinking about how much I admired these godly men. Even though they also were shackled and couldn't protect us, their very nearness took away my fear. I felt safe again. Struggling with our shackles, we managed to maneuver the stairs as we climbed into the bus. Positioning ourselves in our seats while chained together proved even more difficult. I was glad they had given me yet another dress that fit, or I would probably have lost it completely.

"There were over eight hundred of you crazy Christians arrested," our bus driver said, "so they scheduled special court appearances by groups for you late tonight."

As our bus made its way to the courthouse, several women fell into the aisle at the first sharp turn. More clanging, more laughter. They stayed put, seated in the aisle.

When we arrived in the courtroom, the guards removed our shackles. We each took our places on the hard benches. Fighting the urge to sleep, I almost didn't hear when they called my name.

"Here," I said.

Our appointed legal assistant read her own name, then answered, "Here."

The judge was completely confused. "You mean you were arrested too?" he asked.

"Yes, sir."

"And you are representing yourself?"

"Yes, sir. And everyone else as well, Your Honor."

He shook his head in disbelief. "Continue."

I was glad my bench was shoved up against a wall. I knew nothing about court proceedings and was extremely tired. I listened to the judge explain our charges: criminal trespassing, plus felony charges for the leaders. I placed my head on the wall and dozed off, only to be jolted awake by an elbow in my side. Tomorrow we would all be released.

Home at last! I don't remember the carpet feeling this thick. Everything looks so layered, soft and colorful. No jarring lights, no metal seats, tables or beds—no shiny stainless-steel anything. Even the air feels soft and quiet. There will be no angry, shouting voices echoing threatening commands here. Just smiling faces, love, and hugs!

I made my way down the hall to Mom's bedside. Sitting as high as her hospital bed allowed, she was there, waiting for me.

"Welcome home, honey." Her flawless skin and rosy cheeks burst with radiant joy. "I'm so proud of you."

I gave her a hug. How I wished she could hug me back.

"Tell me all about it! Were there any babies saved? Were there?" Raising her beautifully arched eyebrows even higher, she waited for my answer.

"I was told that they canceled all the appointments for the day, so yes, babies were saved, Mom." I reached for a tissue for tears I knew would begin.

Laying her head back, she whispered, "Thank You, thank You, thank You, Lord." With her head now resting on the pillow and her eyes closed, Mom continued to smile, speaking just above a whisper. "I felt like I was right there with you the whole time, honey."

I assured her that she was as I stood in the gap for her.

"And it was so nice to hear the ladies say that they were my arms and legs as well. I wish I could meet them."

Dad interrupted with a voice full of indignation. "I'll tell you who I would like to meet! I'd like to meet those officers that think it is okay to beat up on women and children. Who do they think they are? They treat the pro-life people like criminals and protect the ones who are killing babies! I watched it all on TV. You should see what they did to some of them!"

"Uh, I did, Daddy. I was there, remember?"

His anger mixed with concern for me. "Did they hurt you?"

I turned my gaze to the window. I couldn't meet his eyes. "I'm ashamed to say that I didn't get hurt because I got up and walked, Daddy," I confessed.

"Well, that's nothing to be ashamed of, honey. You could have been seriously hurt."

"No, Daddy, I am ashamed. The babies get more than hurt." The regret that had already grown deep within my soul increased.

"But you went!" Jeromy jumped out of his seat. He picked me up and swung me around. "I'm so proud of you, Mom!" He put me down and kissed me on the forehead. "Way to go!" He nearly knocked me over with his enthusiastic high-five.

Kim stepped forward and gave me a hug. "We're all proud of you, Mom. I still can't believe that you, of all people, actually did that. Weren't you scared? Was jail just awful?"

After answering as many questions as I could, I excused myself to prepare for work the next morning. I had difficulty getting organized. Confused and tired, I went from room to room, forgetting what I was supposed to do. It slowly dawned on me that I had missed a couple days of work. I never expected to be held for days—missing work had not even been a consideration. The Lord had supernaturally prevented worry from entering my mind. *Did you actually forget about work? Oh my.*

On my way to work, I turned up the volume on my radio in my car to listen to Jack Hayford's program, *Living Way*. Pastor Hayford said he was joining other pastors and Dr. James Dobson to answer questions regarding Operation Rescue. With a chuckle in his voice, he stated that they had to address it. Several of their staff had not shown up to work on Monday or Tuesday because of their arrests. I considered my own situation. Facing Jack Hayford or James Dobson for missing work because of a rescue was one thing. What I was walking into might be quite different.

I reached my desk in the personnel department and took a deep breath. As soon as I sat down, the director's assistant appeared in front of me.

"He wants to see you immediately. What were you thinking, girl? You could have lost your job, you know!" She quickly swung around and walked away.

Lose my job? How could any job compare to what I have experienced in the last few days? As I made my way toward his office, I marveled at how the Lord had poured a wealth of spiritual understanding into my very soul, enriching my life by a rescue like nothing else ever could.

The director gave me a firm, professional warning. He emphasized the importance of my position. They had always appreciated the manner in which I shared my faith—however, he cautioned me against bringing this issue into the workplace. I assured him that I appreciated my job and would continue to do my best for him and for the department. Thanks for helping me, Lord. That wasn't so bad after all.

Back at my desk, I was disoriented. I wondered where I had placed my calendar. What was I supposed to be doing, anyway? The office supervisor came over and motioned with her finger to follow her into the break room.

Once inside, she turned and said my name slowly, warning me as she scolded, "As a Christian, I agree with you regarding the abortion issue, but here at work, well..."

I nodded. "I understand."

She filled her coffee cup and laughed. "For someone as shy and quiet as you—who would've ever guessed."

"I know. I'm still having a hard time believing it myself."

She informed me that two recruiters needed to speak to me as well. Mark and Amy were the two recruiters I reported to directly. I walked back to my desk, unsure what to expect from them. Thankfully, my friend Betty was at my desk, waiting for me. I knew I could depend on her.

Across the room, Mark and Amy passed their supervisor, walking stiffly as they headed in our direction and straight for Mark's door.

"Karen, you need to join us in my office right now!" Mark's voice was stern.

Betty and I looked at each other, wide-eyed. I mouthed the word *pray* and turned to follow them into his office. *This is not like them.*

Slamming the door shut, Mark threw his briefcase on the desk and whirled around to face me. "Girl! We just couldn't wait until you got back to hear all about it!"

Amy sat down on the corner of Mark's desk. Leaning over in excited anticipation, she said, "Yeah, yeah! Tell us all about it." Her questions came fast and furious. "Were you scared?"

"Yes."

"Did you get hurt?"

"No."

"Did they handcuff you?"

"Yes."

"How did that make you feel?"

"I cried—"

"Did you actually go to jail?"

"Yes."

"Was it awful?"

"No."

"What did your family say?"

"They're proud."

"Are you going to do it again?"

"I don't know."

"I watched it all on TV," Amy said. "There were thousands of people there. It looked like the police were awful!"

"Well, what do you expect?" Mark said.

Amy made a face at him. "Are you sure you're not hurt?" she asked. She squeezed my arms to be sure. Standing up, she gave me a big hug. "Honey, we're just glad you're okay. I'm pro-choice, but I am so very proud of you for standing up for what you believe."

Mark motioned me toward the door. "Yeah, yeah, now get back to work!"

I returned to my desk and dropped into my chair with a thud. Whew!

The telephone rang. I sat there staring at it, unsure of what I was supposed to do or say. Betty saw that I was struggling. She came to my rescue and answered the call from her desk. I felt completely lost. When asked for a file, I didn't even know where to look. My heart started beating hard, and a tingling sensation ran down both arms into my hands. I suddenly had difficulty breathing.

I rushed into the ladies' room. I stood staring into the mirror. *Get a grip!* Then I remembered that the pastor's wife had told us we might have difficulty functioning after coming home. She had read that it only takes four days to brainwash someone into being unable to make decisions on their own. They would then be easier to control. I thought about the lines on the floor in jail, and the constant commands shouted at us.

At lunchtime, I made my way to the cafeteria. Men were making repairs on a portion of sidewalk surrounded by yellow caution tape. I immediately recalled the yellow police tape at the rescue, and my heart started beating wildly. *This is crazy!* As I stood in line to order my lunch, I felt overwhelmed and had difficulty breathing. All the stainless-steel counters, trays, and kitchen equipment had caused this reaction. I bumped into a uniformed guard on my way to my table. He steadied my tray, then put it down for me. I stood there expecting him to cuff me or something. Instead, he said he was proud of me for rescuing.

Why have I never seen him before? I sat down, feeling weak in the knees. Bowing my head to bless the food, I asked the Lord to take this fear away from me. *You're in a safe place filled with friends and smiling faces. Straighten up!*

After lunch, it surprised me to see a large crowd of people waiting for me at my desk.

"There she is!" a voice called out.

Although I knew most of my coworkers, there were a number of those I didn't recognize. I received hugs and lots of questions. I answered as many as I could and thanked them for their concern for me.

Making my way out of the building that evening, I couldn't help but notice the big sign hanging on the front of a coworker's desk: KEEP ABORTION LEGAL. Oh, my. Glancing back, I saw someone take it down.

Lord, thank You so much for helping me through this first day back. Thank You for going before me and preparing their hearts!

CHAPTER 4

Fear Be Gone!

I succumbed easily to fear all my life, but I hated its grip on me. This struggle amazed me. It certainly didn't come from any sense of childhood insecurities.

I grew up on a farm in Connecticut—the second of six children with five girls, and the last child a much-coveted boy. People said our home life resembled the television show, *The Waltons*. We watched the show faithfully and identified with it completely. We were blessed with loving, affectionate parents who showered their affection on us, as well as on each other.

Dad was a hard worker, both on the farm and in the home. His dedication was reflected in awards won for best milk production, cleanest facilities, and the happiest cows. When he walked in the door after the evening chores, the youngest children and dog alike attacked him. Instantly, one child was on his back, two hung from each arm, and another stood on his shoes while hanging onto his neck. The littlest ones squealed with delight. He moved through the house with his children firmly attached until he found Mom, the object of his search, his treasured wife.

Her George, tall, dark and handsome, would gently shed his small admirers and swoop her into his arms. Surrounded by our smiling, uplifted faces, our parents hugged, kissed, and whispered secrets as we watched. Those secrets—how we tried to search them out. Our childhood guesses would be met with a wink from Daddy and a blush from Mom.

Mom kept busy with housework, managing her frequent pregnancies while caring for children. She was involved in school and church activities, as well as seeing to anyone in need. Each summer, Fresh Air Kids from New York City sent children to spend time in our home. Children filled their days riding high on the hay wagons which rolled across the yellow fields. At the end of their stay, they clung to the trees in our front yard, refusing to leave. Dragged away against their will, they went back to the big city with hopes they'd be chosen to return the next summer.

Our farm was a beautiful place, captured on postcards for its vibrant colors in autumn and fragrant and varied colors in spring. One day, photographers arrived to take pictures for an encyclopedia company. Our farm and children were to be featured in an entry highlighting the rural child. Listening from my hiding place, I heard the excited voices of my younger siblings respond to the attention they received from the photographers.

Alone in my safe place, I wondered what was so wrong with me that I felt the need to hide. I had always been afraid, especially of people. But fear didn't end there. My imagination ran wild as different scenarios coursed through my mind... *of a man who haunted the upstairs of our house ... of monsters hiding in the woods, watching me as I skated alone ... of my recurring nightmares of a dog attacking me in my dreams ... of people who insisted on telling me, "Hi!"*

Now as an adult back in my parents' home, I deeply appreciated how the Lord had allowed me to be raised by such dedicated and loving parents. I marveled at their unconditional love for each other, for their children, and for all those around them. They represented a picture of Christ and His unfailing, sacrificial love. No wonder I found it so easy to feel secure in the Lord's love for me. Certainly, I had no reason for the fear and worry that seemed to always be so close and threatening to me.

That evening as night drew near, my body surrendered to the comfort of my bed. My mind, however, was in great distress. I couldn't stop thinking about how I had walked instead of going limp at the rescue. The regret I felt continued to increase, taking on a life of its own. To be beaten could not compare to what the babies go through. I was disgusted with my fear. *Because you didn't want your arms and legs broken, you stood back and let them pull the children's arms and legs off!* Thankfully, this scenario had not happened, as no abortions took place that day.

I knew the Lord did not condemn me, but my own self-loathing filled me with deep regret. I dropped to my knees and wholeheartedly repented of my cowardice. I asked the Lord to please give me another chance: to die to self and go limp during the next rescue. I realized it was the Lord Himself Who encouraged me to revisit these memories. I needed to see just how long and enduring—and especially foolish and destructive—my fears had been. He wanted me to draw a line in the sand and say, "No more!" I prayed for Him to teach me how to overcome my fears.

But how can He accomplish that in me?

"Not the church, not the state, women will decide their fate!"

Standing in front of the Midland Medical Clinic in Los Angeles, I felt the anger charging the atmosphere as the crowd spewed out their hatred.

"Right to Life is a lie—they don't care if women die!" The chanting continued as more pro-life supporters arrived and joined our ranks. I was grateful. I assumed there was safety in numbers.

Over the chanting, a familiar voice caught my attention. Rich Buhler, a talk-show host from KBRT radio, had announced on his broadcast that he would give his support for Operation Rescue and join the next rescue. True to his word, his large frame now blocked a boarded-up doorway. As he stood on the step, he had an unobstructed view of the activity going on up front. Our eyes connected. He nodded and mouthed, *God bless you.*

I felt safer already. *Surely, they won't beat us up this time with Rich here, ready and able to talk about these events on his broadcast.*

Lord, I asked You to give me another chance to go limp and not walk away, I prayed, *but I feel familiar fear rising in this chicken-hearted child of Yours. Please help me keep my commitment to You.*

Several hours passed, laced with more profanities... spitting... pushing... shoving... chanting. "Two, four, six, eight, you can't make us procreate!"

"Why do they have those clothes hangers on their heads?" a woman behind me asked.

"In the sixties, when they attempted to legalize abortion, feminists perpetrated the lie that thousands of women die every year trying to self-abort with hangers," I said. "Many of those spreading the lie became pro-life and tried to refute their previous arguments but were silenced. This lie is still believed."

"Oh. I wonder if they realize how silly they look," she said.

Amid the noise and confusion, a sense of dread crept over me. I looked at the woman next to me.

Her voice trembled. "I'm getting scared. I'm such a baby; I don't know if I can go limp."

"I understand," I said. "Everyone's scared."

"Are you going to go limp?" she asked.

"I'm scared, but I feel I *have* to this time. I know I have to face my fear to overcome it."

"I'm having trouble breathing just thinking about it." She cried.

I reached over to pat her hand, knowing her fear all too well.

By ten thirty, two hundred police officers had arrived on the scene. Once again, they moved the opposition to a safe place. The police approached us. This time, however, they were carrying more than plastic restraints in their hands.

"They have nunchakus!" a rescuer called out.

People panicked. I tugged on the sleeve of a man in front of me.

"What are nunchakus?" I asked.

"They're martial-arts weapons. They're made of either chain or leather cords with wooden sticks at each end. The goal is to attach them to a body part. The handles are then pulled down, producing a vise-like grip and causing excruciating pain. They can crush bones and severely damage nerves and muscles," he said.

My spirit sank. My neck and back stiffened as tension crawled up my body.

"No! It's against the law for the police to use them!" a voice shouted.

Guttural cries of pain came from some men in the front row. Soon other voices joined the chorus of agonizing sounds that struck terror in my heart. I looked over toward Rich, who stood shaking his head. *Lord, I know I asked You for another chance to go limp—but does it have to be this time with the nunchakus?*

The woman to my right put her hands over her face and wailed, "I can't do this!"

The woman to my left looked at me in terror. "Do you think you can go limp?"

"I don't know," I said.

This was a defining moment in my battle against fear. I recalled the sleepless nights of self-condemnation for not going limp at the first rescue. A wave of disgust for my cowardice washed over me, followed by an inner strength and determination that fear would not win this time. There was a legitimate reason for fear—but if the reason wasn't great, what kind of challenge would that hold? What kind of victory would that be? I commanded my soul, *Fear not!*

The woman to my left pressed me again. "Are you going to go limp?"

"I have to!" As the words left my lips, my victory was nearly won.

Near to us, a blind man was next to be arrested.

"I wonder if the police know he is blind," I said.

Within moments, a nunchaku snapped his upper arm in half, leaving his lower arm swinging. The breaking bone sounded like a rock dropped on concrete. Dazed, he seemed unsure of what had just happened to him.

A unified gasp of horror went through the crowd. The usual quiet respect for these officers was replaced with accusations of police brutality and cruelty. Color drained from the police officer's face at his shock and obvious regret. The other officers were silent. They were equally stunned.

"Where's your God now, little lambs?" a voice taunted from the front.

I shouted back. "Right here, answering my prayer!" I had asked God for another chance to be brave, and He gave it to me.

Ignoring the screams and noises around me, I bowed my head, quoting as much Scripture as I could remember. "No weapon formed against me will prosper . . . Fear not, for I am with you to the end of the age . . . Let not your heart be troubled, neither let it be afraid." I began to sing. "Jesus, Jesus, Jesus, there's just something about that name . . ." Over the next fifteen minutes, I was unaware of anything that happened around me. With my eyes closed and my head down, I thought I was at peace but forgot to inform my heart. Its loud pounding shook my chest.

I kept my head down as two officers approached me. When asked if I would get up and walk, I shook my head no. As one officer placed a nunchaku on my upper left arm, the other officer placed one on my right wrist. Almost instantly, I was in midair as all 107 pounds of me lifted off the ground—then crashed down hard on my feet as they hit the concrete. The excruciating pain caused by the nunchakus demanded that my legs move toward the bus. Wave after wave of pain went through my entire body. My head was spinning, and my legs felt like rubber. *It can't compare to what happens to the babies! It can't compare to what happens to the babies!*

My wobbly legs moved forward. *I did it! I faced my giant, and I didn't die!* The Lord gave me the inner fortitude and strength to do what I needed to do. A significant degree of fear had broken in me.

As soon as I started to walk, the officer to my left released the pressure on the nunchaku on my arm, and the pain stopped. It was a different story with the officer on my right side, however. While I stood in line at the bus, he used the nunchaku to twist my arm behind my back. Wrenching my arm, he forced my hand above my head. I was completely bent over. He continued to twist the handles on the nunchaku, causing indescribable pain to my wrist while pulling my thumb back.

A third officer waited to cuff me. "Cut it out. She's just standing here," he said.

The officer refused to stop. He yanked my hand back down with the nunchaku and continued to apply the pressure while the third officer placed my wrists in a plastic restraint. I heard the terrifying sound of my tormentor's teeth grinding together as he jerked and jerked the plastic restraint to tighten it further. I thought I would pass out.

I lost one of my sneakers as they shoved me onto the bus. As before, the officers tied my right arm to another woman's left arm. Tears streamed down my face from the pain. My breath came in short, rapid gasps.

A woman across the aisle leaned over. "I was right behind you. I saw what that officer did to you. I couldn't believe you never made a sound!"

The disbelief was mine as well. Overwhelmed with emotion, I joined in with the whimpering heard all throughout the bus.

Hundreds of prayer warriors pounded on the windows of the bus, sobbing. Agony filled their faces. They pressed crosses and Bibles against the windows to say what they could not. How difficult it must be to watch, helpless, as officers brutalized us. Many were the parents, spouses, and children of those arrested.

As our bus made its way to the jail, my concerns increased. I could no longer feel my right hand.

Our first stop was the jail for men. Guards put me in the drunk tank with eight other women. The smell of vomit filled the air. Once-white padding hung from ceiling to floor across the bars, which was torn away in many places. Cockroaches roamed freely in and out of the holes. Urine covered the floor. I yearned for my lost shoe as I felt the foul substance soak through my sock. In cells near us, inebriated men used perverted words in their attempt to communicate with "the broads in the padded cell."

I told a guard I couldn't feel my hand anymore and asked him to remove my handcuffs.

He jerked on my arm and spun me around to look, causing a new wave of pain. "Your wrist is bleeding! #%&@#! I'll be right back to cut that off." He disappeared through a door behind us.

Another guard appeared and opened the cell, then shoved us toward a different door to move us out. "You Christians are such #%&@# troublemakers!" he shouted. "Move it!"

I motioned my head toward the direction the first guard had gone. "The other officer said he was going to cut my cuffs off."

"Don't know nothin' about that. Keep on movin'!" When I tried to repeat my plea, he drove a sharp finger into my shoulder blades. I moved toward the door. They placed us on another bus headed for Sybil Brand. I was grateful our time in the men's jail was short-lived.

Hot foul air assaulted my lungs as we entered the women's jail. We made our way down a long hall, where guards ushered us into a large room. Naked women stood along the walls, heads hanging in embarrassment. Others were being rudely subjected to cavity searches. My heart sank—this was completely unexpected. I have always been very modest. I begged, *Lord, please get me out of this!* As I stood in line to be strip searched, I noticed I was the only one still in handcuffs.

Angry female guards told us we were traitors to women everywhere. They intended to demoralize us with the manner and attitude in which they searched us, so the "perfect little Christian ladies" would never come back again. A guard motioned for me to follow her. She led me to a large, clean holding cell. I had escaped the strip search! I thanked the Lord but felt horrible for those who remained behind. I begged Him to help them too.

I saw many familiar faces. One woman asked me if my wrist was still bleeding.

"I don't know, but I haven't been able to feel my hand in hours," I said.

Gently turning me around, she looked at my hands. "The blood has dried, but both of your hands are swollen. Your right hand is huge, almost black, and twice the size of your other hand!"

Other women gathered around, looking and gasping.

A petite woman pushed her way through the others and stood before me. She bore a stern look on an otherwise kind face. "What's your name, honey?"

"Karen. Karen Black."

"I'm Joanna Luttrell. We'll take care of this for you, honey."

Extending every bit of her five two frame, Joanna threw her shoulders back and marched to the door. "Guard! Guard! We need you in here right now!"

A guard appeared at the door and asked what the fuss was about. Joanna pointed at me. "She has been in these plastic restraints for hours and hours. Look at her hand. These need to be removed immediately. She needs medical attention now!"

I turned around so the guard could look at my hand.

"Oh dear, this is not good," she said. The guard called for help. She explained she would hold my shoulders back so they wouldn't fall forward suddenly when the handcuffs were cut. After hours of restraint, the sudden release would be painful. She added, "And I warn you that your hand is going to hurt even more when the handcuff is cut off."

She was right.

Once off, blood rushed into my hand, causing more intense pain than when the officer first applied the nunchaku to my wrist. I felt nauseous and gulped for air. The guard eased my arms forward. Pain rushed from my aching shoulder blades down my throbbing arms and into my hands. For the first time, I looked down at my right hand. It looked like it belonged on someone else's arm.

Joanna instructed the guard to get me to the doctor immediately. "And get her something to eat!"

First, however, they needed to book me into jail. The guard shoved the now cut plastic restraint into my hand and walked away. I pieced the cut ends together. The circle looked like it would barely fit on a toddler's wrist. I couldn't imagine how both of my wrists had been tied by this small piece of plastic. Joanna took me by the elbow and led me back to the bench.

"Thank you so much," I said. "Where were you this morning when I was struggling with my battle over the nunchakus? I could have used some of your grit then."

"Fighting my own battle with fear," she said.

As we sat and talked, an unusual bond took place between us. Joanna was older, wiser, and very brave. I enjoyed my time with her so much that I nearly forgot how awful I felt.

A guard came to take me to the booking department. As I waited for my turn, I stood with my head against the greasy wall. My knees buckled from the long hours, pain and stress. This was so foreign to me. *Who would ever believe that I would be here today? I'm the one who would never, ever break any rules under any circumstance.*

But there I was, waiting to be fingerprinted and have my mug shot taken. I watched in silence as they rolled each of my fingers on the ink pad and transferred it to the card. A guard instructed me to face forward for the camera and then turn to the side. Standing for the picture, I didn't know if I should laugh or cry. *Mom would laugh and then cry,* I thought. I did neither. I was a bit numb as the reality of it all washed over me.

Finally, a guard took me to the doctor in the jail, who examined my wrist. She said it might be broken. I needed to go to the hospital for X-Rays. The guard escorted me back to the cell, where two male police officers waited to take me to the hospital.

I quickly yelled to Joanna, "Make sure someone knows where I am. Don't let me fall through the cracks."

"Don't worry, honey. I'll make sure someone checks up on you," Joanna said.

Separation from the other rescuers made me very uncomfortable. I was confident Joanna would keep her promise and make sure that someone in leadership knew where I was going. I was grateful to the Lord for my new friend and sister in Christ.

As one officer got behind the wheel of the squad car, the other leaned over me to fasten my seat belt. He asked why I needed to go to the hospital. I lifted my cuffed hands, revealing my severely swollen purple hand. His eyebrow lifted in surprise. I was grateful they used real handcuffs to keep my hands in front of my body. The metal caused its own pain on my throbbing hand, but it was better than the plastic restraints.

At the hospital, the admissions clerk informed us the police department did not have an account with them, so they couldn't receive me as a patient. Back in the squad car, the officer refastened my seat belt, and we took off to a different hospital. Once there, we were turned away again. So began a long, tedious night as we tried to find a hospital or clinic that would accept me. *How is it possible they don't know where to go? I can't be the first rescuer they've taken to the hospital.*

I asked about the others who were injured. My inquiry released a tirade of insults, accusations, and profanity. The officer looked at me in his rearview mirror. He argued how stupid our actions were, costing the city a ton of money to protect a fetus.

"It's only a blob of tissue," he said.

I explained that a fetus is a child no matter what stage of gestation. "Besides, abortions are allowed up to nine months of pregnancy."

The officer pounded on the steering wheel and laughed hysterically, denying my claim. I explained how *Doe v. Bolton*, argued on the same day as *Roe v. Wade*, ushered in the right for abortions through all nine months of pregnancy.

"You Christians are just plain crazy! Maybe we should have your #%&@# head examined instead of your #%&@# wrist!"

The other officer just looked straight ahead, not saying a word.

I said, "We 'crazy Christians' desire that men and women everywhere understand how much the Lord loves them." I explained that the Lord wants them to know they can come to know Him and experience both His love and forgiveness. A complete explanation of the cross and its redemptive power was received by only an occasional grunt from the driver. I couldn't believe he just let me keep talking. Only the Lord Himself could have shut him up! I decided I would call one "Angry Cop" and the other "Nice Cop"—to myself, of course.

A call came over the radio with orders for the officers to pick up a man who had tried to beat up a bar owner. We pulled up to the bar, and the officers left me alone in the car. After a long wait, the back door opened. A large, muscular man with a full beard, swollen eye, and a bloodied lip was pushed down alongside me. Unable to sit back with his hands cuffed behind him, he leaned slightly forward.

Buckling the seat belt around him, Angry Cop told the prisoner to "Keep your mouth shut and leave the woman alone."

He turned to look at me and nodded. "Hi."

How does one converse with another prisoner in the back of a squad car? Feeling a bit silly I said, "Uh . . . hi." He sat back as best as he could and looked straight ahead. On cue, I did the same.

The squad car pulled back out into traffic. A call came over the radio again with orders to pick up a drunk man several blocks away. Angry Cop protested that he already had two prisoners—one a woman who needed a hospital—but all the other officers were engaged, so they had to comply. When we pulled up to the edge of the sidewalk, Nice Cop removed my seat belt and told me to move to the center of the seat. An intoxicated man stumbled in, falling halfway across me.

Smelling like he had not bathed in months, he leaned into my face and slurred, "Hi, babe."

The officer slammed the door behind him.

Trying to recover from the stench of his breath, I said, "Aren't you going to cuff him?"

"Nah, that's just Charlie. He's harmless," Angry Cop said.

Charlie lay flopped over me, snoring loudly. When we hit a bump in the road, he woke up, looked at me and said, "Hi, babe" as his hands pawed at me.

I shoved him away with my arm.

In his drunken stupor, he was like a rag doll. He fell over and hit his head on the window. "Help, help! She's tryin' to kill me!" he yelled. "Let me out, let me out!"

The car stopped at the back door of the jail—right where we had started several hours earlier.

Left alone in the back of the squad car, I sat in the dark and listened to my own breathing in the quietness. Oh, how very weary I felt. I hadn't eaten since I left my house at 4:00 yesterday morning, and now my blood sugar was dropping fast. I stared at the shotgun just inches from my face, hanging on the metal mesh barrier that separated officers from arrestees. I couldn't believe how drastically my life had changed since I stepped out in obedience and rescued. I wondered if this night was ever going to end. *Please don't let me fall through the cracks, Lord.*

I drifted off to sleep, only to be jarred awake by car doors slamming. A buzzing sensation engulfed my entire body. The squad car pulled out of the police station, hitting bottom as it bounced onto the road.

Angry Cop complained, "It's almost three a.m. We've gotta get rid of her!" My exhausted brain wondered what that meant.

We arrived at yet another hospital and walked toward the emergency room. I asked the officers if they would please get me something to eat. I was running on pure adrenaline, and my body had started to shake.

"What do we look like, your maids? You've been complaining all night!" Angry Cop said.

Nice Cop defended me. "No, she hasn't. She hasn't complained once!" He told me he would try to find me some food.

Angry Cop walked me through the emergency room, holding my arm tightly. A mother saw me and quickly pulled her child away. I couldn't blame her. I must have been a sight to see—handcuffed, wearing dirty clothes with messed-up hair and smeared mascara, clomping down the hall with my one-shoed foot. Running to catch up with us, Nice Cop reached out to give me an apple.

Avoiding eye contact with me, a nurse approached us and said, "The doctor will see you immediately."

She took us to the back of a large, open area with dozens of empty cots. *How strange that a big city emergency room is so empty. It must be a special area for prisoners only.* A doctor sat waiting for us.

Examining my hand, he shook his head at the policemen with disgust. "Bullies! She has to be all of a hundred pounds. You could have just picked her up!"

"Hey! We're not the ones that hurt her!" Angry Cop said. "It was Metro cops. She told us they used nunchakus, but that can't be true because we're not allowed to use them."

"Only nunchakus could cause this kind of damage," the doctor said. "I watched the evening news. You guys are out of control!"

The doctor noticed the dried blood on my hands and asked how I ended up with cuts on my wrists. I pulled the plastic restraint from my pocket and showed him. He also tried to close the cut ends to form the circle that my wrists had been in but couldn't see how it was possible that both of my wrists had been in that tiny opening. He gave the officers another disgusted look.

Angry Cop threw his hands up. "Metro, I'm telling you, Metro did it! Not us."

Although my wrist was not broken, I learned I had severe contusions and probable nerve damage. The doctor wrapped my wrist and told me to see my personal physician as soon as possible.

The sun rose over the horizon as we made our way back to the jail. It was much quieter now—except for Angry Cop's grumbling about the Metro officers.

They put me in a cell to await my release. A kind guard informed me that all my other friends had gone home hours earlier. She smiled at me and gave me a bag of trail mix to eat. After devouring the food, I lay down on the bench in the cell and fell into a deep sleep until a fellow prisoner shook my shoulder, waking me up. She nodded toward the door. A guard had been calling my name as I slept. The guard said it was time for me to go and to follow her. I stumbled after her.

"I'm releasing you through the back door," she said.

"Just like that?"

"Yup."

"What if no one is there to pick me up?"

"That's your problem. That's why you get this quarter. Here, call someone!"

Outside, I blinked as the bright light stung my eyes. When my eyes could focus, I saw Jeromy—all smiles, standing with his thumbs in his pockets. He wrapped me up in a big hug.

"Whoa, Mom, you're a mess! Where's your shoe? What happened to your wrist?"

"It's a long story," I said. "Just take me home!"

Climbing into his souped-up yellow truck, I noticed several guys waving to us, revving the engines of their souped-up trucks. "Are those guys waving at us?" I asked.

"Yeah, Mom, all my friends came with me to pick you up. We're all so proud of you," Jeromy said.

Jeromy's friends honked their horns in celebration of my freedom. I waved at them and laughed as our caravan pulled away.

"How did you know to pick me up?"

"A lady named Joanna told somebody the officers took you to the hospital. When she found out you were back at the jail about to be released, she called Grandpa, and Grandpa paged me."

"God bless Joanna," I said. I dropped my weary head onto the headrest. *Thank You, Lord, for caring for me today and helping me to overcome my fear.*

CHAPTER 5

Only If God Says So!

Two months had passed since my encounter with the nunchakus, but even with a brace on my hand and wrist, the pain continued. That didn't stop me from attending every rally, picket, prayer vigil and rescue that I could. Each experience moved me one step closer to understanding how abortion hurts God's heart.

I was encouraged by the increasing number of participants at each event. In the late sixties, so few people had joined us in this battle. The church rejected us when we tried to recruit their help to prevent abortion on demand. At the time, abortion was classified as murder and was against the law. Many Christians thought it was crazy to think abortion would ever be allowed. They called us "fear mongers." Many years later, we were left trying to stop something that would have been easier to prevent in the first place.

On January 22, 1973, I watched the news and learned that the Supreme Court had passed *Roe v. Wade*. I called my mother, but Daddy said she didn't want to talk. He told me she was just sitting, shaking her head and crying. She grieved for the children who would die.

Daddy choked up as he spoke. "What is wrong with this country? God help us, the United States is heading straight for self-destruction! If we can legally kill children, what will be next? Will they euthanize invalid people like your mother? Mark my words, child abuse will increase. They'll be killing each other in the streets. We're on a slippery slope. You just wait and see!"

My parents were greatly influenced through the writings of Francis Schaeffer in his book *A Christian Manifesto*. Francis warned us not to confuse the Kingdom of God with our country or wrap our Christianity in our national flag (Crossway, 121).

"It's not our country that you should be angry at, Daddy," I said. "You should be angry at the church. They are two separate things. We haven't been the salt and light that we should have been. We haven't treasured and fought for the things that are close to the heart of God."

Mary Ann Kreitzer was one woman who did treasure and fight for the things close to the heart of God. In 1977, she courageously chained herself to an abortionist's operating table in Washington, DC. The caption under a picture of her sitting on the table read, "There! That Oughta Do It!"

Now, twelve years later, I had my first experience outside an abortion clinic—and my resentment toward the church began to grow. As I remembered Mary Ann's example, however, I struggled with my resentment and judgment toward the church. I chose to confess my sin.

An urgency to serve the Lord remained with me constantly. Day after day, I begged Him to take my whole life and give me a full-time ministry. "Lord, I don't know what kind of ministry I'm looking for, but please bring it soon," I said out loud. My level of frustration was persistent and tangible. For two years, I had been asking for a ministry. I thought He'd be glad that I wanted to serve Him so desperately. Gee whiz!

On my fortieth birthday, I realized that nearly half of my productive life was over. I always had a conscience awareness of the need to make the most of my life. Every day of my childhood I would read the plaque that hung over Mom's kitchen sink: "Only one life 'twill soon be past, only what's done for Christ will last." I believe that plaque contributed to the fact that I loathed the thought of a wasted life.

My life was being enriched by the hidden things of the Spirit—lessons learned while I took a stand amid spiritual battles at abortion clinics and in dark holding cells. Operation Rescue provided Minute Man Rescues as a new opportunity for volunteers to save children. I committed to be ready at a moment's notice on any weekend. When a call came, I'd leave immediately for the clinic. Many times, children's lives were saved without arrest because the police agreed to keep the clinic closed.

During one Minute Man Rescue, I sat on the sidewalk with a group of rescuers in the heat. A police officer stood in front of us, scanning the crowd.

"Martha, where are you, honey?" he said.

An older woman waved her hand. "I'm over here."

"Are you okay, honey? Can I get you some water?" Responding to the puzzled looks on our faces, he told us Martha was his wife. He shouted to her, "I'm real proud of you, honey!"

Folding tables arrived with Dixie cups and water for everyone. We figured we wouldn't get arrested that day, and we didn't. The police agreed to keep the clinic closed, even though they performed abortions on Sundays. Not *this* Sunday!

One day, an attorney contacted me for permission to hold a meeting at my house. He wanted to invite a group of women over to discuss concerns about the strip searches. When the women arrived, they were excited to meet my mom, Rita, the woman they'd been praying for since the first rescue.

"We love you, Rita! We're *all* here to be your arms and legs!"

Mom was equally excited to meet the ladies. The Lord had answered her prayer to meet them. That's why He arranged the meeting at my house. The Lord never fails to cover every situation and answer every prayer.

As a result of our meeting, the *Orange County Register* reported strip searches would no longer be conducted for a misdemeanor. Shortly after this meeting, another female rescuer and I were ordered to serve a five-day sentence at Sybil Brand for one of the rescues. We were given copies of a letter from Sheriff Sherman Block that we would not be subjected to a strip search. At the jail, the guards obeyed his instruction. Praise God!

Our five-day sentence was whittled down to just a few hours in jail. During this time, the guards separated me from the other rescuer, placing me in a holding cell with many other inmates. One distraught woman explained to the guards she was not supposed to be held there. She was arrested in Chino, miles away from Sybil Brand. The guards ignored her pleas to make a phone call and arrange for someone to take care of her little boy, Jeremy.

I sat down beside her. I told her I also had a son named Jeromy, but he wasn't little anymore. Instantly, we shared a bond. She told me she regretted not taking good care of her son. The day before her arrest, she begged God to help her change her life. She asked other people if it was possible for God to be a friend to people, even to a person like her.

"Everyone told me they think He's supposed to be your Savior, not your friend." Her beautiful green eyes welled up with tears. "But I need Him to be my friend too. I don't have a friend. I'm such a sinner. I guess He could never be a friend to me anyway."

Unable to contain my joy, I told her about Jesus, the *friend* of sinners, and of His great love for her. She was so ready to receive this friend and Savior! She threw herself face down on the floor and cried out to Him for forgiveness. She acknowledged His death, burial, and resurrection in the simplest, most heartfelt way I ever heard.

When she stood up, her entire countenance had changed. She reflected pure joy. Both of us began crying. I hugged her as my brand-new sister in Christ and shared about the Lamb's Book of Life. I explained that she was now royalty. She was not only a friend of God but a child of God Himself. She was so ecstatic that she jumped up and down.

Her joy quickly turned to horror. She clutched my hands tightly. "What if they hadn't brought me here today? What if *you* weren't here today?"

"The Lord would have used another way to answer your prayers," I said. "He will answer your other prayers now too."

Exhausted from the intensity of emotion, she fell asleep with her head on my shoulder.

A guard approached us and woke her up, saying there had been a mistake. "They're looking for you in Chino," the guard said.

Mistake? I thought. I couldn't help but smile. As she turned to leave, she threw me a kiss goodbye. I prayed the Lord would give her new godly friends as well.

It was now my turn to be released from jail, and I was grateful to be let go so quickly. They usually couldn't process and release us fast enough, which caused me many Mondays of missed work. My vacation and sick time reserves were rapidly depleting.

I sat in my supervisor's office on Monday morning, listening as she explained that my vacation and sick days were all used up. She got right to the point. I would lose my job if I missed one more Monday because I was stuck in jail. I told her I understood and thanked her for the patience she had shown me time and time again. As I stood up to leave, reminders of all the Lord had been pouring into my soul came flooding through my mind. How could I regret losing my job after all He'd done?

"Remember, you *will* lose your job!" she threatened.

Only if God says so! These words came crashing through my senses. My spirit responded in immediate agreement, affirming the fact that He had shown Himself incredibly faithful to me. My days, my hopes, my dreams—and His will—were tightly held in the hands of the Great I Am. Right then and there, I decided that "Only if God says so!" would be the creed I would live by.

That day a letter arrived in my mail from Operation Rescue, highlighting an upcoming three-day event of rallies and rescues in Washington. They called it "The DC Project." Immediately I was drawn to go, but I didn't have any workdays off available to me. I would go "Only if God says so!"

The next morning on my way to work, I wondered how the Lord was going to work it out so I could go to DC. I turned up the radio to listen to Jack Hayford.

"Many can testify about how the Lord gave them back the years the locust had devoured after disobedience," he said. He shared stories of people who asked the Lord to give them back very *specific* years of their lives—years lost to rebellion and bad decisions. Through a set of the same specific number of years, the Lord multiplied new life experiences to restore their hearts.

Sharp pains ran from my stomach up into my chest. I thought about my disobedience to the Lord when He repeatedly told me not to marry my second husband, resulting in terror and abuse that reigned in our home. I wasted seven years just trying to survive. For so long I carried horrible regret and deep grief over those wasted years. So often I wished I could turn back the hands of time and make a different decision. I knew the Lord had forgiven me, but forgiving myself was much more difficult. I couldn't bear to think of the pain that I caused my children and how my disobedience had hurt the heart of God.

The pain of regret washed over me afresh, like a great tidal wave. Tears stung my eyes as intense grieving sank further into my soul. My head pounded as I tightened and twisted my fingers on the steering wheel.

Pastor Hayford asked, "How about you? Can you name your specific number of lost years? How many are there? Two . . . ten . . . perhaps fifteen . . . or even a lifetime?" His voice continued to prod into the painful places of my heart. "Do it! Do it now! Take those wasted years to the cross. Name those specific years and ask the Lord to give them back to you, pressed down and overflowing. Do it *now!*" he commanded. "Don't delay. Put Him to the test. Trust Him that He will keep His promise and you will experience the restoration of those years. Stop what you're doing and name those years!"

Unable to hold back my need to go to the Lord, I swung my car into a parking lot. I leaned hard over the steering wheel as deep, mournful sobs racked my body. With every fiber of my being, I pleaded,

"Please, please give me back those seven years I wasted because of my foolish, faithless disobedience to You."

When I lifted my head, I felt the tension leave as peace rested on my body and in my soul. My lungs suddenly filled deeply with air. It was as if I had not dared to fully breathe, perhaps for years, until that very moment. I wiped my eyes and tried my best to repair my makeup before pulling back into traffic. I believed that somehow, out of His great mercy and grace, the Lord would indeed restore those years to me.

As soon as I arrived at work, I was summoned once again to my supervisor's office. All the secretaries were already gathered there. My supervisor announced the staff would need to attend an out-of-town conference for four days—the exact days I needed off for The DC Project!

"We don't need all the supporting staff to work while we are gone. Would someone mind taking those days off, without pay?"

Like an overly enthusiastic schoolgirl, I nearly threw my arm out of its socket as I shot my brace-bearing hand into the air and waved it frantically.

She pointed to me and said, "You got it!"

The others moaned at their missed opportunity.

All day I couldn't keep from smiling. I was becoming more fascinated with the Lord every day as I experienced His marvelous provision in so many ways. I knew without a doubt He would move mountains to meet my needs. *Washington, DC, here I come!*

Sitting in the back of the room, I was overjoyed to see the mass of pro-lifers gathered in this place. Thousands of attendees had registered, coming in from all over the nation. Occasionally, I'd glimpse someone I knew waving to me through the crowd—fellow rescuers who'd held tightly to my hands as we sat together on the sidewalks in California, crying with me as officers beat fellow rescuers in front of us. What sweet fellowship came out of our mutual experiences.

I whispered to the Lord, "Thank You so much for making a way for me to be here."

As I folded fliers one by one, the brace on my hand and wrist slowed down my progress. Listening to the speakers share their burden for the unborn, for their mothers, and for our country, I was confident the Lord had something special in store for me during this time. I was so grateful to be a part of this movement—to be among people who cared so much about others that they were willing to stand in the gap for those they didn't even know.

I wore my Operation Rescue T-shirt proudly. Though many tables at my first rally were filled with pro-life shirts, this was the shirt that caught my attention. On the front was a picture of four women raising an American flag in the same manner as the iconic picture of soldiers raising the flag at Iwo Jima. One woman holds the hand of a toddler, while another cradles a newborn. Another woman has a baby on her back in an infant carrier, and the fourth woman is pregnant. Written alongside the flag was this verse: "Rescue those who are unjustly sentenced to death; don't stand back and let them die" (Proverbs 24:11 TLB). Below the picture, in bold letters were these words: "We pledge our lives, our fortunes, our sacred honor."

I wanted to be identified as a woman who would fight not only for unborn children but also for their frightened mothers who might otherwise be robbed of the joy of their motherhood. I wanted to stand against the lies that Satan was perpetrating through feminists that motherhood was something to be detested instead of desired. I first became aware of these angry women in the early sixties. I watched how they gave up everything, vehemently fighting long and hard for the right to abortion on demand. I realized that as godly women, we needed to be filled with the Spirit of God, integrity, love, and the same determination. I wondered if I could ever become such a woman and be able to live up to the promise on the T-shirt I wore.

Enjoying the speakers as they shared from their hearts, I was relaxed and at perfect peace. The atmosphere began to change when a new speaker was introduced. As if by supernatural means, a sense of mental and spiritual alertness came over me. I felt my brow tense. I questioned the Lord, "What's going on?" The Lord impressed me to pay particular attention to this speaker. I sat up higher in my seat, waiting in anticipation for what he had to say.

Pastor Joe Foreman walked toward the podium slowly and deep in thought. He spoke without hesitation. He said that for months now, many pastors had been in agreement with each other through prayer and fasting. They were seeking the Lord for direction concerning a particular rescue outreach. "This isn't like anything you've experienced before, and it's not for everybody," he said. "We're not talking about doing an occasional rescue once a month. Instead, it will be an all-out effort of rescues as a full-time, pro-life missionary."

He let us know the pastors had considered many cities, but the Lord always redirected their prayers back to Atlanta. "Some are calling this 'The Siege on Atlanta' or 'The Call to Atlanta.' Again, this isn't for everyone," he said. "You must earnestly seek the Lord's face before answering this call. You'll need to quit your jobs, sell your homes, leave your families, church, and friends, and buy a one-way ticket because you're not coming back!"

I realized I had been holding my breath. My heart started pounding fiercely in my chest. I could hear my pulse in my ears. Without warning, strength drained from my arms and legs. Deep in my spirit, I sensed the Lord speak. *This is what you have been praying for.*

My response was immediate. "No! I don't know what I've been praying for, Lord, but it's certainly not this," I said.

Haven't you been praying that I would give you a full-time ministry?

"Yes, Lord, but I never once considered anything like this. Maybe something like a woman's Bible study, or a ministry to children right at home with my own children. You know, something like that."

But didn't you say you wanted to give Me your whole life, your all?

"Yes, Lord, but . . . leave my children, my aging father and invalid mother? What are You thinking? What are You asking of me?" I was completely distraught. I quickly put my spiritual fingers in my spiritual ears, deciding I would have none of this conversation.

My mind kept spinning for hours. Driving through the city with others back to our hotel for the night, all I could think about was the call for full-time missionaries to rescue in Atlanta. I feared the Siege on Atlanta would end up as Seize Karen in Atlanta. I continued my silent argument with Him. "Lord, my children have already lost one parent through divorce. I'm all they have. Besides, what about Mom and Dad? How can I leave them with the added responsibility of caring for Kimberly? That would be so irresponsible of me. You gave my children to me to raise, not to my parents."

But they raised you well.

So began the mental gymnastics of arguing with the Lord with all the reasoning I could muster. The driver pulled up to the curb to let us out.

At that moment, I heard a preacher on the car radio quoting Jesus's words from the book of Matthew: "You're not worthy to serve Me unless you are willing to leave father and mother and son and daughter, take up your cross, and follow Me."

My heart began to sink.

At early dawn the next day, I was back on a sidewalk somewhere in our nation's capital, unaware of what was going on around me. My mind was still preoccupied as I bantered back and forth with the Lord in a heated debate. "But Lord, I can't leave my children . . ."

A voice crashed through my struggle with the Lord. "Everyone down, and crawl across the street!"

"Crawl? Why would we do that?" I asked.

No one answered. They were already on their knees, so I dropped to my knees as well. All around me, a mass of people crawled like ants across the wide street. I felt foolish, but I soon discovered we were crawling toward an abortion clinic. I had been so absorbed in my mental battle that I hadn't seen where we were going.

Several police officers tried to contain us, but we kept moving despite their efforts to hold us back. One officer placed his right hand on a rescuer's back while stretching to reach another rescuer to his left. As his hand lifted off the one on his right, the first crawler proceeded to move forward, out of his grasp.

"Hey!" the officer yelled.

With his attention diverted, the rescuer on his left side crawled away as well.

We inched our way forward, one hand and knee at a time. The officers continued to perform what I called "The Rescue Dance." They reached for some and stepped over others, only to spin around and find another had escaped. It was comical! Some officers gave up and stood still with their hands on their hips as our group of swarming ants continued to outmaneuver them.

The officer directly in front of me was not giving up so quickly. He had managed to capture two crawlers, one on either side of him, by grabbing onto their coats. He stood there with his feet spread far apart, holding onto his prey. Meanwhile, a woman crawled right between the officer's feet.

I can't believe she did that! I wondered if I could make it through with as much ease as she did. As my head ducked under his legs, the officer quickly grabbed hold of me, with his lower legs pressed firmly against my skull.

"Stay put! You're under arrest!" Feeling quite jubilant at his success, he called out to his comrades, "I got three!"

"Now how're ya gonna cuff 'em?" One of them laughed back.

I kneeled with my head in his vise, unable to look at anything but the ground. I had deservedly lost every shred of dignity. I found myself reaching around the officer's leg to brush the dust off his shoes with the cuff of my sweatshirt.

"Look! This one's polishing my shoes," he said.

Good night, Karen! You do tidy up a bit too much, I thought. Released from my head lock, I got up and faced the officer as he shook his head at me.

"Sorry," I said.

He nodded across the street and told me to join the others.

The officers handcuffed us with plastic restraints. Mine was so loose, I was able to take it off and hold it in my hands—until an officer noticed what I had done. Raising his eyebrow, he gave me a look that said, "Put that back on!" As I slipped on the restraint back over my wrists, I marveled at how different this rescue was from what I had experienced in Los Angeles.

As women rescuers filed into the paddy wagon, I took a seat on the crowded metal bench. The officer drove so fast we couldn't help but slide back and forth on the slippery benches. Our bottoms lifted off the seat multiple times as he hit speed bumps much too fast. Several of the women fell to the floor on their faces. Others landed hard on their shoulders. I simply took my cuffs off again and braced for a fall. By the time we reached our destination, most of us were plopped on the floor.

As we walked through the jail toward our cell, an aging, overweight guard held the door open for us.

"Welcome, ladies," he said with a big smile. "We're filled up everywhere else, so it looks like the rest of you will spend the night here with me."

Twenty of us entered this cell with metal bars. Its appearance looked like a scene out of a cowboy movie.

We threw our coats on a top bunk and began our usual routine of cleaning and tidying up.

"See, Lord, I'm not the only one," I said out loud.

"I'm sorry, were you talking to me?" a woman asked.

"Oh no, I was just talking to the Lord."

Another woman piped in. "She does that all the time. You did that all day while we were sitting on the sidewalk, you know."

"Did I? I'm sorry. I talk out loud to the Lord all the time."

"It sounded more like arguing to me," she said.

"Well, it was," I confessed.

"What were you arguing with the Lord about?"

"Atlanta."

Her face went blank.

"Atlanta," I repeated. "You know, the 'Call to Atlanta' that Joe Foreman talked about last night?" Afraid to acknowledge the next thought out loud, I whispered, "I think the Lord is trying to get me to go."

"Yes! I knew it! I thought of you immediately when he started talking!"

I turned around to face a dear friend from home.

"Well, you have been praying for a full-time ministry," she said. "And you know that you have been begging Him for over two years now."

"Oh no, here we go again." I sighed.

"Don't forget how frustrated you've been, waiting to hear from Him. So you're gonna go, right?" Her face flushed with excitement.

"No, I don't think so. You know . . . my kids . . . my mom and dad . . ." I fully expected her to understand.

She rested her hand on my shoulder and reassured me that the Lord would make His will clear.

My body ached all over from the day's activities. Desperately needing to relax, I climbed onto the empty top bunk and stretched out on the coats. Unknown to me, our coats hid the fact that the bunk had only a few slats and no mattress. I promptly fell through the opening and landed on the women sitting on the bottom bunk, filling the cell with laughter.

My spirit lifted, but just for a moment. Even the *possibility* of going to Atlanta weighed heavily on me. Needing a good distraction, I tuned in to the conversations around me. One woman's family was upset by her involvement with the rescues. They didn't understand and were making her life miserable.

Another woman pulled out her New Testament to encourage her friend to remain in rescue, if she felt it was God's will for her. "Jesus says in Matthew 10:36 that 'A man's enemies will be those of his own household,'" she said.

I knew what was coming next, and I didn't want to hear it.

"He said you're not worthy to serve Me unless you are willing to leave father and mother and son and daughter, and take up your cross and follow Me."

My soul began to sink into utter mourning.

Our guard stood in front of the bars chatting with the women. One thanked him for being so kind to us. Another mentioned how most of the officers were very patient with us at the rescue.

"Oh, they're just used to it 'cause this is Washington, DC, and everyone comes here to protest something or other," he said. "No one has ever cleaned the cell like you ladies though."

Most of us surrendered to the exhaustion brought on by the long day. A few, however, decided to watch television. Our guard leaned back in his chair and put his feet up on his old wooden desk. He turned the TV so the others could see from the cell, sharing his snacks with them. *This place is more like Mayberry R.F.D.* I laughed. *If he were skinny, the guard could pass for Barney Fife.* Between the noise of the TV and the battle raging in my heart and mind, I braced myself for a long, fitful night.

Loud banging on the bars shocked me awake.

"Ladies!" the guard said. "Rise, and shine, and give God the glory, glory," he sang in a loud, booming voice.

I couldn't believe it. It felt as though I had just fallen asleep. I heard others moaning as well. The guard encouraged us to hurry up and get ready. We were being released. Since they hadn't fingerprinted us or taken our mug shots, I wondered if they had really arrested us at all. The guard told us we didn't want to miss the rescue scheduled in Maryland this morning. *How did he know about that?*

That evening when we gathered back at the auditorium, I was restless and exhausted from lack of sleep and fighting with the Lord. I couldn't focus on much of what was shared, although my ears perked up when I heard someone quote Matthew 10:37. *"Really? Doesn't anyone know any other Scripture around here?"*

A man turned around, annoyed.

"Did I just say that out loud?" I asked.

I was embarrassed when he said yes. I need to learn to keep my conversations with the Lord to myself . . . or at least whisper.

To top the evening off, Pastor Foreman emphasized the 'Call to Atlanta' and the foreboding siege. If we were going to come, we needed to communicate with them as soon as possible. They were scheduling rescuers to arrive in Atlanta on the fifteenth of every month. The first wave of rescuers would leave soon. Someone shoved a brochure into my reluctant hands. I grimaced when I read the title: "Come to Atlanta to Die." This was a quote taken from John 12:24: "I say to you, unless a grain of wheat falls into the ground and dies . . ." I almost died on the spot! How many times over the last few years had I asked the Lord to help me to die to myself?

I wanted to be completely available to Him for that full-time ministry I had regularly begged Him for—and now I was arguing with Him.

CHAPTER 6

Losing a Grip on My Will

On the flight home, I was acutely aware that in spite of all my fussing and fighting, a "knowing" had begun to settle into my spirit and mind. I could feel the iron grip of my will start to loosen, however reluctantly. It would be horrible if my children didn't agree with my decision to consider the possibility of moving to Atlanta. I could never bear it if they begged me to stay with them. My spirit cried out to the Lord, pleading, *If You indeed want me to do this, Lord, please work on the hearts of my children. I will need them to send me off with their blessings!*

I walked in the door from my trip and drew in the aroma of dinner simmering on the stove. It was the day before Thanksgiving, and I was thankful to be home.

My mother could always sense when something was bothering me. From the time I was a little girl, I would come home from school and sit with her while she rested. We would listen to classical music together and talk about theology. She was my ultimate role model, and she could read me like an open book.

"You look like you have the weight of the world on your shoulders," she said in her bedroom where my family had gathered. "Now tell me what's wrong."

"Not the weight of the world Momma, just God's hand on me. It's terribly heavy." I described the upcoming "Call to Atlanta" and told my family I felt the Lord had put a call on my life to go there as a full-time missionary.

Jeromy rolled his eyes. "Here we go again. You're always up to something, Mom." Though he didn't want to hear what I had to share, he sat back down at the foot of the bed when I asked him to stay. "Let's hear about your latest plans," he said sarcastically.

"They're not *my* plans!" I said. "One thing I do know for sure is that the 'Call to Atlanta' is not my idea."

"What's that other thing you said they were calling it?" Daddy asked.

"'The Siege.'"

"Yeah, I like that. You should call it 'The Siege,'" he said.

I shrugged. It made no difference to me.

As best as I could, I explained what moving to Atlanta would involve. I'd purchase a one-way ticket, as I might not be back for a very long time. Jeromy bristled. We seldom saw each other now since he had moved away from home, so I knew that he wasn't concerned about me being gone for a long time. Rather, it was the idea of full-time rescuing that disturbed him. He had been skeptical of my involvement with the rescue movement ever since I had become injured.

"You think God wants you to go?" Jeromy said, glancing at the brace on my arm. He shook his head, refusing to make eye contact with me. "You've gotta be kidding me!"

During this interchange with Jeromy, I was aware of Kimberly's silence in the corner of the room. Daddy stood exercising Mom's arm, listening quietly. Mom never took her eyes off me. I searched her face for a clue as to what she was thinking. She just smiled at me, deep in thought.

I felt hurt by Jeromy's disapproval, but I understood his resistance.

Jeromy nodded in his sister's direction. "What about Kim?" he asked.

My heart started to break again at the thought of leaving my daughter. I turned to look at her and saw big tears rolling down her cheeks. My heart sank even further. *Please, Lord, don't ask me to leave without both my children and my parents being in full agreement. Please, Lord, please.*

Kimmy bit her lip as she brushed away a tear. "Mom, I love you, and I will miss you terribly, but I would rather have you twenty-five hundred miles away from me *in* God's will, than here with me and *out* of God's will. Just be sure you know what the Lord wants you to do."

Overwhelmed by her maturity and selflessness, I hugged her until I heard Mom say, "Honey, don't worry about the kids. They're not little anymore. Jeromy is on his own now, and Kim is so grown up."

"Your mom's right, honey," Daddy said. "The kids will be okay. Don't worry about your mother and me either. You know the Lord always takes good care of us. You just obey God. That's the only thing you can do."

Jeromy picked me up and gave me his usual kiss on my forehead. "Well, at least I won't have to go to LA to bring my mother home from jail anymore." He put me down and affectionately tousled the hair on top of my head.

"Remember now, I'm not entirely sure about this yet," I said. "I just wanted you to know what *might* happen. I'm still praying about it. I might not be going!"

As I left the bedroom, I saw Daddy wipe away Mom's tears.

The Lord had answered my prayer—my family did give me their blessing. Rats! Secretly, I hoped they would have been adamant for me to stay with them. I could barely breathe just talking about it to everyone. *How am I going to actually do it?*

Word spread through our community that I was considering moving to Atlanta for The Siege. Many friends called to share their counsel. I loved and appreciated each one for their godliness and spiritual maturity. Their advice, however, left me with more questions than answers.

Some said, "You can't do that, Karen. God didn't give your children to your parents to raise; He gave them to you."

Others said, "Your parents did okay in raising you. Your children will be all right."

One friend sounded alarmed. "Your children's lives will be ruined!"

Another friend encouraged me. "Karen, the best thing for your children is for their mother to be in the center of God's will. Don't you disobey God!"

One woman warned, "The Lord would never ask any parent to leave their children to serve Him."

The next caller said, "The Lord has required many missionaries to leave their children behind. Some for years."

Then came the argument I dreaded most. "How could you possibly consider leaving your mom and dad with the struggles they have? You'd put the responsibility of your children on their already burdened shoulders."

I knew the Word of God says there is safety in a multitude of counselors, but not when each one gave conflicting advice. Discouraged by their words, I decided not to accept any more calls or listen to any other voices—not even my own. I couldn't risk making this life-changing decision based on emotions. I desperately needed to hear from God.

The Holy Spirit reminded me it is always best to ask Him to confirm His will through His Word. He had already spoken to me through the verses in Matthew, but I wanted something more certain. Awareness of my past disobedience to the Lord created an ongoing fear that I might slip into disobedience again. I dreaded the consequences that disobedience had brought into my life. Now I was facing a difficult decision unlike any other I had ever had to make. I needed to be absolutely positive it was His will, beyond a shadow of a doubt. I prayed for a crystal-clear verse directly from His Word to confirm whether I was to go to The Siege. This prayer was constantly in my heart, night and day.

As my struggle continued, a growing sense of knowing filled my heart—I would go to The Siege. Still, I held out for that decisive verse I could cling to later. Though this request was a tall order, one that even God Himself would have a hard time pulling off, I fully trusted that the Lord's will would come through His Word.

Early one morning I awoke to Daddy's voice telling Mom he'd be right back. The front door slammed closed. I poured myself a cup of tea and joined Mom in her bedroom. Mom was awake and eager to talk about my adventures. I was the least likely of her six children to have experiences like these.

"You always were the one who could hear from God. Do you remember how that started, honey?" Mom asked.

How could I forget? It began in the summer, when I was six years old. While other children played, I spent every moment I could swinging on a rusty swing set, enjoying spectacular views overlooking the fields, mountain, and sky. My hands would be stained with rust from sitting on the swing for hours, yearning to hear the voice of God and receive His wisdom. How that burning desire started, I do not know, but it never let up. Every night I'd run into the house in tears, begging Mom to help me hear from God.

Three years later, I heard the voice of my Savior when I accepted Him as Lord. At that very moment, I could hear His clear, abiding voice. Though not audible, His voice was something I experienced deep in my spirit, something I just knew. Jesus said, "My sheep hear My voice" (John 10:27). When He speaks, it always falls in line with the written Word of God. This keeps me accountable to what He has shared.

Mom enjoyed recalling this story as much as I did in retelling it. "That reminds me!" Mom pointed to the bookcase. "When you were in DC, Daddy and I saw a Bible advertised on TV. We both felt you should have it, so Daddy went out and bought it for you."

Why do I need another Bible? I walked to the bookcase and picked it up, puzzled. It was the Living Bible in Kwikscan. "What kind of Bible is this?"

Mom didn't reply. She was falling asleep.

Raised a Baptist, I was very suspicious of this new Bible. I had only owned a King James Version. Thumbing through the pages, I noticed that every few verses were in bold print. If someone read just the bold print, they could read through the passage quickly. It was different from any Bible I'd ever seen.

"If you are involved in rescue, you need to read from the Book of Jeremiah," a pastor from DC had said.

I entered my room, closed the door, and got down on my knees. I placed my new Bible on the edge of my bed. Opening to Jeremiah, I reminded the Lord of my need for a confirming verse if He wanted me to go to The Siege. I read only what was in bold print, but was frustrated. I could twist the meaning of the first few verses either way—to encourage me to go or to stay.

"Lord, please!" I insisted. "I need a crystal-clear verse if I'm to go to The Siege!"

My eyes fell on the next verse in bold print: Jeremiah 10:17. It read, "Pack your bags, He says. Get ready to leave now; the siege will soon begin."

I yelled out loud. "What? Are You kidding me?!" Goose bumps ran down my arms. I reached for my King James Bible and opened it to read, "Gather up thy wares out of the land, O inhabitant of the fortress." The Lord's confirmation would never have been clear to me had I not read this passage in my new Bible.

I woke up Mom and read the verse to her. With tears in her eyes, she said, "I think you better do what it says, honey. You better pack your bags."

I rushed into the living room and read it to Jeromy. "Whoa, Mom, you better get out of here now!"

I returned to my room, half laughing, half crying. A burden for my parents came over me once more. Would I ever see my mom alive again? I reached for my new Bible. I understood I should never just open Scripture and point to a verse to seek God's will. I felt led to do it anyway. "Lord, can You do it again? Can You give me a verse that will encourage me about my parents?"

As I opened my Bible, my finger landed on Psalm 45:10. In bold print it said, "I advise you, O daughter, not to fret about your parents." Tears flowing, I dropped to my knees in awe and wonder. "Okay Lord, I'll go, but I'm taking this Bible with me!"

I shared the news with Daddy and Kim when they came home. They were amazed too.

"I'm really going to miss you, Mom," Kim said, "but those verses give me so much peace. I know for sure that it's God's will for you to go."

I thanked the Lord for giving those two verses to my family and me. We would have them to anchor our souls for the days ahead. It made me laugh to think of how the Lord orchestrated everything I needed. He was just plain showing off! How marvelous the feeling of peace that comes from knowing for sure what the Lord wants you to do. The verses He gave to me supernaturally instilled great confidence. I didn't need to worry about anything else. He had gone ahead of me and had prepared the way.

Wow, Lord! You are so incredibly, unbelievably awesome. How great Thou art and greatly to be praised!

Balloons, cake, and casseroles filled the table at the farewell party thrown by my coworkers. One by one, these dear friends stopped by my desk to say how much they would miss me. Hugs and tearful goodbyes punctuated the day.

I was so grateful for my years at this workplace; employment provided by the very hand of God. I marveled at how men and women alike had responded so quickly to my Jesus. Many had eagerly invited Him into their lives. How very close I felt to each of them. I would miss their faces at our Bible study group that met every Thursday—faces that winced when I talked about police brutality; faces that glowed when I shared of the Lord's faithfulness to me.

When I was ordered to report for sentencing five days after my scheduled departure for Atlanta, these were the friends who prayed.

I insisted I would leave as planned, but they believed I would have to stay for the trial.

"Only if God says so!" I said.

Their faces filled with joy when I shared the good news from Operation Rescue's attorney: the district attorney had dropped all charges against me. They had lost my paperwork and couldn't find video evidence of me in attendance at the rescue. I was free to go to Atlanta! Although no one else saw the tears of these faithful friends, their cheers echoed loudly down the hall.

Everything was ready for my departure. In the two weeks since I surrendered to the call on my life, I had sold all that I could sell and had given away the rest. I emptied my savings, paid off my bills, and made the financial arrangements for Kimberly's care. I tucked away my one-way ticket and remaining hundred dollars into the one and only purse I was taking with me.

I communicated with Pastor Foreman that I would soon join him and the others in Atlanta. He told me to bring very little and to carry only a small suitcase. The suitcase was sitting in the corner, already packed, but it felt like something remained unfinished.

Contrary to my hopes, I had received no support or encouragement from my home church in Orange County. They didn't believe I had heard from the Lord, thinking instead I was being rebellious and irresponsible. They laughed when I said I was going to Atlanta as a full-time pro-life missionary. "That's foolish," they said. "Atlanta isn't a foreign country!" They said I had not been anointed or commissioned as a missionary. Their lack of support hurt deeply. I felt uncovered and unworthy to be called a missionary.

Later that evening, I went to a pro-life meeting in Long Beach, held at Pastor Al and Judy Howard's church. I was glad for the opportunity to say goodbye to my closest rescue friends. The Howards had a maternity home called His Nesting Place, which housed many grateful women. This gracious couple poured out unconditional love on these women and their children. I admired Judy for her faithful, effective sidewalk counseling at the clinics over the years. I felt especially close to Pastor Al. We had suffered much together at many rescues.

At the close of the meeting, I told them I was leaving for Atlanta soon. Without hesitation, Pastor Al invited everyone to pray for me. The crowd gathered around and laid their hands on me. Pastor Al anointed me with oil and said he was commissioning me to be a pro-life missionary to the babies of Atlanta.

The Lord was the One Who encouraged Pastor Al to anoint and commission me. Pastor Al didn't know that the Lord had used him to destroy the lies spoken over me, restoring my joy. Now I was convinced. I was indeed a pro-life missionary, chosen and commissioned by God Himself.

CHAPTER 7

Saying Goodbye

I didn't know how I would be able to bear the pain of leaving my children. They meant the world to me. How could I turn my back on them to follow God's call on my life?

Mom understood the difficulty I was facing. "Karen, your desire has always been to be greatly used by the Lord." She reminded me that A. W. Tozer once wrote, "It's doubtful whether God can bless a man greatly until He has hurt him deeply" (*The Root of the Righteous*, Christian Publication, 1995, chapter 35). Those words echoed in my mind.

Mom was too weak to get into her wheelchair that morning to see me off, so I said my goodbyes to her and Daddy through tearful prayers and hugs.

Kim waited for me in the living room with my bag in her hand. Thinking about Mom's words seemed to make each step I took away from the house and toward the car become increasingly more difficult. As my sweet Kimmy Kay backed the car out of the driveway, I looked over at her. My heart ached. How I would miss that beautiful face and darling smile she so freely gave to me.

"Why couldn't you be a brat or some hateful, rebellious teenager?" I said.

She laughed, knowing full well what I meant.

Ours had always been the sweetest of relationships. Kim was so delightful, thoughtful, and kind. Never could I remember an argument or an act of disobedience or disrespect toward me in all her sixteen years. My heart ached as I thought of how much I would miss hearing her sweet voice and finding her "I love you" notes in my lunch bag, under my pillow, and taped to the steering wheel of my car. I couldn't stop my tears from flowing.

Kim pressed a fresh tissue into my hands. "It's going to be okay, Mom."

I swallowed hard. "I know, honey," I said, "but I'm going to miss you so much. I feel like I'm abandoning you."

"Now stop that, Mom! I know how much you love me. You would never leave if you didn't feel without a doubt it was God's will for you to do so. I hate to tell you this—because I don't want you to think I won't miss you—but somehow the Lord is making this okay for me. He really is! And He'll make it okay for you too, Mom. You'll see."

Listening to her share, I believed the Lord was making it okay. In the last six months, Kim had kept herself busy with two after-school jobs. Slowly, she had moved away from her need to be my constant companion. I thanked the Lord for how He had so beautifully prepared her heart for our separation.

My heart, however, was a different story. The bleeding had begun again. I wondered if Jeromy would make it to the airport in time to say goodbye. Kim and I stood near the departure gate when I caught sight of him, all smiles and out of breath. Jeromy rushed up to me, lifted me up, and planted a kiss on my forehead.

Boarding started, and I had only a few minutes to convey my love to my children. I didn't want to waste a second—but the words would not come. Our eyes filled with tears. "I love you so much," was the most that we could say. With a final call from the gate agent and our last group hug, I moved toward the gate.

"I'll see you in three months, Mom!" Kim said.

I turned around and rushed back to her. "What did you say, honey?"

"I'll see you in three months," Kim said matter-of-factly. "Last night I asked the Lord to let us see each other every three months. So, I'll see you then."

"All right!" I tried to cover up my doubts and not take away from her prayer of faith.

I was grateful that my seat was by the window so I could see my children standing in the terminal. I watched Kim push Jeromy's hand away as he teasingly messed up the hair on the top of her head. Then Jeromy put his face against the window and made a pig nose at me. Sitting there, I laughed, I cried, I laughed, I cried.

"Hi, Karen, may I sit with you?" A perky voice interrupted our silent, extended goodbyes.

I looked up into the young and pretty face of Ruthanne Tedman, who also had answered the Call to Atlanta. She sat down in the seat beside me as the plane pushed back from the gate. I pivoted my attention to the window once more, afraid to miss a single moment. Jeromy and Kim were both standing still with their hands pressed on the window. Although Jeromy is six feet tall, and Kim is taller than me, they looked like toddlers in my eyes.

I'm abandoning my babies! I could no longer hold back my sobs.

Ruthanne knew how I felt about leaving my children. With incredible compassion in her voice she said, "Aww, I'm so sorry."

My shoulders shook. I looked in my purse for a tissue and wiped my eyes, blinking hard to see more clearly. Right behind the tissue packet was an envelope. Recognizing the familiar handwriting, I quickly opened the envelope to read the note Kimmy had left for me: "Momma, stop crying! Always remember that you're not leaving us. Rather, we're giving you to the babies of Atlanta, so they will have a chance to know the love of their mothers in the way we have known the love of ours." The maturity, graciousness, and love of my little grown-up girl overwhelmed me. My sobbing became noticeably loud. Many people turned in their seats to stare at me, but I didn't care.

"This is a terribly difficult day of my life, and I'll cry if I want to!" I told Ruthanne.

As I felt the plane lift off the ground, I realized I was flying into a brand-new life. I wondered what was waiting for Ruthanne and me. I had been in many rescues with Ruthanne and her mother. What a caring young woman she was, so dedicated to her pro-life efforts. I watched her talk to other passengers, all bubbly and enthusiastic. This was not just a call that she had answered but an exciting adventure to experience. Her mother, though, could understand the pain I was going through. I saw her tears at the airport too. In that moment, I felt something like a warm blanket enveloping me. It carried a sense of, "It's going to be okay, honey." I welcomed this tender message from the Lord. I knew by His grace I would indeed be okay.

On our descent, my heart skipped a beat when the pilot announced we were approaching Atlanta. The Siege was upon me. I reached into my purse to remind the Lord I only had one hundred dollars. He was the One Who had made it clear He wanted me to take a complete step of faith. He would have to take care of me.

Twelve of us sat on the floor of a Motel 6 room as Pastor Joe Foreman welcomed the first wave of rescuers to Atlanta. *This is the wave? This is all that's coming?* The look on Ruthanne's face told me she couldn't believe it either. In California, I had grown accustomed to thousands of pro-lifers working together at the rescues. I couldn't imagine what we could accomplish here with so few.

"You are all probably wondering what we can accomplish with just twelve rescuers," Joe said, "but let's not forget the twelve disciples Jesus used to turn the world upside down."

Joe looked around the room and asked us to introduce ourselves. How did we get involved in the pro-life movement? How long were we planning to stay? Some rescuers were willing to give six months. Others were not sure—it depended on circumstances back home. A few thought it might be a year, since this was the jail term Atlanta officials threatened per rescue.

When it was my turn, I said, "I guess I don't understand. I thought we were just to come. I figured the Lord would decide how long. I just know absolutely, positively that I'm supposed to be here." I teared up when I talked of my children and how my heart ached when I left.

"How were you able to leave them?" a rescuer asked.

"That verse! God told me clearly through His Word, 'Pack your bags . . . get ready to leave . . . the siege will soon begin.' I'll never forget it."

Joe threw back his head and laughed. Now everyone knew I was supposed to be here, and they wouldn't let me forget it.

As a parent, Joe knew the anguish I felt over my children. With concern in his voice, he asked the group to gather around me to pray. An outpouring of compassion for my mother's loving concern for Jeromy and Kim freely flowed. Their prayers melted my heart. A great sense of appreciation and love for them was pressed deeply into me, which could never be stolen. Each of them had made their own sacrifices, leaving behind families and careers.

"Tell your children not to worry. We'll take good care of their mother for them," a rescuer said.

I fell into place as the "little mother" of the group, the one who was most in need of protection—even though I was older than most in the group. So began their daily commitment of looking out for me.

Every day that followed, we engaged in a flurry of activities. Shivering in bitter cold temperatures ranging between five and twelve degrees, we picketed and held prayer vigils outside of abortion clinics. We counseled on the sidewalk and went to churches to explain our mission, asking for prayer coverage and pleading for others to join us.

Late in the evenings, several of the men would go dumpster diving in the dark alleys behind the clinics. They gathered up information, such as hours of operation, and found written communication regarding injuries that occurred to several women. I wondered why these reports weren't shredded.

Other rescuers posed as clients, sitting through the counseling process at the clinics. They hid their cameras, and tape recorded the advice they received. Some of us quietly went into the waiting rooms and sat down alongside the women, to encourage them to choose life for their children. Sometimes we were able to leave on our own; other times we were arrested.

The police followed us everywhere, but they treated us very well. No one was injured or hurt.

Our funds for hotel expenses depleted rapidly. Since we assumed we would be in jail most of the time, the need for housing was not considered. We did not expect to be so quickly released each time. Members of different churches opened their homes to us on a temporary basis until something permanent could be arranged. Our days were spent together, but nights we slept in different homes.

One night I was hosted by a gracious family, who arranged for me to sleep in their small attic bedroom. I settled in with a thick quilt for comfort as the wind howled above my head. Deep within my spirit, I became aware of silent footsteps approaching my heart and mind—a sound made familiar through the times His Spirit drew near. The sound of His footsteps, heard only by my heart, alerted me to the message He carried. He would come to me with solid, firm footsteps to give a command and new marching orders. He would come to me with gentle, soft steps that brought Him near when I needed comfort and encouragement.

These steps sounded strangely familiar, and I felt myself shrinking back from them. They carried with them a bitter message and a beckoning, painful question. I turned away from the encounter I feared.

"Good night, Lord," I prayed, hoping He would quietly tiptoe away, but my finite power dissipated into thin air.

Deep within my spirit, I sensed Him inquire, *Are you willing to never see your children again?*

"What? I already gave my children back to You. Didn't I leave them behind in California?"

As my soul was open and laid bare, I felt the Lord accusing me of not fully surrendering my children. It annoyed me that I couldn't hide anything from Him. I questioned if I would really be willing to never see them again, if the Lord asked that of me.

No wonder these footsteps sounded familiar. I struggled in California when He first asked me to leave my children. My spirit sensed Him say, *The level of surrender you made then enabled you to leave your children. Now, are you willing to never see them again?*

I jumped out of bed, and paced back and forth. I had convinced myself that I had entirely given my children to His care. But He was right. Expertly hidden in the depths of my soul, I was holding on and cleaving to my children. I marveled more at how *nothing* is ever hidden from Him. Or was that anger I felt? I hugged my abdomen to somehow lessen the gut-wrenching pain centered there. I shook my head to displace the piercing question reverberating relentlessly in my head. Will this never end? This letting go, this giving up, this dying to self? I knew the Lord wanted me to love my children—just not more than my love for Him. I wondered if I had made my children idols that stood between the Lord and me.

I knew the Lord would never leave me or forsake me. My desperate, burning desire to please Him and be used by Him in a great and mighty way could only be accomplished through complete surrender and obedience. I could not allow anyone or anything to come between the Lord and me. If I did, I would not be able to be used by Him in the way that I wanted, and certainly not in the way required for this battle.

My heart broke as I thought about how this would add even more pain to my children. It felt so unfair to them! Why should they have to pay a price for my obedience?

Remembering a similar line of thought from Oswald Chambers's devotional, *My Utmost for His Highest*, I quickly reached for my old, worn copy.

What My Obedience to God Costs Other People:
If we obey God, it is going to cost other people more than it costs us, and that is where the sting comes in. If we are in love with our Lord, obedience does not cost us anything, it is a delight, but it costs those who do not love Him as much. If we obey God, it will mean that other people's

plans are upset, and they will gibe us with it—"You call this Christianity?" We can prevent the suffering, but if we are going to obey God, we must not prevent it, we must let the cost be paid.... We can disobey God if we choose, and it will bring immediate relief to the situation, but we shall be a grief to our Lord. Whereas if we obey God, He will look after those who have been pressed into the consequences of our obedience. We have simply to obey and to leave all consequences with Him. Beware of the inclination to dictate to God as to what you will allow to happen if you obey Him. (Barbour, 1963).

I knew if my willingness never to see my children again was something He required of me, then this was what I needed to commit to, even though I would acutely feel the sting of pain. I also knew He would somehow make it okay for my children and me. I hoped the pain would ease with the passing of time.

Wiping the tears from my eyes, I once again surrendered my will. "Yes Lord, I'm willing to never see my children again. I'm now completely turning them over to Your tender care."

This pain of relinquishing my children crushed my will into a fine powder. Hopefully, He would now remake me into the vessel of His choosing.

Early the next morning, I learned that an additional seven missionaries had arrived in Atlanta during the night. Both newspaper and television reporters said they couldn't believe the tenacity of our ragtag army of rescuers.

Our work continued into the holiday season. Several days before Christmas, we were arrested at a clinic in DeKalb County. The police treated us with respect. The guards applauded as we filed into the jail. They admired us for the stand we were taking, appreciating our courage and godly behavior. In a few hours, we would be released. I wondered where we would go. The homes we had been staying in were now filling with relatives coming in for the holidays.

To our great surprise, a friend named Holt Hudson arrived at the jail to pick us up. Holt had a loud, gruff exterior that nearly obscured his kindness. Every day he would follow us around at the clinics, bringing us hot coffee and breakfast on his way to work. He didn't want us to spend Christmas there, so he stuffed all nineteen of us into his large work van and took off for his house. Heavily burdened with its many passengers, the bottom of the van hit the street hard and scraped loudly as we pulled into his steep driveway.

We pressed into the warmth of his small, cheerful home. Holt introduced us to his three children and the sitter. We missed meeting his beautiful wife, Linda, who was away visiting her mother. That evening we occupied every bed, as well as the open areas on the floor. Someone even slept under the Christmas tree.

The next morning, Holt went off to work and left us alone with his children. When Linda arrived, she was shocked to find nineteen people in her house. In her delightful Southern way, she welcomed the strangers who had invaded her home. I was amazed at how well she handled finding nineteen strangers, all fresh out of jail, alone with her children. Holt had told her about us but assured her we would all be gone before she came back.

Hopefully, she'll remember that she's pro-life and won't kill Holt when he comes home tonight, I thought.

By Christmas Eve, nearly all the missionaries had found places to stay. When I inquired where I was to go, a pastor answered me with prophetic confidence, "You're to be with the Duffys." I didn't know anything about the Duffy family, so Linda was quick to fill me in. Dan and Melissa were a great couple from their church who wanted to be my host family. I was disappointed because I had looked forward to getting to know Linda better. She had a special way about her—feminine, gracious, and truly delightful.

"You'll just love them," she said.

When Dan arrived to pick me up, his six-two frame and warm smile filled the doorway. His coat was open, revealing a plaid shirt underneath. As I looked up into his friendly, red-bearded face, he reminded me of a burly lumberjack. I returned his smile. Feeling completely safe after a welcoming bear hug, I knew I would forever treasure the friendship of this wonderful man.

On the way to their home, Dan shared how he and Melissa participated in the 1988 rescues in Atlanta. I was amazed.

"You were part of the group that my mom was praying for. I can't wait to tell her!"

When we pulled up to their house, the Duffy children jumped up and down, unable to contain their excitement. Meghan and Brian, ages ten and six, were like-minded in their enthusiasm.

"We get our very own missionary!"

Melissa stood behind them, sharing in her children's joy. I quickly found out that warm bear hugs were a family thing, and I was unmistakably made to feel welcomed. The children tugged on my sleeves, full of questions. Melissa reminded them it was Christmas Eve and assured them tomorrow I'd be able to answer anything they wanted to know.

Christmas morning arrived with more squeals of delight from Meghan and Brian. During the night, two other rescuers had arrived at the Duffys' home. I was shocked to find that Melissa had placed gifts under the tree for each of us. I was about to learn that Melissa could do just about anything she set her mind to at a moment's notice. On this bittersweet day, I was grateful the Lord had placed me with them.

With each gift opened, each display of affection shared between children and parents, my heart ached more and more for my own children. Before I left California, I knew this day was going to be tough—but I had completely underestimated the pain. I wondered what my children were thinking and if they felt abandoned.

Later that morning, I talked with Jeromy and Kim. They reminded me I had made a point of having an early Christmas with them before I left and said they didn't feel like they missed out on anything at all. They thanked me for the additional gifts I had asked Daddy to put away for them for today, the *real* Christmas morning.

As Christmas Day went on, I responded to rapid-fire questions from Meghan and Brian. I joined them as they played with their new games, making every effort to appear lighthearted. I didn't want to expose my broken heart and heavy spirit that might spoil their festivities. This cover-up could not be hidden from Melissa, however. My new friend was keenly perceptive.

After dinner, when we had washed and put away the last dish, Melissa put her arm around me and invited me to sit down with her for a cup of hot tea. Closing my eyes, I breathed in its delightful aroma. I traced the unique shape of the delicate china cup with my finger, admiring the exquisite design expertly etched in blue. The beautifully flowered linen napkin lying alongside it finished the picture that spoke so warmly of home. I choked back the tears from yet another wave of homesickness. As I thought about my own teacups I had sold before leaving, it dawned on me that I had nothing left. Nothing of all the years of homemaking or of the beautiful things I had acquired that made our house a home.

Melissa reached over and gently touched my hand. "I'm sure today was terribly difficult for you, missing your children and all," she said compassionately.

I appreciated her tender understanding, then quickly changed the subject. "I love your teacups. They make me wish I had saved at least one for myself before selling them all."

"Wow! So you don't have anything anymore, not even your children? Well, that's the pits! It's a good thing you're dead, or that would really hurt!"

"Excuse me?"

"You're dead anyway, so it doesn't matter, right? 'Come to Atlanta to die.' Didn't Joseph Foreman invite y'all out here by saying this? Well, if you're dead, what difference does anything make?"

Stunned, I looked at Melissa. I had no words to say.

"All right then. Every time I see you're feeling down, I'll just say, 'Suck it up! You're dead anyway.' Now don't you feel much better?" Melissa laughed, patting my hand.

I sat back, staring at her. *She's the most insensitive person I've ever met!* I thought. But then I had to admit I somehow did feel better. After all, I had agreed to "go to Atlanta to die." Pastor Joe had used this phrase in reference to Jesus's words, "Unless a kernel of wheat falls to the ground and dies, it remains only a single seed. But if it dies, it produces many seeds" (John 12:24 NIV). For years I had begged the Lord to help me die to self. If I truly let the Lord accomplish that in me, then the complete loss of loved ones, friends, and things should hurt a great deal less.

Alone with my thoughts that night, I smiled thinking of her words to me. Melissa was right. If I was never to see my children again, how could I ever survive with a heart that bled every day? How could I ever stay focused on this weighty call on my life if I had a divided mind about teacups and the earthly possessions I had sold and given away?

When I closed my eyes to pray for my children, a familiar hurt invaded my heart. At that moment, Melissa walked by my door and whispered, "Suck it up! You're dead anyway." As her laughter and footsteps faded down the hall, pain was supernaturally lifted from my heart—replaced with a swelling gratefulness for Melissa, this rare gift from God.

The Lord had gone before me to prepare the way. He had chosen the perfect family for me.

CHAPTER 8

Pretrial Detention Center

The guards stuffed us into the holding cell at the Pretrial Detention Center, shoulder to shoulder, back to chest. It was standing room only when a guard called my name.

"Black. Out!" He opened the door and escorted me into the cell next door.

Light from the hallway shone briefly into the dark cell, illuminating an empty bench. There didn't appear to be anyone else in the cell. As my eyes adjusted to the dark, I noticed a woman in the corner. Dressed up in a business suit, heels, and jewelry, she sat on the sink with her feet placed on the toilet. I wondered why the guards had allowed her to keep her jewelry and high heels.

"You don't look like you belong in here," I said.

"You don't look like you belong in here," she replied. She pointed to my T-shirt and asked, "What does that mean?"

I was wearing an Operation Rescue T-shirt which read, "Be a hero, save a whale; Save a baby, go to jail." I explained who we were and what we were doing in Atlanta. I felt a distinct impression to talk to her about fetal development.

While I was sharing, she raised her hands. "You've said enough! Now I know why I'm here today."

Her daughter was pregnant. Furious, she'd made an appointment for her to have an abortion—an abortion that was scheduled for tomorrow.

"When I left for work this morning, my daughter was crying uncontrollably. She told me she was going to be praying all day for God to bring someone to make me change my mind about the abortion."

That morning as she drove to work, an officer pulled her over for speeding. It didn't make sense.

"In rush hour traffic in downtown Atlanta?" she questioned.

The officer asked to see her license, which had expired. When he asked for her registration and proof of insurance papers, she couldn't find them anywhere. The papers were not in her wallet or in the glove box. The officer gave her three tickets—one for speeding, one for driving with an expired license, and one for not having proof of insurance or registration. With three tickets, they towed her car and took her to jail.

"You're why I'm here!" she said in shocked surprise. "God wanted me to meet you. He knew you'd be here today, and He knew my daughter needed someone to talk me out of the abortion."

Earlier that morning, she believed the pregnancy was only a mass of tissue. When I explained fetal development, she knew she couldn't kill a baby. She called her daughter and told her she would help all the way through her pregnancy.

She hung up the phone and told me, "I promise you this child will not die!" She gave me a hug. "Thank you for being here today."

The guard came to the door. "Black. Out!"

He returned me to my original cell, slamming the door behind me without saying a word. Soon after, a guard went back to release the woman. They had found the proof of insurance paper right in her wallet, where she knew it was all along. It was evident to her God had blinded her eyes so she wouldn't find these papers, as an answer to her daughter's prayer. When the computer showed no record of her license being expired, they let her go.

I hadn't been in her cell for more than fifteen minutes, but those were fifteen minutes appointed by God. I thanked the Lord for answering my prayer to be used by Him. I need to make myself available, and He does all the rest.

Most of the abortion clinics we targeted were in downtown Atlanta. Attitudes there differed significantly from those found in surrounding counties. Volunteers stood outside on the sidewalks to escort the pregnant moms past us into the clinics. These clinic escorts were angry men and women who pushed, yelled, and cussed at us. Daily they called the police to lie about our activities. Often the police took the escorts at their word, and we would find ourselves in trouble for things we had not done.

There were many others passing by who encouraged us. One couple with young children made their way across the street to shake our hands. Another woman stopped to give us hugs, saying we were "angels sent from heaven." The best encouragement of all came from a motorcycle cop. He pulled up alongside the sidewalk and told us he admired our dedication to be there day after day. Although many officers didn't favor us, he said there are more that do, and they're on our side.

Nodding toward the clinic, he acknowledged they don't like what goes on in there either. "Someone needs to stop it," he said.

Though the holidays were over, our activities had not slowed down a bit. Each day we struggled to keep warm as we braced ourselves to battle the wind, snow, or freezing rain. My greatest struggles, however, were with my low blood sugar and fibromyalgia. Due to our unpredictable activities, I could never count on regular meals. The damp, cold weather significantly increased the pain I experienced throughout my entire body. I was constantly tired and quickly fell prey to colds and sore throats.

One morning, I woke up with a severe sore throat. My team encouraged me to sleep in until later in the day, when they expected to return. They were going to Feminist Women's Center, a very busy abortion clinic on Fourteenth Street. No one returned from the center that day. They were all arrested, and I was left alone.

Soon a second wave of rescuers arrived, and I joined them for their first rescue. It was easy to get to know each one. We carried the same heart for the Lord and shared the same concern for women and their unborn children. Their dedication and courage were inspiring. At this rescue, we were arrested. This was their first arrest and my fourth. The Fulton County Police threw us into a smelly paddy wagon with their usual angry disdain. With our hands cuffed behind our backs, we struggled to adjust to reasonably comfortable positions.

"Are you ready for this?" a fellow rescuer asked as we made our way to the Pretrial Detention Center.

"I don't know about my readiness, but I am expectant," I told him.

"What're you expecting?" In the short time since meeting him, I'd learned that Bob Roethlisberger had an insatiable need for facts, but I was not able to give any specifics.

"This morning I sensed the Lord was going to release me through this rescue," I said. I had a feeling I was in for an unusual experience.

We arrived at the jail, ushered in through the back door. We took our positions alongside the walls of the crowded hallway and went through the normal pat-down searches and property check in. I could already feel my blood sugar dropping. All I could think about was getting some food to eat. I knew they served breakfast at 3:00 a.m., lunch at 10:00 a.m. and dinner at 2:00 p.m. We had missed breakfast, but they would serve lunch in a few minutes. The guards placed me in a noisy, crowded cell with four other rescue women. As the tumult increased, so did my hunger and accompanying headache. I was glad to see a guard appear at the door with our food trays. Right behind him, however, was another guard to take us away for the booking process. When we returned several hours later, our lunch trays were gone.

With the booking process completed, we were now ready to be called upstairs to housing where we would receive a mat and could finally lie down. Instead, the guards began a long and arduous process of moving us from cell to cell throughout the night. Every cell was hot and stuffy, dirty and foul smelling. They filled each one to capacity with tired—and sometimes angry—inmates. Most just wanted to be left alone in the dark. As they moved us yet again to another cell, I noticed empty trays stacked outside the door. We had missed dinner as well.

I was hopeful to get a spot on the bench since I was at the front of the line. Other inmates pushed me away. This forced me to remain vertical, hour after hour with my head resting against the filthy wall, my body shaking, my head pounding. The long night hours dragged on. My back was at the point of breaking. My knees buckled as my eyes grew heavier. Sleep tried to invade my exhausted body. I couldn't believe there wasn't any space on the floor to sit on. Everyone was lying down, and I was the only one left standing up. One inmate even rested her head on my feet.

I marveled at how my fellow rescuers could sleep so soundly on the floor. Dena was curled up in a fetal position, unaware that her beautiful long blond hair was hanging in the floor's drain. It was wet with urine and vomit.

"Bless her heart," I whispered. I was so exhausted. I would do anything to trade places with her right now. I wondered if anyone would notice if I just laid across the whole pile of them.

I looked longingly again at the fully occupied bench. In past arrests, angry inmates coming down off their drug-induced highs would knock me off the bench so they could lie down. I was so tempted to do the same to them now. I knew, however, that it wouldn't fit well with the name they had given me and the other missionary women: "Church Lady."

Soon the guard took a few inmates away to be fingerprinted. Even if I captured a spot on the bench, a more assertive and equally exhausted inmate would push me aside. As the crowd shifted a bit on the floor, I spotted a small opening at my feet. I slid my body down the wall into a crouching position. I felt a questionable liquid on the floor soak through my clothing. I hugged my legs to my chest, making my knees a makeshift pillow for the night. Sleep. Blessed sleep.

A horrific sound assaulted my dulled and sluggish senses. A woman in a cell across the hall was kicking at the metal door and screaming out of control. I opened my eyes and looked at the other rescuers. I couldn't believe they were able to sleep through the incessant noise of her loud voice spewing out obscenities, accusations, and murderous threats.

"Black! Church Lady! Where are you?" a guard yelled into our cell. He motioned for me to follow him.

As I made my way through the twisted maze of sleeping bodies, my head started to spin. I told the guard I had missed all my meals and was feeling strange. With complete disregard for my plight, he grunted and opened the cell door across the hall as the inmate continued to scream. He shoved me in.

"Calm her down—now!"

My nerves were shot, and my head was splitting. I simply did not have any patience for her.

She had exhausted herself and was sitting on the bench in the dark cell, leaning over. With veins bulging from her neck, she strained to continue her screams through a hoarse throat, threatening to kill the next person she saw.

Great—that's me! I thought.

Her body was covered in blood and reeked of alcohol. Blood from her nose dribbled into her mouth. Thick slobber drooled down her chin and chest. She looked up at me through swollen black eyes like a wounded, hurting animal.

Nothing I could say would help at this moment. She needed quiet understanding and compassion, and I didn't possess an ounce of either. Not knowing what else to do, I sat down next to her and put my arm around her shoulder. Immediately, she laid her head on my chest. Clinging to me like a child, she let out a horrible, mournful cry. Falling into a deep sleep, her body slumped down until her head was in my lap.

Feeling myself nodding off as well, I yearned for the comfort of the cement floor. I tried to ignore the pungent smell of blood, alcohol, and body odor assaulting my senses as I slowly shifted away from her. I placed her head on the bench. When I pulled her legs up onto the bench, she turned onto her back. For the first time, I could see her abdomen, hugely swollen from an advanced pregnancy.

I dropped down hard onto the floor in front of her. She took in air with big, noisy gulps. Bloody foam made its way down the side of her battered face and jaw. I held my blouse away from my chest, hoping that the putrid dampness caused by her blood and foul spittle on my clothes would dry. Then I looked at her belly again. Did her child get injured during the beating she received? Questions continued to race through my mind. Where does she live? Is there anyone in her life able to help her raise her child?

Breaking through the quiet, I heard a voice say, "It would be better for this child to die than to be raised in these horrible circumstances."

The words echoed off the walls. I sat in horrified shock—not by the words, but by the fact that they had come out of my mouth! I gasped in disbelief. Forcefully, I cupped both my hands over my mouth as if to stuff the words back in, forbidding others to escape. I was amazed at the depth of the wickedness of my heart. I rocked back and forth on my knees, bowing to the floor alongside this mother. I reached over to touch her child.

"I'm so sorry, sweet baby," I cried.

Tears streamed down my face. I begged the Lord for His forgiveness, too, for the words I had spoken. This was the argument I heard from others all the time—from those going in for abortions and from many other well-meaning people. They didn't want to see a child mistreated and abused by their mother's difficult lifestyle. How can I have succumbed to that kind of mentality in one exhausting day? I tried to blame it on unclear thinking due to my lack of sleep and low blood sugar, but my excuses fell to the floor.

What little remaining strength I had left drained out of my soul. I lay prostrate before the Lord on the floor. With my wicked heart open and bare before Him, I felt the Holy Spirit prod me further.

He asked, What if you knew for sure this child would be raised in filth, abuse, crime, and horror, only to end up right here like its mother someday? Would you have encouraged her to give life to her baby? Would you have risked arrest for this child this morning?

Angry that He had insulted my intelligence as well as my theology, I yelled out loud, "Of course, Lord!" I could not, however, deny the fact it was me who had spoken those words.

With every fiber of my being, I believe every woman and every child should be spared the horrors of abortion. I believe that abortion for any reason, at any stage of pregnancy, is premeditated murder, carried out in a most heinous and painful way. If there was even one exception to this, then the entire basis of my belief in the sanctity of life would be meaningless!

I did question, however, if this experience had revealed a murderous heart within me.

The Lord responded, A murderous heart is not what you have, Karen. It is a doubting heart that spoke those words.

For one second, I had believed these circumstances were beyond His power to transform. I realized it is a heart full of doubt that says that He could not redeem the life of this woman and her unborn child. I felt so ashamed.

"Lord, please don't give up on me. Take away my doubt and self-righteous pride. Fill me with Your faith and humility," I prayed.

An incredible sense of peace poured over me. I now had a greater understanding of those who repeat the words I'd said. I felt a greater compassion for the women who feel overwhelmed and compelled to abort under these very circumstances. My spirit yielded to the promise of the cleansing and forgiveness that comes with the confessing of my sins. Surrendering to His Peace, I drew in a deep physical and spiritual breath and asked the Lord to help me get some sleep.

I was numb. At least twenty-six hours had passed since I had last eaten or gotten any proper sleep. Fibromyalgia caused my body to throb. Electric shocks went buzzing throughout my entire body. The hard cement floor would significantly increase the pain, but I desperately needed to lie down. I stretched out, thankful for an empty floor.

Before I could fully drift off to sleep, a guard unlocked the door and demanded I follow him. He was taking me back to my cell to get ready for court. It was 5:00 a.m., and somehow, I had missed another meal. Reluctantly, I picked myself up off the floor, leaving the beaten pregnant woman behind. I didn't even know her name. She never spoke a word to me, yet through her the Lord had spoken volumes to me. *Lord, please meet her needs, and never let me forget the lesson learned here in this place tonight. Thank You for Your faithful, loving rebuke.*

Standing outside the historic Fulton County Courthouse, the public would never guess what was hidden behind those doors. The holding cell area was a miserable place. It reminded me of the Pirates of the Caribbean attraction at Disneyland where desperate pirates try coaxing the dog to give them the keys to their cells. The guards would hold us in these filthy cells for hours before bringing us before the judge.

The cells were not without amusement, however. On a previous visit to this lovely place, we invented a game called Bull's-Eye to pass the time. Using wet paper towels, we drew a perfect bull's-eye on the wall. We shaped the mystery meat served daily for lunch into a sticky dart. Due to its high fat content, it stuck right to the wall until removed, leaving no doubt who won the game. We waited for our mystery meat sandwiches to arrive so we could begin playing, but the food never showed up. We had missed another meal.

As the hours dragged on, stomachs growled and nerves became frayed. It wasn't long before the inmates began fighting and arguing over who was going to sit on the benches. As if on cue, the rescue women began teaching the inmates their favorite praise songs—and as usual, they immediately quieted down.

When the inmates stood holding hands and singing in the middle of the room, I saw my opportunity. With the stealth moves of a cat, I snuck behind them as they swayed back and forth. Quietly closing in, I crouched low to avoid being seen and slowly eased my bottom onto the wooden bench. I was too late. Like a ghost, Sheneeka suddenly appeared. Her colossal frame towered over me, threatening me with the look on her face. I was too tired to care. Giving Sheneeka my best Cheshire Cat grin, I raised my legs onto the bench, folding my arms over my head and accentuating a long, drawn-out stretch. I knew she could squash me like a bug. Instead, she laughed.

"You're okay, Black!" she said, playfully punching me in the ribs before she turned and walked away.

Ouch, that hurt!

I settled into the bench and felt delightful sleep enfold me like a welcoming down comforter. Five minutes later, an inmate rudely interrupted my bliss when she tripped playing hopscotch and fell on top of me.

You've got to be kidding! I screamed inside my head. Pain shot through my hip. Sleep changed back into a slippery, evasive reality that refused to be captured again. I kept my face to the wall, tracing every crack, chipped piece of paint, and squashed fly. Exhausted and quaking from hunger, I had crossed over to that place where adrenaline causes the alertness that prevents sleep altogether. I tried to will myself back to sleep.

The singing had stopped, replaced by a constant, ever-increasing barrage of vile profanity. I stuck my fingers in my ears, but it wasn't enough to eliminate the noise. My teeth clenched together when I recognized the voice of another rescuer, interrupting my attempts to sleep. *Does she have to read every verse in the entire Bible out loud to every inmate in this place every minute? And if they sing one more praise song, I'll scream!*

Finally, a guard came to the door and called for Operation Rescue. I shook off my frustration as we filed out into the hall. I told the other ladies to walk down the center of the hall and keep their eyes straight ahead. We would have to walk between the rows of cells containing male inmates. As soon as they saw us approaching, we received the usual onslaught of perverse comments, propositions, and wolf calls.

I smacked the hand of the first one who grabbed me through the bars and dodged the second one's attempt.

Standing by the door to the courtroom, I saw the male rescuers from our group. They looked so rested and not bedraggled like us—or at least like me. My heart swelled with pride and appreciation for them. So often I had watched them sit in front of abortion clinics praying, offering no resistance or defense when taunted and abused. Though battered and bloodied, they would lay down their lives for women they didn't even know and for their unborn children they may never meet. No one can compare to the heroes I found in rescue!

When they saw us, their faces lit up, happy to see us as well. Everyone started talking at once, wanting to know if we were okay. Our reunion was short-lived.

"Shut up!" the guard yelled as he ushered us into the courtroom.

Sitting in the prisoners' box, we tried in vain to communicate with each other regarding our case. We had to represent ourselves, and that was the worst part of rescuing for me. I knew nothing about court procedures. It scared me to death. How I managed to plead my case, I'll never know.

The guards moved us back into a holding cell at the Pretrial Detention Center as we waited to be taken upstairs to housing. Hours passed. Occasionally, a Dixie cup of water would bring temporary relief from the hot, dry air. Guards offered a strange colored liquid with white particles floating on the surface as well, but still no food. At least, not for me.

Separated from the other missionary women, I was put in a cell with another crying pregnant woman. She said she couldn't continue her pregnancy under her present circumstances. I assured her I knew many people desirous to help her. I encouraged her to choose life for her child. Using her remaining quarter, she let me call a pastor for her. He and his wife were willing to come immediately, pay her bond, and take her home with them.

When I returned to my cell, I learned the others had received their trays. The guards had refused to leave one for me. My fellow missionary women, however, had each saved a piece of bread for me. I was determined to be grateful for the massive lump of bread that eased the pain in my empty stomach. After eating, I sat cross-legged on the floor next to the bench and rested my head on my arms. I felt drugged. I wondered if it was just from sheer exhaustion or if the suspicious substance that floated in our drinks had drugged us. This would explain why everyone could sleep so soundly. Everyone except me, of course. With my head on my arms, I sat in the dark, listening to everyone's heavy breathing and occasional coughing.

Forty-eight hours had passed since our ordeal had begun. Finally, the guards called us out of the holding cell to go to housing. My legs had fallen asleep from sitting with them crossed for so long. I hobbled to the door. More electrical shocks ran through my body as we made our way to the elevator.

Upstairs in Quad A, the usual roaring noise made by the vast number of women shouting greeted us. The excessive volume of voices echoed off the walls of the large open room. It added to the buzzing feeling in my body. Not even this kind of noise could keep me awake. If only I could find a space on the floor for my cockroach-filled mat.

While waiting for a space on the floor, I noticed three inmates sitting at a metal table. It felt like I was walking through thick mud as I forced my heavy legs toward them. With my eyes already closing, I plopped down onto the metal seat. The inmates complained about how the guards wouldn't respond to their pleas to go to the hospital. I squinted through my tired eyes, trying to focus on them. One inmate was on the verge of miscarriage. Another had an ugly, infected cut on her shin. A third was in active labor. I breathed a weary prayer for each one as I dropped my heavy head onto my arms that rested on the metal table. My heart was beating in a strange, painful way. My pulse throbbed in my ears. Every part of my body screamed for sleep and sustenance. I felt myself being sucked down into a dark black hole. I offered no resistance at all.

"Get up, Black!" a voice screamed into my head.

Stop . . . shaking . . . my . . . shoulder. My thoughts came slowly, as if I were in a dense fog. Leave . . . me . . . alone.

"I said, 'Get up!'"

A female guard hovered over me. She told me I had passed out, and they were taking me to the hospital. That couldn't be right! "I just fell asleep . . . from exhaustion." I yawned.

"You have diabetes. You're going to the hospital!"

With eyes still closed, I said, "I don't have diabetes. I just need to eat. I'll be okay as soon as I eat something. Anything."

Frustrated and angry, the guard would not take no for an answer. As we made our way to the door, the inmates who had been sitting at the table with me stood up and followed us. They begged to go to the hospital too. "We've been asking to go to the hospital for days, and you won't take us. She's only been here a few minutes, and you take her when she doesn't even want to go!"

The guard pointed to the inmate in labor. "You! No one else."

I looked back at my fellow rescue women. They assured me they'd be praying and would let the Operation Rescue leaders know where they took me. The pregnant inmate began moaning and rubbing her back. I put my arm around her and asked for her name. In between moans, she said her name was Tamika.

"Don't touch her!" the guard said.

Tamika screamed out in pain.

A male guard met us in the hall. He walked us to the back of an elevator, where we joined six male inmates. Our guard asked the other guard which button to push.

"Push 'escape'!" I quipped, as a bit of humor rose from my foggy mind.

The inmates laughed. The other guard chuckled. Our guard fumed.

Outside the elevator, she slammed me up against the wall and warned me that another outburst like that would find me in solitary confinement. Oh, how deliciously tempting, I thought. The word "solitary" suddenly held great fascination for me. Solitary would mean all by myself, completely alone, no one else. No screaming, no foul language, peace and quiet—and sleep, sleep, and more sleep.

For a moment, I fought the temptation to make that one more outburst and earn the much-coveted prize, but I chickened out. I nodded in agreement. I would behave myself.

CHAPTER 9

Grady Hospital

The guard drove to the back door of the hospital and took me to the holding cells reserved for prisoners. *How strange to have holding cells in a hospital. Why am I here? I don't have diabetes. What's going on, Lord?*

Thankful for permission to use the restroom, I knew as soon as I finished and walked out the door I was in for an unpleasant experience. As a female guard frisked me, a male guard roughly handcuffed my wrists and shackled my feet. She explained to him that I was with Operation Rescue. There was no reason to treat me harshly.

"Operation Rescue is a #%&@# nuisance, and you're no #%&@# better than any other prisoner." He taunted, shoving me toward a cell.

I stumbled with the shackles. My shoulder hit the doorframe hard as I fell. The female guard bent down to help me, but he held her back as I struggled to get up on my feet again.

"I'm so sorry," she said, disgusted with her coworker's behavior.

"It's okay. I don't need special treatment."

"That's good," he said, "because you ain't gonna get any here!"

Once in the cell, he shoved me toward the bench. Two steel pipes ran horizontally along the entire wall. One pipe was just above the bench, and the other pipe was underneath the bench, near the floor. The guard stretched my left arm out, handcuffing my wrist to the pipe behind my back. He shackled my ankles to the pipe beneath the bench. When he turned to leave, the heavy metal door slammed shut behind him.

I took in my new surroundings. The room was big with long benches, but I was alone. Not only was this a holding cell but an overflow storage room for hospital equipment. Wheelchairs, piles of bedpans, and rows of crutches lined the far wall.

My body demanded sleep, but the hard floor was beyond my reach. With the pipe digging into my back, it was impossible to rest my shoulders on the wall. Only my head could rest uncomfortably against the wall. The pipe also prevented me from being able to sit back on the bench, forcing my bottom forward and moving my legs further from the edge of the bench. This new position pulled on the shackles restraining my ankles. As soon as I started to fall asleep, my body would relax and my backbone would slide against the pipe. The pain in my back joined the pain in my ankles, waking me up. Chest pain and nausea added to my misery.

Hour after hour, I fell in and out of fitful sleep.

The heavy door opened, nudging me out of my drowsiness. Over fifty hours had passed since I had last slept, and I was starting to wake up. Unfortunately, I was also waking up to the pain caused by the handcuffs and shackles. My skin hurt terribly from the rubbing of the restraints, and I desperately needed to stretch my bent knees.

The guard escorted a petite young girl to the bench beside me. Her arms and clothing were stained with blood. I watched as the guard handcuffed and shackled her to the steel pipes.

"My name is Tina," she whispered.

I smiled at her. "Hi, honey, my name is Karen."

With that simple introduction, Tina burst into tears and poured out her story. The police brought her to Grady Hospital after she was arrested and injured during a drug raid. Speaking through her sobs, her arrest story turned into her life story, one of incredible neglect and abuse. It amazed me how much she had suffered at such a young age. As I listened to Tina describe her life of misery, I soon forgot my own physical discomfort.

Tina felt worthless. She knew no one could ever love her. At five years old, her parents gave her away to strangers at a rest stop. They pulled away and never came back. The strangers brought her to the police, who put her into foster care. At seven years old, she was adopted by parents who gave her back when she turned ten. She went from home to home. When she aged out of the foster system at sixteen years old, she started to live on the streets.

"I must be a horrible person for two sets of parents to give me away like that. My life will never change. I'll probably die of an overdose someday."

"Tina, there's One Who loves you so much that He died for you, to give you life and life more abundant," I said. "He can give you a beautiful life and joy like you've never experienced before."

"Really, an abundant life?" Tina acted as though she had never heard of Jesus before. She stopped crying and wiped her nose on the sleeve of her free arm.

"If you'll trust Him, He'll write your name on the palm of His hand. You'll be spiritually born again into the family of God. He'll adopt you as His very own child, and you'll become royalty," I said. "You know, Tina, the Lord never gives back His adopted children."

Tina fixed her eyes on me as her tears streamed down her face.

I described the life in Christ that would be available to her if she gave herself completely over to Him. I was not talking about jailhouse religion and emphasized what "giving your life completely" meant. I refused to encourage her to pray the sinner's prayer, leaving her to think that she would then be okay with God. I didn't want her to think that her life would miraculously change just because she trusted what Christ did *for* her on the cross.

Tina kept her eyes on me as she repeated back the words of the Apostle Paul: "I have been crucified with Christ; it is no longer I who live, but Christ lives in me" (Galatians 2:20).

"Do you understand that you must be crucified with Him? There can't be any spiritual growth for any of us without the desire to die to self. You need to come to Him as Lord and Master, not just Savior, if you want to experience a transformed life."

Tina needed to know how very serious and life-changing this decision would be. I encouraged her to count the cost. A Christian's life doesn't suddenly become all rosy when we trust Christ. If she did trust Him, she would no longer be alone to live her life. Jesus would never leave her or forsake her.

Tina asked me question after question. She wanted answers to everything! She explored every possible outcome of trusting Christ as opposed to turning from Him. Clearly, Tina was a brilliant young woman. She knew herself well. "If I don't come to him as Master, I will quickly take Him for granted and misuse His love. I won't change at all if I make Him only my Savior."

Tina became quiet. She turned to gaze across the room, as if she were staring through the wall into her future. She nodded her head as she contemplated her decision.

After what seemed like an eternity of silence, she turned back to look at me. I knew from her radiant smile she had already decided to follow Him.

Now it was my turn to cry. I listened to her heartfelt prayer of confession and commitment to Jesus, her Savior and Lord. With clanging handcuffs and shackles, I gave her an awkward, one-armed hug. I welcomed her to the family of God and told her she was now my sister in Christ.

"You mean I am really part of a family now?" She beamed at the thought.

A guard entered our cell to take Tina to the doctor for her injuries.

As they led her away, Tina looked back at me, smiling. "I'll never forget you. After all, you are my sister."

Delight and stress come while encouraging someone to trust Christ. They are choosing between eternal life in heaven and eternal life in hell. I had felt the tug and pull of the battle for her soul. *Thank You, Lord, for the victory won through Your never failing, wonder-working power. Please raise up someone to disciple her.*

I was more awake than I had been in hours. I wondered why I was even there. The Lord does nothing unless there is a good reason. It was evident I needed to be there for Tina—but I knew there was something more; something I needed to learn. He always uses an object lesson to teach me something He wants me to *never* forget. I prayed He would show me soon. I wanted to learn it and get it over with. I couldn't wait to get back to jail.

After five long hours in the holding cell, the mean guard came back to take me into the emergency room. His harsh manners still intact, he forcibly removed the handcuffs and shackles from my inflamed ankles and wrists. He jerked on my arm and dragged me through the cell door, then shoved me toward a gurney. I sat on top of the gurney and rubbed my wrists and ankles, relieved to have the restraints removed.

My relief was short-lived. The guard slammed me down on the gurney and handcuffed my left wrist to the bed railing, then yanked my legs down and attached the shackles on my ankles to the bottom of the gurney. It was impossible for me to lie down. To support myself, I had to lean on my elbows. A second guard took pity on me and raised the back of the gurney, patting me on the shoulder.

As the angry guard pushed me down the hall, I heard the sounds of a riot growing louder. A group of rival gang members had just been brought to the emergency room—shot up, stabbed, and still fighting. At first, I was indifferent. They had nothing to do with me.

Quickly, we entered the hall where the gang members were fighting. Gurneys lined both sides of the hall with prisoners who had their left wrist handcuffed to the railing and their feet shackled to the bottom of their stretchers, just like me. There was no mistaking the anger on the men's faces behind their swollen eyes and bleeding lips. Some were covered with so much blood it was hard to see their wounds. They spit out both blood and foul language back and forth at each other in ever-increasing decibels of animal-like sounds. The noise was deafening.

Without warning, my gurney stopped. Right there in the middle of the hall, in the middle of the gang—in the middle of their ensuing war. I waited for the guard to start pushing me again, but the gurney didn't move. I leaned on one elbow to look behind me and saw the guard walking away. He left me there on purpose because I was a Christian and a rescuer.

A bloody hand reached out angrily and pushed my head down. The gang members on one side of the hall were trying to get to the gang members on the other side of the hallway, and I was in their way. They grew increasingly annoyed at me. With a free hand, one prisoner pushed my gurney down out of his way, while using my gurney to pull himself across the hall. Then he swung his bloody fist at the nearest rival gang member just feet from him.

The next prisoner down the row became annoyed that they had pushed me in front of him. He used his free hand to push me back where I came from and likewise took a swing at the prisoner nearest him. Back and forth, they pushed my gurney up and down the hall. I felt blood splattering on my arms and face as they tried to reach over me. The loud clanging of all the metal bed rails, handcuffs, and shackles added to the horrific bone-jarring noise.

Sucking in the hot, foul-smelling air, I yelled at the top of my lungs, "Lord, help me!"

No human could have heard me scream over the utter confusion in that hallway, but praise God, He did. My gurney started to move. It picked up speed down the hall, approaching two wide doors without hitting a single obstacle on its journey through that jumbled-up mess. My gurney pushed through the double doors with a loud crash and swung around, bumping up against the wall as it came to a sudden stop.

Instantly, I felt fresh cool air hit my face. I now faced the double doors I had just passed through. I watched them close, shutting out the utter confusion in the hall. I turned to thank the person who rescued me and pushed me out of there. I wanted to congratulate them on their skillful maneuvering in the obstacle course of gurneys, but no one was there.

"How did he get away so fast? Where did he go?" I said out loud.

As I raised myself up for a better view, I noticed my gurney was sandwiched between two inebriated patients. One patient pulled back the curtain and glared at me with his bloodshot eyes, insisting I was his long-lost girlfriend, Shirley. With spit flying, he sputtered how cruel I had been to him. I used my free hand to pull the curtain shut. He tugged it open; I pulled it closed. He opened the curtain again, this time reaching for me. I pushed off against the railing of his bed and headed straight into the reach of the other drunken, woman-hating patient.

Grabbing me by the hair, he screamed, "You're a mean old woman, Shirley-girly!"

As I pried his fingers from my hair, he pulled off his mask, coughed, and spit in my face. "There! Now you have TB too, Shirley-girly."

I wanted to yell out to the doctors and nurses at the end of the room to move me. *I'm not like the rest of the prisoners in here. I'm with Operation Rescue! Shouldn't they treat me better?* Wiping the spittle from my face, I remembered the Lord. Wasn't He sinless, pure, and holy? Yet He was spit on by people like me. If the Great I Am could be spit on, just who did I think I was?

At that moment, Melissa's gentle rebuke echoed in my mind. "Suck it up. You're dead anyway." I smiled. Unfortunately, I could not agree—I was still very much alive to myself. As the drunken patients shoved my gurney back and forth between them, I closed my eyes, letting my head roll freely from side to side. I pretended they were rocking me to sleep. Eventually, my tormentors were the ones who nodded off first. Peace and quiet at last.

Imprisoned on the gurney in handcuffs and shackles, a new sense of understanding flooded my spirit. I needed a serious attitude check. The persistent progression of multiple sclerosis in my mother had left her imprisoned in her body for years, only able to move her head slightly. She never complained about her arduous situation. Instead, she glowed with the love of the Lord. Thankful for her godly example, I drew strength from her testimony.

Thud! A tray of food landed in my lap. What a delightful surprise! The orderly who brought my tray rushed off, avoiding eye contact and refusing to respond to my thanks. I was grateful he did not wake up my roommates. With the tray resting precariously on my lap, I used my free hand to steady it. I would have to eat in a half-sitting, half-lying position. Most of the food had already slid onto the bed, but I didn't care. I laughed with joy. At long last, I had food!

The cold mashed potatoes, anemic looking green beans, and burned chicken looked like they were prepared and displayed by the finest chef in all of Atlanta. I savored the exquisite mixture of delicate flavors that delighted my palate. Sipping on the ruby-red vintage that had also stained the bed linens, I was fully satiated in both body and soul. I quietly laughed with gratitude and thanked the Lord.

Almost immediately a different orderly appeared, removed my tray, and replaced it with another one. I told him I had already eaten, but he ignored me and walked away. This time it was pressed ham, boiled potatoes, and greens. When I finished the plate, my stomach was full, and my eyes were heavy. I felt myself drifting into a pleasant sleep while wondering how much longer I could wait before they would allow me to use the restroom. I had been in restraints for hours.

Startled by a bump to my bed, I opened my eyes. Two nurses stood next to a gurney turned sideways at the bottom of my bed. "Undetermined cause of death and no identification," one nurse said to the other, who wrote the information on her clipboard. They walked away, leaving her corpse with me, without a sheet to cover her up. She was an attractive young woman, perhaps in her thirties, and neatly dressed. I was impressed with her shiny, perfectly groomed blond hair.

The questions came fast and furious to my mind. *What happened to her? Does she have a family? Is she married? Does she have children wondering where she is? How will they feel when they learn their mother is gone?*

I watched her lifeless body while listening to the heavy breathing of the two men on either side of me. Time and abuse had taken their toll on them. I looked at the deep crevices on their faces, their dry, calloused hands, gawking bones, and sagging skin. They had experienced much of this world, but had they accomplished anything special? And what about that young woman? She looked pulled together, but now she was dead. What had she accomplished with the time given to her?

These thoughts stirred up questions of my own. *What about me, Lord? What have I done with the time You've given me?* I thought about the moments and years squandered. So much wasted time and opportunities had been lost forever. I breathed a heartfelt prayer that the Lord would enable me to live out the rest of my life for Him.

As the nurses wheeled the young woman away, it reminded me how much death was in this place. Grady Hospital trains doctors to perform abortions. Some testimonies from these doctors had been used to argue before the Supreme Court, helping to usher in abortion on demand. Down here in the basement, I felt like I was in the bowels of a monster.

Morning brought a new orderly and another tray of food. More needful than food, I had an urgent need to use the restroom, but the orderly rushed away, ignoring my request for help. I didn't get it. I had gone for hours with nothing to eat, and now they couldn't stop feeding me. This time they served me cold grits, eggs, and warm tea. I wasn't hungry, but I knew it was best to eat whenever food was served. I didn't want to risk the possibility of a repeat performance when I returned to jail. Even though my legs were stiff from holding the same position for hours, and my skin rubbed sore from the shackles, I finished my breakfast and fell fast asleep.

Lord, what is the lesson You want me to learn? Please tell me. I'll do or say whatever it is. Just hurry up and get this lesson over with so I can get back to jail.

Twelve long hours had passed since they brought me here. I had only used the restroom once when I first arrived. Both my bladder and shackled ankles were crying out for release. The nurses refused to help me.

"You'll just have to wait for the next shift of guards, to see if they can find the key to your shackles," a nurse said as she walked away.

I cried out to the Lord again to explain why I was here. Just then, a new guard I had never seen before stood at the foot of my bed with keys dangling between his fingers. He unshackled my legs and pulled them to the right side of the bed, then released the handcuff from the bed as it dangled by my side. Stiff and sore, I felt pain shoot through my ankles as I stood up. The guard shackled my feet together again, and I slowly made my way to the restroom thirty feet away.

"Move it!" he yelled.

Still shackled, I tried to quicken my baby steps but tripped and fell.

"Get up!"

As I struggled to my feet, he yelled at me to move faster. I tripped and fell again.

Like a drill sergeant, he stood over me, shouting. "You better hurry up or else!"

This time when I hit the floor, I welcomed the pain in my knees that made me forget the pain in my ankles. His voice boomed out again, demanding I stand up and walk.

I hobbled my way to the restroom, leaned against the sink, and choked back tears. My feminine feelings were injured—not because he yelled at me but because he never once offered to help me up. Wiping away my tears, I looked in the mirror and thought of Melissa. "Aww, suck it up," I said.

Leaving the restroom, I looked at the space between the bed and me, dreading the trip back. Mr. Congeniality leaned against the foot of the bed with his hands on his hips. *That big bully won't make me cry again.* I stood up straight and tall and took a deep breath. I stumbled with my first step and fell flat on my face. Tasting blood, I almost lost my resolve not to cry.

I continued to struggle with baby steps, only to fall repeatedly while he used his booming voice to intimidate me. It didn't work. His voice was overshadowed by revelation from the Lord. Now I realized why I was here and what He was trying to show me.

It was the shackles!

The Lord showed me it wasn't only my ankles that were shackled. I was spiritually bound by invisible shackles which hindered my heart, mind, and gifts. He showed me how I had allowed lies from the Deceiver, myself, and others in the church to shackle me. Their lies and discouragement kept me bound and unable to walk with the freedom He intended for me.

At last, I made it across the room and climbed into my bed.

I rejoiced as the invisible shackles fell from my heart and mind. Cold, heavy shackles forged from lies that told me because I was a woman, there was a limit to how the Lord could use me. *They fell!* Weighty, painful shackles that held me down and tripped me up, binding me with thoughts which said because I was a divorcée, I was damaged goods and unfit for the King's service. *They fell!* Loud clanging shackles that echoed disapproval from lies which said the Lord was so disappointed in me and would never use me because of my disobedience. *They fell!* Shackles forged from the persistent lie that fear would always rule my heart. *They fell!* The Lord and I were having a serious encounter, and He was setting me free.

I blinked away tears of joy to focus on the face of a doctor standing over me.

Smiling at me, he said, "You're perfectly healthy and free to go."

"Yes, I am. God and I are out of here! I've learned my lesson. Now I can hurry up and get back to jail."

"I thought we learn lessons to keep us *out* of jail," the doctor said, puzzled.

I smiled as he walked away.

The guard stood watch at the foot of my bed. Suddenly, I *saw* him. His sternness was gone, leaving his countenance completely changed, almost glowing.

With a tender voice and a beaming smile, he said, "Now you're ready for the race!"

Immediately, this Scripture verse flooded into my mind: "Let us lay aside every weight, and the sin which so easily ensnares us, and let us run with endurance the race that is set before us" (Hebrews 12:1). I couldn't run my race with my feet in shackles!

Stunned, I wondered if this man was an angel in disguise. Isn't it the drill sergeants who prepare men for battle? I needed the reminder that I was in a battle as well. *Lord, help me to never pick up another spiritual shackle. Please help me learn to always walk in Your free and abundant grace.*

He walked away as another guard brushed past him, holding up keys. "I'm here to let you out of your shackles, Black." Surprised to see me freed from my shackles, he took me by the elbow and escorted me down the hall, then put me back in the holding cell with another inmate. Handcuffed and shackled to the metal pipes, I was reminded that these chains were a reminder of my spiritual shackles that were now gone. After hours of talking and laughing together, I rejoiced when the other inmate trusted Christ.

The twenty-one hours I spent at Grady Hospital were no coincidence. The Lord used these unusual means to teach me and set me free.

CHAPTER 10

Forbidden to Pray

Many from our first wave of rescuers remained behind bars at the Fulton County Jail. A third wave of rescuers arrived to help with our efforts in rescuing, picketing, sidewalk counseling, and attending prayer vigils. For eight weeks, I worked from early morning to late every night in the snow and freezing temperatures. The lack of sleep and stress took its toll on me.

One morning, I woke up with a horrible sore throat, a pounding head, and body aches all over. My temperature rose to 102 degrees. There was a prayer vigil planned at the Feminist Women's Center that morning, and I was in no mood to go. I hobbled to the kitchen on my aching feet, surprised to find our leader, Joe, with several rescuers already in the house, ready to carpool to the vigil. Joe saw that I was sick and understood if I wanted to stay home. It was going to be a long day. He suggested I come for the prayer vigil only and return right back home. I reluctantly agreed.

At Fem Center, Joe instructed us to spread out, leave gaps of space between us, and keep our knees on the edge of the sidewalk. Even though women would not be coming for abortions on this day, he wanted to make sure we could not be accused of blocking any portion of the wide sidewalk. A familiar, overwhelming sense of grief came over me as I knelt to pray. On this day, my grief was heavier, and I felt deep sorrow for the Lord. I wondered how He could bear to see His precious gifts thrown back into His face every day, the little ones He miraculously weaved in the womb. His plans for their lives would never include a brutal death at the command of their very own mothers.

A loud voice interrupted my thoughts. "If they're going to be out here praying every day, we might as well give up right now!"

I looked up and noticed the assistant director standing at the top of the stairs, her face filled with anger. *Wow! She understands the power of prayer.*

Weeks earlier, I had been praying in front of this center by myself. Five angry clinic workers surrounded me, screaming at me to leave. A few were crying, letting me know they were witches and needed the babies' blood. They, too, understood the power contained in our prayers.

I put my head back down and continued with my thoughts and prayers. Every inch of my body ached. I confessed my desire to hurry up and get home. Except for the chirping of the birds and one man who occasionally read quietly from his Bible, everything was very still.

"Karen, you need to get up and leave." I was surprised to see Officer Summers standing over me. He was a kind, older officer I had come to appreciate.

I argued with him that we were only praying, but he insisted I leave. I looked around and saw police in riot gear, handcuffing some of our men. On the backs of their jackets were the words: Crime Scene Force.

How appropriate. Horrible crimes are committed here, but not by us, I thought.

"We're not blocking the clinic or the sidewalks. Are you arresting me for praying?"

"No, just get up and walk away. Please. If you just get up and walk away, you won't go to jail."

"You are arresting us for praying! I don't believe it! We're actually being arrested for praying here in the Bible Belt!"

All at once I felt sicker than I had all morning. I ached terribly. I desperately wanted to get up and go home. A song I learned as a child in Sunday school came into my mind with its lyrics, "Dare to be a

Daniel, dare to stand alone." When Daniel was forbidden to pray, he went home and threw his windows open for everyone to see. I clearly heard an officer say that we couldn't pray there. I knew I had to stay. If he just hadn't said that! To obey the officers would be a form of denying Christ.

"I need to be a Daniel!" I said.

Officer Summers understood. Noticeably disturbed, he nodded and moved away from me, keeping his head down, his hands behind his back. Another officer stepped in to cuff me. Usually when I am handcuffed, a strange sensation comes over me and I start crying. This time I started laughing. As soon as the cuffs were on, all the aches and pains left my body. I no longer had a sore throat. I tried to swallow hard and couldn't even make my throat hurt. My ears and eyes felt perfectly fine, and I could tell my fever had left.

I started laughing and couldn't stop, even when the officers lifted me up and threw me into the back of the paddy wagon. My chest slammed hard against the metal floor—but for the first time, that didn't hurt either. Others were thrown on top of me, but all I could do was laugh. The door slammed shut. In the dark, we began the task of detangling ourselves, trying to sit up with our hands cuffed behind our backs. I heard the others calling for me to see if I was okay, but I couldn't answer them—a shoe was pressing on the back of my head, pushing my face onto the floor of the van. Finally, I was able to scramble out from under everybody and sit upright.

"Hey guys, I'm not sick anymore! As soon as they put the cuffs on me, I was completely well. Can you believe it? Praise the Lord!"

"Operation Rescue this side of the hall, common criminal, other side," an officer said as he separated the inmates.

That's not very nice, and it won't help our relationships with the other inmates in the cell with us, I thought.

We were standing together in the Pretrial Detention Center, its hallway as noisy and smelly as ever.

Guards led us away to the holding cells. They placed me with four other rescue women in a cell across from our men. Noise could be heard coming from other cells, even through the thick doors. As was our custom, we began singing hymns. As soon as the men could decipher what song we were singing, they joined in. Then they would choose a hymn, and we would join them. Back and forth it went, song after song, while the hallway and cells became remarkably quiet. Inmates from other cells would shout out requests.

"Let's hear 'The Old Rugged Cross,'" a guard asked as he passed by.

So it went, hour after hour. I marveled at how singing about the Peacemaker brought sweet quietness, even to a place like this.

I remembered how preachers would often emphasize the fact that Paul and Silas sang hymns in jail. I discovered that when you take a stand for righteousness and end up in prison, singing happens naturally. The Lord meets with you in ways unlike anything you have ever experienced before. Under these circumstances, the force of His presence is overwhelmingly powerful. Songs can't help but burst out from your very soul.

Eventually, our voices gave out, and sleep took over our weary bodies. I laughed in wonderment at how I still felt so completely well.

During the night, guards called us out for booking and put us in an overcrowded cell away from our men. The cell was hot and filled with smoke. I couldn't believe they let the inmates smoke in such close, crowded quarters. Three of the prisoners argued over a "Cadillac," an unsmoked cigarette. I was glad there was no light in the cell. The darkness helped most of them to sleep instead of filling the air with more smoke. Inmates who were awake asked us if we had been singing earlier in the day. They wanted to know what we had done that caused our arrest and put us in jail. Eventually, they wanted to know about our Jesus. Hour after hour we shared about the Lord and the pro-life cause. Many confessed their abortions, wishing we had been there the day they lost their babies. Others opened their hearts to trust the Lord and receive His forgiveness for aborting their children—forgiveness they had once believed was impossible for their sin.

In the morning, I was moved to a new cell that had a telephone mounted on the wall, which was rare. I quickly used this opportunity to make a call to my parents.

Usually when I'd speak with them from jail to let them know why I was arrested, they would say, "That's nice honey. We'll be praying for you." This time Daddy got upset.

"Are you sure you were just praying? Was anyone blocking the sidewalk?"

I assured him it was just a silent prayer vigil. I told him we were frequently accused of things we didn't do, so we had someone across the street recording a video of our prayer vigil.

"Happy Valentine's Day, honey," Daddy said as I hung up the phone.

The reminder of Valentine's Day brought me back to an idea I had two nights earlier, when I encouraged everyone on our team to make signs that looked like valentines. I thought that on this Valentine's Day, we could all hold up the signs to the women who stand outside the Surgi Center porch every day, waiting for their abortions. Most of the rescue men protested. They didn't want to make silly valentines with heart-shaped doilies. They finally consented, getting down on their knees to work on their poster boards on the Duffys' basement floor.

Dale didn't wait for Valentine's Day to bring his valentine to Surgi Center.

"Valentine's Day is tomorrow, Dale," I said, annoyed when I saw his sign.

He told me he felt led to bring it anyway. The rest of our team carried their usual signs. It began to rain heavily, and all our signs started wilting—but not Dale's valentine. One mother saw Dale's sign and believed its message of love. She came down from the porch to tell him how much she appreciated him. She chose life for her child.

The Lord knew we wouldn't be at Surgi Center on Valentine's Day. I was ashamed of being annoyed with Dale for not doing things at the proper time. I asked for his forgiveness, as well as the Lord's. Because of Dale's obedience to the Holy Spirit's leading, a mother and child were spared the horrors of abortion.

After thirty hours at Pretrial, we were brought to the courthouse for the judge to hear the charges against us. I dreaded the agonizing process of representing ourselves before the judge again. I wished we had someone to fight for us. To our surprise, we were met by several attorneys who wanted to defend us. My father had called Jay Sekulow, an attorney with CASE (Christian Advocates Serving Evangelism). My parents had supported this ministry for years. Dad had reached Jay by phone to tell him of our arrests.

The district attorney charged us with disorderly conduct with blocking. He requested for us to be held on a three-hundred-dollar bond, even though our attorney argued we were nonviolent. We were all penniless, so to us it may as well have been a three-hundred-thousand-dollar bond. Either way, we wouldn't pay, so we would be held over in jail until March 3, to give the prosecutor time to prepare his case.

Before I was sent back to Pretrial, Jay requested to meet with me to tell me about Daddy's telephone call. Jay laughed and said he had been sure my father was mistaken. We must have blocked the door to the clinic leading to our arrest. My father had insisted he watch the videotape evidence. Jay couldn't believe what he saw and made immediate plans to come to our aid.

"You can thank your father for this," he said.

Jay offered to make arrangements for my bond, but I refused. I would be just fine with the Lord and all the other rescuers.

"They'll take you back to Pretrial and then on to Key Road Prison. March 3 is a long way off," Jay said with concern in his voice. "A lot of bad things can happen in that amount of time."

I smiled, confident of this one truth. "Only if God says so!"

After many long hours waiting in holding cells at Pretrial, we were escorted by the guards to the housing quads upstairs. The heavy door opened to Quad A, assaulting us with the horrific noise.

"Tell me again why it was we were so anxious to get back up here?" I asked a fellow missionary.

"The mats!" she said.

Oh yes, the dirty mats. After hours without sleep in the holding cells, the mats were as inviting as exquisite cushion-top mattresses from the finest bedding store. As soon as I laid my weary body down, my prayer of genuine appreciation for the mat was quickly followed by, "And Lord, please encourage the cockroaches to stay inside." Using my sweatshirt as a pillow, I fell into a short, but restful, nap.

Feeling someone trip across my mat, I opened my eyes and noticed a cockroach moving in and out of its hiding place within inches of my face. I lay there quietly, watching it scamper about. I thought about what it must look like on the inside of the mat and wondered just how many others were in there. I laughed when I realized it was the cockroaches who made the funny noises I'd hear when holding my ear to the mat. I was no longer creeped out by our regular morning routine. We would stand in a row with the other inmates, picking broken cockroach legs out of each other's hair. No wonder the Lord didn't answer the prayer to keep them inside my mat. He knew it wasn't necessary. I had overcome yet another fear.

The Pretrial Detention Center had a well-deserved reputation for its living conditions. It was no place for the faint of heart. On one of my previous visits, I was met with filthy toilets whose contents spilled out onto the floor, leaving no place to step without encountering the putrefied sludge. The showers didn't work. Spoiled, unpalatable food was doled out in tablespoon-sized portions. Forcing inmates to live in these conditions infuriated me. No matter what they were arrested for, the women brought here should not be treated like animals. Not even the guards wanted to step foot into the stench of the Quad, leaving this place in undisciplined chaos. The hot, overcrowded conditions spurred on the hungry, thirsty, already angry women to violent fights. In a flash, they would be punching, kicking, scratching, biting, screaming, cussing, and pulling each other's hair like a scene out of a bar fight on TV.

I contacted my coworkers at Operation Rescue, giving them a vivid description of this vile place. Other rescuers joined me in writing letters to the appropriate authorities, spelling out our grievances. Several illiterate inmates sat near us, impressed by the speed with which we wrote, asking us to tell them what our letters said. We were glad to be a voice for them, especially in here. Our letters of protest produced an immediate response. Within one day, all our grievances were addressed. The restroom areas were hosed out and made clean, hot water returned to the showers, our dorms were sprayed for insects, and our food was nutritious and plentiful.

I was grateful Pretrial was cleaner than before, but the overhaul hadn't touched the turmoil and despair written across the faces of the women here now. Some managed to maintain their tough exteriors, but I could always catch a glimpse of someone crying. Recognizing some familiar faces, I walked over, asking if I could sit with them. I inquired about their children, having made a point to remember their names. Like all mothers, they talked about new teeth for their babies and first days of school for their older children. My heart broke for them.

"Thank you, Church Lady," they said as they gave me a hug, touched by my concern and prayers for their children.

Frieda was the inmate who needed love most. So tough and cruel, with anger and agony written over her face, she never let anyone come close. I touched her shoulder lightly as I walked past her, like so many times I had done before in other jails. This time, however, Frieda reached back and grabbed my hand, jerking me down in front of her, asking for a hug. Her large frame began shaking as her sobs increased. A deep, agonizing pain spilled out from her fractured heart. For the first time, she opened up and poured out an all-too-familiar story of neglect, abandonment, and abuse.

The women who had steered clear of this formidable, calloused woman now began to gather around. Curiosity on their faces, they circled to find a juicy tidbit of gossip to share. Their hearts softened when they saw my tears as I cried with her. Kneeling down next to her, they reached out to touch her, slowly, cautiously, to see how she would react. Frieda's stiffened body relaxed. Tears broke through the dam of pent-up emotions, held back over years. Her sobbing turned to loud wailing, and the room quieted in response.

Others stood and stared in her direction. I saw them nodding in agreement with her pain. I knew they were now reflecting on their own dreadful life experiences. A great anger grew in my heart for Satan and his accompanying evil. The evil that had invaded their lives, leaving destruction in its path, was always so evident here. My mind went outside the walls of the jail. Yes, evil displayed itself differently out there, but it was no less destructive than what I found in here.

Frieda wiped her tears and calmed her emotions. "I just want some peace in my life," she said.

I told her true peace, lasting peace, can only come from the Peacemaker Himself. For the first time since I had met her, Frieda welcomed the Lord's story of grace, mercy, and forgiveness. Many others joined in with her prayer as she trusted Christ as Lord and Savior. I laughed with joy, watching the woman who was once cold, hard, and unapproachable begin to freely give and receive hugs, perhaps for the first time in her life.

CHAPTER 11

Key Road Prison

Reunited with our men on the bus to Key Road Prison, we filled each other in on our experiences during our five-day stay at Pretrial and rejoiced over those inmates who trusted Christ.

As we neared the prison, Joe prayed, "Lord, use us to share the gospel. Please keep us encouraged and fortified for whatever awaits us now."

Guards separated us when we arrived, leading our men away to a different section of the prison. They handed out blue men's uniforms to all our women. I noticed the other women inmates wore cute, light-green pinstripe uniforms.

"Why do we have to wear these blue uniforms?" I asked our guard.

"Because you're political prisoners. Now shut up! Just be glad you came here and not the farm down south they have prepared for you. You don't want to go there. It's not fit for animals!"

Political prisoners?

Another guard frowned and told her to be quiet, as though she had let out a secret we were not supposed to know. "Move it, Black!" she yelled into my ear. "Find a cot and stay out of trouble!"

I had never met this guard before. *How did she know who I was?* Following her direction to find an empty cot, I walked into the open housing area. I was delighted to see so many inmates that I knew but felt sad that they had been arrested again for other offenses.

"The Church Ladies are here!" A few inmates jumped up and ran to greet us. "We knew they'd bring you here. We saw the news on TV. You were arrested for praying."

I had learned from Daddy that our arrests had received national coverage.

I surveyed the room and found two empty cots together near the windows. I had made a promise to our youngest rescuer that she could stay close to me. Dena was a pretty blonde from California, just nineteen years old. I knew her mother and felt responsible for her. Dena called me her "Jail Mom." I admired her godly attitude and pro-life commitment. We claimed the two cots as our own. Alongside each cot was a plastic milk crate, ideal for holding our street clothes, Bibles, and devotionals. Under the windows was a large empty area, perfect for our five rescue women to gather for Bible reading and prayer.

Calling out to the inmates over the noise, I invited whoever wanted to join us to come. I was surprised at the immediate response. So many women came over that we had to shove some cots away to make more room for them. We started by teaching them our favorite praise songs. As the women started singing and clapping their hands, even more joined in. Soon there was standing room only. Inmates who had been brought up in church raised their hands and their voices in praise to the Lord. When they prayed, they used great swelling words, mimicking what they had heard in church. Unfortunately, many of them had no knowledge of a personal Savior.

The next morning, much to our surprise, the guards led us outside into the crisp cold of February. We didn't mind. We were happy to visit with our men through a chain-link fence and breathe in the fresh air. As our men described their section of the prison, it was apparent that their living conditions were much different from ours. They had freedom to walk around the entire top floor, which included a recreation room, a lounge area with a TV, two pool tables, and a Ping-Pong table. They were allowed to play basketball, volleyball, and football outside. Gee whiz!

The guys got all the fun.

We filled our days with Bible studies and prayer, morning and night. On our third day in prison, all the missionary ladies were summoned to meet with Officer Branson in her office. She was a very pleasant guard, who began our meeting by letting us know how much she appreciated each one of us. She was particularly grateful for how we kept the girls quiet with our Bible study and prayer times.

"As a Christian myself, I respect you for the stand you are taking regarding abortion. I hate doing this, but I've been ordered to tell you that you are forbidden to meet for prayer anymore. If you continue, you will go to solitary confinement. I'm so sorry." Officer Branson was noticeably embarrassed and avoided eye contact with us as she spoke.

"We understand you're only doing your job," I said. "Do you realize we're in here because we were told we couldn't pray out there?"

She nodded. "Sorry."

"I'm sorry too, but I can't abide by that order. I know I can pray silently, but to be told that I can't pray publicly means that I have to pray now."

Before I could ask the others what they wanted to do as individuals, they all voiced their agreement. They also would go to solitary confinement before agreeing not to pray.

"I understand," Officer Branson said.

I guess we'll have to be Daniels in here too, I thought. A half-dozen girls had stood outside the door eavesdropping. They followed us down to our cots, spewing out stories of the terrible things that have happened in solitary confinement.

"They mean it. They'll put you in there," one inmate said.

"Only if God says so!" I said. "Besides, if He does, it will be for a good reason."

We ignored them and their horror stories as we prepared. We were told there was no heat. They wouldn't allow us to bring our sweatshirts, so we put them on under our uniforms. We shoved our toothbrushes and New Testaments into our pockets.

As I was preparing my belongings, a guard called me out to the visitation room. I was delighted to see Dan and Melissa sitting at a table with Joe Foreman. Our visit was brief. Dan and Melissa filled me in on news from home. I shared that the women were being threatened with solitary confinement if we continued to meet for prayer and learned our men also faced the same restrictions. Joe wondered if solitary confinement was as bad as everyone made it out to be.

All too quickly, the guard yelled, "Time's up!"

Melissa shoved yet another devotional into my hands. "Here, I almost forgot to give you this."

I hated seeing them walk away.

Back in the women's dorm, I went straight to our special corner and showed the other missionary ladies my newest devotional. "You know, we use one devotional in the morning and the other one at night," I said. "I think we should add a third time to meet at noontime and use this newest one."

The ladies all agreed. We sat down in our circle, and I turned to the first page. Instantly, we were joined by the usual crowd of inmates. As I began to read out loud, five male officers in full riot gear marched into the room. They stomped their army boots in an apparent effort to intimidate us. The room fell completely silent. Without looking up, I continued to read.

The officer in charge declared, "You've been forbidden to pray!"

"I'm not praying."

"Are you going to?"

"Well, I'm sure I will be praying..."

"Even though you have been told not to?"

"We don't mean to be disrespectful, sir, but as Christians, we can't stop praying because you tell us to."

Motioning to just the five of us, he continued, "If you insist on meeting for prayer, you will go to solitary confinement!"

Just then, one woman who had refused to join us before walked up with her hands on her hips.

"If you take them, you'll have to take all of us!"

Every woman in the room joined together in agreement. They would back us up. Those who sat on the floor stood up, folding their arms across their chests.

The officer in charge looked around at the defiant women and threatened, "We'll be back!"

The guards turned around and marched out.

"They'll be back with more guards, and next time they'll hurt you!" an inmate warned.

"Only if God says so!" I said and closed our meeting in prayer.

The next morning, I woke up sensing a shift in the spiritual atmosphere. I was soon to find out that a new guard had been assigned to our section. Officer Stanton was a large, angry woman and seemed to have it out for me immediately. She came over to my cot and warned me to stay away from her two girls, Clara and Mia. These two lifelong friends did everything together—including prostitution—and now they were in jail together with me, as new sisters in Christ whom I had led to the Lord the night before. Throughout the day, I spent time with these girls, encouraging them to make different decisions as they lived their new lives in Christ.

"Stay away from them!" she repeated. "And I don't want to catch you doing your Jesus thing around here with anybody else either!"

Sharing Christ was much like breathing for me, especially in this place, so I figured I would be in constant trouble with her.

Once we were alone, I asked the girls why Officer Stanton was so angry that they had gotten saved and learned that she was their pimp on the outside. She was afraid I would influence them to stop prostituting themselves. She was right to be afraid! From that moment on, whenever I spent time with Clara and Mia, Officer Stanton would try to undo everything I had taught them by teaching them how to use men and prostitute themselves without getting caught. In turn, I would meet with them and try to undo everything that she had taught.

The days went by, and I continued to encourage Clara and Mia in the Lord. One morning, Officer Stanton threatened to hurt me.

She leaned close and whispered that she could call me out and no one would ever know what happened to me. As she walked away, I muttered under my breath, "Only if God says so!"

Clara and Mia began to avoid me when she was around but would come to me in the evening with all their questions. They were afraid of her and didn't want to make more trouble for me. Even so, Officer Stanton found various ways to harass me. Every morning, she would come in with her massive ring of keys, banging them as loudly as possible on my metal headboard as she berated me. She watched me as I stood in line for the telephone for terribly long periods of time. When it was finally my turn, she would walk over and push the receiver down, laughing in my face.

Another day, Officer Stanton moved Frances to the cot directly across from me. Frances was a lesbian and a leader other inmates obeyed. While she may have thought this action would disturb my "delicate Christian feelings," I saw it as a great opportunity to reach Frances, who had been so aloof to me. Frances could have easily hurt me as she had done to others. She towered over me, outweighing me by a hundred pounds, but she never touched me. I would frequently catch Frances staring at me with a puzzled look on her face while she remained silent, distant, and unapproachable.

That night, Dena pulled the covers over her head and begged me to chase a woman out of Frances's bed. I walked over and assured Frances I was not against her, just the behavior. I told her about the Lord's great love for her and the special plans He had for her life. She stared at me, never saying a word. I said her *friend* had to leave and return to her own cot. Fances kept her eyes on me as she pulled the covers back and motioned for the woman to go. She left in a huff.

Night after night I would get up, walk over, and tell yet another girl to leave her bed. Because of Frances and her visitors, I was not getting much sleep.

After several weeks in jail, they would give us access to makeup and a small dressing table with a mirror. It was such a change from Pretrial. There we would use the color from M&M's candies as our eyeshadow, lipstick, and blush—and it was there that I learned how to make hair curlers out of toilet paper.

One morning, Ruby asked if she could braid my hair. Sitting down at the dressing table, she asked me for suggestions about how she could do her makeup differently.

"Maybe just tone it down a bit. You don't want to be mistaken for a prostitute."

"Girl, I *am* a prostitute!" she said.

"I'm so sorry. Do you enjoy your lifestyle?" I asked, immediately regretting my choice of words in my apology, as she began to describe in detail just how much she *did* enjoy it.

My heart was breaking for her. I couldn't hold back the tears, and Ruby began to comfort me. I conveyed to her my sincere desire that she learn to treasure the beauty that the Lord so generously gave her. I explained how tremendously valuable she was to the Lord and how He had special, unique plans for her life.

With my hair only half braided, she took me by the hand and walked me over to her cot. Sitting me down, she sat on the floor at my feet and asked me to tell her more. An hour later, Ruby trusted Christ.

She walked over to the sink and washed off both her tears and her overdone makeup. "Only Jesus could wash the inside of me, but I can wash the outside."

She was glowing. I was able to see just how beautiful she was.

Ruby paused as a new thought came to her. "I have training as a bookkeeper," she said. "That's what I'll do from now on."

To my surprise, at that very moment, she was called to the office to check out. I didn't know that this was her day to be released. With a hug and a thank-you, she was gone.

Officer Stanton stomped over, then stood in front of me with her hands on her hips. She had caught me doing the unthinkable—again—of leading someone to the Lord. She pulled me by my one and only braid toward the day room and told me to stand. I wasn't allowed to sit down all day. This punishment of standing up was much better than my previous punishment of sitting, because the round metal seats had two large bolts that really hurt.

"And don't lean on the wall!" she said, then left the area.

Pulling out my braid and thanking the Lord for Ruby, I looked over at the large bookcase along the wall. There was a stack of books, magazines and old newspapers strewn about in a mess. Thankful for something to do, I walked over and busied myself straightening up the bookcase. I pulled everything off the shelves and onto the table. Then I found it—a journal that I had written during one of my previous visits to Pretrial. It had been stolen from me there, along with the special socks Melissa bought for me. I had been praying that the Lord would somehow bring these items back to me. The journal contained details about the events of a prior arrest as well as all the names and stories of the women I met at Pretrial. Someone had made a blue cover for it out of construction paper with these words written across the front: "For Everyone—Do Not Remove!"

"It's my journal! I can't believe it!" I was so excited to finally find my journal, I couldn't help but yell.

"It's not yours," one girl said. "It belongs to all of us!"

Unable to convince her the journal was mine, I shared some thoughts I had written, but she wasn't satisfied. As others looked on, she read some of my words back to me, making me write them down to compare my handwriting with the journal entry. Reluctantly, she agreed that it was mine. Some of the other girls said they had fun reading it because they knew most of the girls in the journal. They read it out loud to the women who couldn't read. It made them both laugh and cry.

Tired from standing most of the day, I was relieved that my punishment was over. I returned to my cot and dropped down hard. I huddled under the blankets, attempting to keep the cold wind and rain that blew in through the broken window off me. No wonder the cots had been removed from the large area next to my bed. Fewer and fewer women were joining us now for Bible studies, due to the puddles of rainwater in our meeting area. Only the serious ones would attend. I wished we didn't have to have our evening Bible study later. I didn't feel like sitting on the cold, wet floor. I pulled the blanket over my head, hoping to dull some of the noise. Both the volume and pitch of the ever-present shouting seemed especially irritating today. And the cussing. Always the cussing. I was horrified at the fact that sometimes I caught myself repeating the words in my head. I was scared that they might actually come out of my mouth someday.

My nightly surveillance with Frances and her friends, coupled with shaking all night from the wind and rain blowing on me, resulted in a severe lack of sleep that left me feeling less able to cope with the stress. With Officer Stanton's daily harassment and homesickness hovering over me, I began to feel a bit down. I couldn't help but think of my mother. I had learned from Daddy that she was in the hospital with a collapsed lung. The doctor said I should probably bond out and come home.

Ever since I was a child, there were many times when the doctors would say, "This is it." Every time, however, she pulled through. I prayed and felt confident she was going to be okay. I needed to stay where I was, even though my children weighed heavy on my heart. I missed them so much, sometimes it felt like the weight of the pain was going to crush me. I knew I could end the pain by simply getting on a plane and leaving Atlanta for good. Instead, I had to intentionally place them on the altar afresh each day. I remembered a saying that when God wants to do an impossible task, He takes an impossible person and crushes him. Relief would come only when I would focus on the awesome fact that the King thought me worthy to serve Him. Perhaps He could use me then. Amazing!

I only intended to rest a bit on my cot, but instead, I fell sound asleep.

Officer Stanton's keys pounded on my metal bedframe, jerking me awake. It was morning, and she was back. Shaking the keys at me, she taunted me with the fact that she was the key holder, able to come and go as she pleased.

"You're stuck, Black. You couldn't leave if you wanted to. How does it feel to be in prison, unable to leave this place—huh, Black?"

I smiled at her, pretending that I was unaffected by her words. I wasn't about to let her know she was really getting to me. I started to get up, but she yelled at me to stay put until she told me I could get up. I looked around the room. Almost everyone else had left. I was very uncomfortable being with her by myself. I had seen her hurt a girl's wrist when she wouldn't pick up a Styrofoam cup fast enough.

I heard her footsteps leave the area. I stayed in my cot, feeling overwhelmed by the need to be with my children—to touch them, to hear their voices. Knowing Officer Stanton wouldn't even let me call them made me feel truly confined and bound. I asked the Lord to please give me some encouragement.

I looked up and saw a small bird flying outside the rows of tall, dirty windows. With great ease, it flew high into the air, then swooped down through the razor wire on the top of the wall. It flew through the broken window and torn screen, as well as the bars on the window right in front of me, then flew around inside the room and landed on the foot of my bed. It looked at me, cocked its head, and took off fluttering around the room again.

Leaning up on my elbows, I watched it head for the outside, once again making its way through the bars, screen, and broken window. Skillfully maneuvering through the razor wire, it rose high in the sky, soaring around with ease as if showing off for its audience of one. Then, with greater speed than before, it took the same path through the potentially dangerous obstacles. Making its way inside, it flew around my head, again stopping and standing on my footboard before returning to the outside.

For the third time, the bird flew back inside, circled the room, and rested once more on the foot of my cot. It began flapping its wings rapidly and chirping loudly. Cocking its head, it looked at me as if to say, "Do you understand what I am trying to tell you?"

"Yes! I understand!" I said, laughing out loud. I fully believe that this bird was sent by the Lord to show me what I already knew. Officer

Stanton was the one bound and imprisoned. My spirit was free in Christ, and no one could take that from me unless I willingly relinquished it. I remembered my experience with the shackles in Grady Hospital. *Thank You so much for yet another lesson, Lord,* I prayed. *Please don't let me pick up any new shackles. Instead, help me to cling tightly to the joy that comes from You.*

I shouted out loud, "My body is imprisoned, but my spirit is free!"

"Shut up, Black, and get up!"

I jumped at the sound of Officer Stanton's voice.

"You've got laundry duty all day!"

Ignoring the unpleasant aroma of the men's dirty clothes, I welcomed the heat from the massive dryers. It had been a long time since I had felt warm. I started the task of folding the first of many mountains of white clothes. Then I saw it, lying right on top—one of the special socks Melissa had given to me. This pair of long knee-highs had a hidden pocket on the inside of one of them. I'd used the socks to smuggle much-needed lip gloss into jail many times. There seemed to be only one sock in the pile, but it was the one with the hidden pocket. Now a dingy gray, it was right in front of me.

I jumped up and down and laughed out loud. Officer Stanton thought she was punishing me by sending me to the day room, where I found the journal. She thought she was punishing me with laundry duty, where I found the missing sock. If she hadn't felt the need to punish me, I wouldn't have discovered these answers to prayer. That evening, my sock joined my journal in the ever-increasing stash of items in my milk crate.

The Lord used what Officer Stanton meant for my discouragement and He turned it into a blessing for me. During this time in Key Road Prison, He showed Himself faithful, keeping me safe during many potentially dangerous circumstances.

One morning, I woke up at four to take my shower away from the others. As the spray washed over me, I realized I was not alone. Three women stood side by side, looking me up and down. As they started toward me, suddenly a huge figure appeared between us, facing the inmates with arms stretched out wide. Even with water in my eyes, there was no mistaking the look of terror on their faces. Another blink and the women were gone. Was it an angel? I don't know for sure, but I thanked the Lord for rescuing me.

He showed Himself faithful in the little things too. One morning, I wished I had a Walkman and a praise tape. Later that day, Melissa came for a visit, bringing me books, some curlers I'd requested—and a Walkman with a praise tape! He gave me my heart's desires before I even formed them into words. *God, You are so good!*

How I needed that encouragement during the times gloom settled over the women. One evening, a girl tried to hang herself and was taken to the hospital. The women were upset, talking with each other and wondering if she would have gone to heaven or not had she died. These women who were usually closed down and uninterested in spiritual things were now openly discussing eternity, and I told them how they could be sure where they would spend eternity. They knew I didn't trust jailhouse religion, as the decision to follow Christ was serious and meant giving oneself over completely to Him. As I was explaining the importance of this decision, one inmate interrupted me.

"I *am* dead serious! I want Jesus and a new life *now*!" she said.

I choked back my tears, overwhelmed with joy because the one who spoke these words loud and clear was my very own Frances! I sat in amazement at how the Lord never seems to tire of redeeming us and our rebellious lives. He turned one suicide attempt into an opportunity to bring new life for another.

Night after night, Frances continued to keep me from getting sleep. This once aloof, former lesbian woman wouldn't stop talking and asking me spiritual questions for hours on end. Now I was the one who would sit and stare at her. My heart was filled with thankfulness to the Lord. How great Thou art and greatly to be praised!

During my stay at Key Road Prison, I decided to change my life verse to Philippians 3:10: "That I may know Him and the power of His resurrection, and the fellowship of His sufferings, being conformed to His death." I hoped I wouldn't regret claiming this verse or try to run from its truth someday. My heart's prayer was that He would make me beautiful for Him.

Nearly three weeks had passed since we first knelt on the sidewalk praying at Fem Center, and our court date finally arrived. Before we left, I took time to walk around, fixing faces and names into my memory. I knew I would miss many of these women. I hoped to never see them again—at least not in another prison somewhere.

As we said our goodbyes, there were many hugs and tears for each of us. We were especially touched as the women crowded into the day room and sang their favorite chorus to us.

As the door was closing behind us, a woman yelled out, "We'll never forget you!"

On the bus on the way back to court, we wondered if they would require us to serve the one-year sentence they'd threatened us with. Joe prayed for wisdom for Jay Sekulow as he represented us and for the Lord to join us there.

When I leaned down to pick up my Bible that had fallen off the seat, I realized the journal was missing again. I shook my head, wondering who took it *this* time. I prayed it would be a continuing source of laughter and encouragement to the women we left behind.

Our bus pulled up to the courthouse, and we were ushered directly inside. Our arrest had been covered by both secular and Christian television nationwide. People came from surrounding states, packing out the courtroom. Many had to go upstairs to an overflow room.

When the proceedings began, the district attorney asked the police officers to identify the people they arrested, but the officers had difficulty doing so. The judge allowed them to go outside in the hall to look at the pictures they took of us that day, but they returned to the courtroom even more confused, giving conflicting testimonies.

The judge turned to Officer Summers. "Tell me, sir, in your professional opinion, just what these people were doing."

"Praying, Your Honor."

Jay demanded the video be shown. The judge appeared to be upset as he watched the footage.

He turned to address the prosecutor. "I hope you have more than this! It's the police who are blocking the sidewalk."

Jay questioned the prosecutor too. "How could you let these people stay in jail when you knew they did nothing wrong?"

The prosecutor didn't respond.

The judge was visibly angry that we had been held in jail for a prolonged time and that these police officers blatantly gave false testimony contradicting the video footage. "They were peaceful, they were on the sidewalk, and their demonstration was constitutionally protected. It was the police who were blocking the sidewalk!"

A cheer went up in the courtroom when he dismissed all charges against us.

The judge turned to the prosecutor with one final question. "What did you learn today?"

The prosecutor was shaken. He tried to explain how hard he worked to prepare the case against us.

"When your battleship is sinking, don't try to fight it with water wings," the judge said. "You weren't even close."

I looked behind me and saw Dan smiling, towering above the crowd.

Giving me a hug, he said, "Come on. Melissa and the kids are waiting for you at home." On the way home, Dan drove by Fem Center, the place of my arrest. Suddenly, my throat was sore, and within seconds, my whole body ached. My head was pounding. By the time we got home, my ears hurt too. Melissa took my temperature. I had a fever of 102 degrees.

I know that I know the Lord supernaturally lifted the severe flu symptoms I had the day of my arrest. Now that I was instantly sick again at the precise location where it lifted, I was further convinced of

His great power. He can do whatever He wants, whenever He wants to, and in whatever way He wants to! I don't usually rejoice at being sick, but this time I was praising Him, for indeed my faith was increased due to the flu coming back.

I thought about Mom, who had been released from the hospital. Multiple Sclerosis is no more difficult for Him than the flu. Surely, her cure will come, but "Only if God says so!" Praise God!

As evening came, my sore throat and aching ears prevented sleep. I reflected on the events of the court that morning. I was grateful for the Lord's deliverance, but I was troubled by some comments I had heard. Many who came to support us during the trial were patting us on our backs. They called us heroes, thanking us for standing up for what is right. Others, referring to our pro-life activities, thanked us for our tenacity to our cause. These well-meaning people made me wonder. Do they think that we are doing what we are doing because we are merely committed to a cause?

Lord, help me to always follow You, my Hero, the One Who rules the universe, and not just simply be committed to our cause. Please help me to demonstrate tenacity in serving You, my perfect Hero.

CHAPTER 12

Blessed Beyond Measure

Kimmy was arriving for an eighteen-day visit! She had asked to come, but I didn't have the money for her flight. Without my knowing it, Dan mentioned our need to a gentleman I had briefly met after church one day. Mr. Mercer was one of the nicest men I had ever met. I was delighted and surprised when I learned he had mailed a ticket to Kim. I hoped she would be able to meet him while she was here.

I rushed through the crowded terminal and approached her arrival gate. I could hardly contain my excitement when I saw her—all tan and beautiful, with new blond highlights and two earrings in each ear. I relished the warmth of her hug as she begged for air. Nearly crushing her in my arms, I didn't want to let go.

"Mom, do you know what day this is?"

"A fantastic one!"

"Mom, today is March fifteenth. Exactly three months to the day since you left California." Her face had a sweetly perfect "I told you so" look. She had prayed that the Lord would allow us to see each other every three months, and now she was here.

"Oh my goodness, yes! Thank You, Lord, for answering her prayer!" I yelled out loud.

I stopped abruptly and stood still as the realization of what had just transpired sank in. I had completely forgotten about Kimmy's prayer. When He asked if I would be willing to never see my children again, He already knew He was not going to require it of me. My heart swelled with love for the Lord when I realized what He had done.

Kim wanted to be a part of everything I did. She joined me and the other missionaries early the very next morning at Fem Center for prayer. They were all glad to meet her since they had been praying for her and Jeromy every day. Next, we went to Surgi Center to sidewalk counsel. My heart sank at the thought of my sweet daughter having to go through the experiences I knew were waiting.

After warning her about the clinic escorts, I gave her the option to stay in the car. Kim assured me she was a big girl, reminding me as she stepped out onto the sidewalk, that it was nothing compared to what happens to the babies. With a collected surge of demented energy, the clinic escorts surrounded their newest victim. As they spewed out their vile filth at my precious daughter, I was pierced to my very soul. Sensing my anguish, Kim stood tall and smiled at me, mouthing words for my comfort. *It's okay.*

We moved on to the nearest MARTA station, and I watched as she enthusiastically passed out pro-life literature to those stepping off the trains. Late in the afternoon, we went to court in support of our fellow rescuers. The judge punished them with unreasonable sentences for saving children.

The evening ended with us kneeling in the dark in front of Midtown Hospital. Once a children's hospital, it was now a place where women from all over the United States came to terminate their late-term pregnancies, even when fully nine months pregnant. No wonder Atlanta was known as the City of Blood! The front of the building looked much like a Southern mansion, complete with large white pillars on the front porch. It was nothing more than a facade covering the ugly three-story brick building behind it and the grotesque activity hidden within its walls.

I thought about the first prayer vigil I attended at Midtown. I had prayed the Lord would either turn it into a maternity home someday or that He would take it apart, brick by ugly brick.

As the days went on, Kim and I cried together, trying to intervene for the little ones on the sidewalks of numerous clinics downtown. I watched her come to a fuller understanding that these were indeed places of child sacrifice.

One day, she shared a realization with me. "Mom, before you left California, I was concerned you might get killed out here. After seeing how the Lord is blessing you and protecting you, I believe it will happen—as you always say—*only if God says so!*"

Even though her experiences here were difficult, she was glad to be a part of our activities. It made her more certain than ever that I was exactly where I was supposed to be, in the center of God's will.

I came to a greater understanding also. I realized why it was necessary for me to be fighting this battle here and not in California, near her. I simply could not have done what I had been doing while at home. Each day since she arrived and joined us for all the pro-life activities, I was under constant stress. I feared that one of us would be arrested and separated and not able to spend this special time together. I realized that in California, I wouldn't have the freedom to make myself completely and unreservedly available for the Lord's service.

Here, I could truly say each morning, "Here I am, Lord, use me."

I was glad that I had scheduled fun activities for Kim as well during her stay. We spent hours laughing and enjoying each other's company. While at the Duffys', Meghan set and combed Kim's hair relentlessly, with Brian trying to get as much attention from her as possible. They always raced to see who could sit the closest to her on the couch or at the table. They finally agreed to one on each side.

With her visit drawing to a close, I dreaded the thought of yet another goodbye. Taking her back to the airport became a family affair. Meghan and Brian clung to her and cried so badly that consoling them was a great distraction for me. To calm them down, Kim bought them each chocolate ice cream cones. Now that she knew where I lived and who I was living with, she was able to picture me in the surroundings the Lord had prepared. She felt that the Duffys were now her family too, and she couldn't wait to come back.

As she walked toward the gate to board the plane, she looked back, threw kisses, and in her best Southern accent said, "See y'all in three months!"

This time, she was the one sitting on the plane, and I was the one standing in the terminal window watching her leave. I waved until I could no longer see her. Swallowing hard and wiping away my tears, I looked down and saw that Brian's ice cream cone had dripped all over my shoes. Then I noticed that he had left a perfect chocolate ice cream kiss on the window. This six-year-old boy thought it was hilarious. I thanked the Lord for Brian's contagious laughter. It eased the ache in my heart and the lump in my throat.

I glanced back toward her departed plane. Accompanying the pain of my sweet daughter's farewell was a comforting certainty. I knew the Lord would be faithful to answer Kim's prayer. I was confident I would see her beautiful face again in three months.

The horizons of my life now opened to things I never dreamed possible, with great richness pressed into my soul. I could barely recall my once narrow existence.

The number of missionaries from the third and fourth wave of rescuers diminished considerably, as they arrived in ripples rather than waves. Each one carried new energy, hope, and vision, and their enthusiasm for sharing Christ was just as mighty. Although rejected at the abortion clinics, their love for the Lord and others was eagerly received in jail. Even the guards at Pretrial welcomed us warmly. One guard completely changed her mind about Operation Rescue.

Another male guard had been watching us, knowing our Jesus was the difference between us and other inmates.

A female officer knelt down on my mat, hoping I would be back soon as she confided in me, "I know I can trust you to speak the exact words that will convince me to have this baby and not an abortion."

God gave me the words, and she chose life.

Almost all the guards, male and female, helped me now whenever I was detained in Pretrial. They repeatedly sought me out and placed me alone in cells with pregnant women who had scheduled abortions. Every woman responded and chose life—whether it took fifteen minutes or four hours. The Lord used those guards, who always put me in a cell with a telephone. I made countless calls for someone to bond the pregnant women out and get them the help they needed.

I was grateful I no longer had to pick the locks between the quads to meet with inmates in need. It first began when Sarah, one inmate with me in Quad B, had been crying over her friend, Adrianna, who was locked up in Quad A. Adrianna was seven months pregnant and was scheduled for an abortion at Midtown Hospital the next morning. Sarah insisted her friend really didn't want the abortion, but she didn't have anyone to help her with the baby. Frantically, she begged me to talk to her. I was more than willing to speak with Adrianna and arrange help for her.

There was one problem, however. A big steel door in the wall separated the quads. The only way through was if someone picked the lock. Sarah suggested that one of the inmates could show me how to do it.

"Pick the lock? I could so get in trouble for that! Why don't *you* learn how to pick the lock?"

"Oh no, I couldn't stand going to solitary confinement!"

Hmmm, here's another opportunity for solitary confinement and peace and quiet, I thought.

Picking the lock was necessary if I was to have the chance to save this child's life. Asking a guard to let me go over there was out of the question. The guard on duty that day refused to answer even simple questions, turning her back to us.

It was difficult for me when I first joined Operation Rescue. Breaking the rules was something that I found almost impossible to do. And yet, by using civil disobedience, I was able to rescue and save children numerous times.

A group of girls taught me how to pick the lock. I encouraged them to do it for me, but they refused. Using a smuggled-in hairpin,

I was frustrated with each failed attempt and ready to give up. I was surprised when the lock finally turned. As if I was some authority around there, I told the girls not to let anyone in or out. I imagined all kinds of chaos breaking out.

With one inmate as my lookout, I stepped into Quad A and quickly made my way to Adrianna, who was heavily pregnant. I sat down on her mat with her, sharing the help available to her. I showed her pro-life literature that described the reality of both early- and late-term abortions.

She was disturbed by the pictures but was still not convinced she wanted the baby. I discovered that Adrianna was more in favor of abortion than Sarah realized. Convincing her to have her child proved difficult, even with the promise that with one phone call, I could connect her with someone to bond her out of jail. Before I could finish talking to her, my lookout whistled, warning me that the guard was returning. I left the pro-life literature with her, along with the name and number of someone she could call for help.

The next morning, a guard called out my name to release me from jail. While I was standing in line out in the hall, I heard knocking on the thick window of Quad A. Adrianna stood there, holding up the pictures of the aborted babies. She pointed to them and shook her head: "No." Then she folded her arms in front of her and rocked an invisible baby back and forth, nodding her head: "Yes."

I smiled and thanked the Holy Spirit for the work He had done on her heart during the night.

On my return to Pretrial a few weeks later, I picked the lock to Quad A repeatedly. One time I didn't make it back to my Quad quick enough, and the door closed on me during roll call. When there was one too many inmates in Quad A, and one inmate missing in Quad B, I fessed up. But darn it, *still* no solitary confinement! The guards simply told me to let them know when I needed to talk to someone next door.

A new pattern emerged in the way I was treated by the jails, courts, and even the police. It was different from the way they responded to other rescuers. I would go to the same clinics with the other missionaries and get arrested with them. Sometimes I would be held with them, but more often I would be the only one released—even though I never paid a fine or bond. On three occasions, I was the only one who did not receive a date for arraignment. When I inquired about my arraignment, the officer said there wasn't any record of my arrest.

After one rescue at Surgi Center, I was the only one left sitting in front of the door. The police had arrested everyone else and placed them in the paddy wagon.

I didn't want to be out by myself again, so I yelled, "Hey, what about me?"

The police ignored me, and both paddy wagon and a squad car pulled away.

At another gathering, the opposite happened. A police car pulled up while we were picketing. I didn't recognize the officer. He told me I was needed in jail. He took me by the elbow and put me in the front seat of the car, leaving everyone else on the sidewalk. I looked back and saw my fellow rescuers continue to picket as if nothing had happened. I wondered if they even saw me leave.

The officer bought me a hamburger and Coke at the McDonald's drive-through after I mentioned I was hungry. Refusing to answer my questions, he pulled up to the back door of Pretrial. He again took my elbow and walked me down the hall and directly into a cell with a pregnant woman.

"She's scheduled for Midtown tomorrow," he said, then closed the door.

Nancy was immediately relieved that someone cared. She believed me when I shared that there was help available and burst into tears, thanking me. She hadn't wanted the abortion. She had begged the Lord to send someone to help her.

Handing me a quarter, she asked me to please call the people who would help her. I have always been frustrated because my brain usually seems unable to retain or recall names and numbers. At that moment, however, I had complete recall of the telephone number of a pastor and his wife. They had stopped by the clinic just the day before to introduce themselves. They said to call them for anything, at any time.

As I started dialing the phone, I was amazed. Me? Remember a telephone number I only glanced at once? Now that was God!

I gave Nancy a hug and pounded on the thick, heavy door. When the same officer opened it, I said, "Mission accomplished!"

With a nod, he turned around, leaving her door completely open. "Follow me."

I walked behind him. Glancing back, I saw Nancy sticking her head out of the still opened door. She saw me and shrugged. I said hi to a couple of guards I knew who were ordinarily very friendly. They just looked right through me. I swear I was invisible or something.

On the drive back to the clinic, the officer was totally silent. I kept glancing sideways at him because he looked like he had makeup on his face and hands. I had never seen him before, but I sure remembered seeing that makeup! When he dropped me off at Surgi, the rest of the rescuers were still there. They never even saw me leave, but they certainly saw the stack of hamburgers the officer brought for them!

The first time I encountered officers who looked like they were wearing makeup was also at Surgi Center, a few weeks earlier. As I was sitting on the front steps during a rescue, a young woman couldn't get past us. She began crying and backed away. After a few minutes, she motioned to me and asked me if she could talk to me. She turned and walked up the hill toward her car. I followed her to the parking lot, hoping she would listen to me and choose life for her child.

She had already changed her mind. "You all were willing to get arrested for protecting my baby. I'm its mother. I need to protect it," she said. She just wanted to hug one of us to say thank you.

As I walked back down the sidewalk to rejoin the rescuers, the paddy wagon passed me going up the hill. Everyone else was arrested, and I was out by myself again! In front of the entrance to Surgi, three officers stood between me and the front door, fixated on the clipboards in their hands. They looked completely out of place, as it seemed they were pretending to write on their clipboards. I didn't recognize them, and never had I seen an officer with a clipboard before. Even stranger was their appearance. It appeared they had heavy makeup on their faces and hands. I moved toward one of them to look closer at his face, but he slowly turned his back to me.

When the large group of men on the porch—those who had been taunting us during the rescue, spewing out their vile contempt for us—now saw that I was the only one left, their harassment intensified, as would be expected of a bunch of bullies. I didn't mind the names they called me and the things they said they would like to do to me. Obscene profanities flew out of their mouths as they described their unborn children as useless mistakes. They laughed about all the other ones they had already gotten rid of. One hoped for the baby's mother to die in there too. A wave of grief from the Lord came over me. He not only loved and died for these children but also for their mothers and, yes, for each one of these men as well.

One man pointed up to heaven and mocked. "Even your #%&@# God couldn't love my #%&@# woman and #%&@# kid!"

That was when I lost it! With volume I didn't know I had, I yelled at them, saying they didn't have the right to call themselves men. They were all overgrown bullies, cowards, and weasels. They just laughed. I looked at the police officers, expecting them to tell me to be quiet and get off the property. Instead, they made an obvious point of moving out of my way, still looking down at their clipboards. Their response was strange and totally out of character for the police.

Clearly trespassing, I marched toward the front porch and started up the stairs. I had no idea what I thought I was doing getting in the faces of nine angry men, but there I was, filled with an awareness of the Lord's empowering presence that caused my fear to evaporate. As soon as I was face to face with the largest, loudest man, I burst into tears. When I looked into his eyes, I saw a child. Not a big, bearded, foul-mouthed coward, but a little boy. A boy probably neglected by his own father, knowing nothing about how to be a man.

I thought my heart was going to burst inside me. I began to sob. I said I was sorry—sorry they didn't know how special they could be as men, protecting women and unborn children. I was sorry for the neglect and abuse they received as children themselves. They just stood there in silence, staring at me. Some began to tear up. Others apologized for the things they said to me. I told them about the Lord's desperate love for them, as well as their children and their children's mothers. The tallest one, with his hands still in his pockets, began hitting his forehead on the side of the building several times.

Instinctively, I turned to my right and made eye contact with one man. "You need to go in and bring her out. She needs a hero and so does your son," I said.

Without making any attempt to wipe away his tears, he immediately went inside. Another one followed quickly behind him. Two other men walked off the porch and up the sidewalk. One leaned over the railing and stared at the ground. The tall one was still resting his head on the side of the building. He was now sobbing. The rest sat on the stairs with their heads in their hands.

I told them of God's forgiveness for even something as horrible as abortion and about His great love and sacrifice that purchased heaven for them. I told them they could agree in prayer with me if they wanted that forgiveness and salvation. As I prayed aloud, they mumbled in agreement. When I finished, they all hugged me. I told them it was time to go in and bring their women and children out.

As they started for the door, I looked for the police, but they were gone. I never heard a car or a motorcycle leave. That was so odd. I walked toward the building across the street but was stopped by the sound of a woman's voice.

"Wait!"

I turned in the direction of her voice and was nearly knocked over as she threw her arms around me.

"Thank you, thank you, thank you!"

Standing behind her was the first man I had encouraged to go in and be a hero to her and his son. He was beaming with joy. We stood in the middle of the street as he hugged me as well. All lanes of traffic on the one-way street had stopped to watch us, and not one person even honked the horn! As we went to separate sides of the road, I yelled out one last question for him.

"Did you see where those police officers went?"

"What police?"

"You know, the ones who were standing out front?"

With an "I don't know what you're talking about" look on his face, he shrugged and walked away.

I was confused. If the police officers had really been angels, they shouldn't need makeup. Who were they? I will always wonder about them.

CHAPTER 13

A Shift in Direction

Exactly three months had passed since Kim's first visit. Now she was back, just as the Lord had promised. Kim picked up where she left off, jumping in to help our efforts. She joined Youth for America, a group of young people who had planned three days of pro-life activities. Joe's wife, Ann Foreman, assisted the group as they picketed, engaged in sidewalk counseling, and organized rallies in the evening.

Bravely, they decided to rescue at Northside Women's Clinic in Chamblee. When the police started moving four and five young people at a time, some adults joined in to help them hold the door. Before the women arrived for their abortions, over thirty adults had been removed with the young people.

I was careful to stay down the hill and out of trouble. I was on probation in that town for two previous arrests at this clinic. As the first woman drove up for her appointment, Kim ran over and knelt down in the driveway in front of the oncoming car. With my heart in my throat, I frantically ran to the car and counseled the woman. As I turned back around, I saw the police carrying Kimmy away. It hurt my heart to see her arms bent backward over her head.

Then they pointed at me. "Take her too!"

The officers placed me in the paddy wagon with Kim.

"Kim, kneeling in front of that car was so dangerous. What made you do that?"

"I *had* to, Mom," she said.

Big tears filled her eyes. If only we all understood the urgent need to intervene for a child about to be brutally murdered. I drew on Kim's courage that day, and it has since enabled me to have more boldness. We later found out that the woman in that car decided to have her baby.

As I sat in custody with my daughter that day, I praised the Lord for the opportunity of sharing in a rescue with Kim, rather than going to the mall as we had planned. Our day was better and far more productive when we joined others to save babies.

The court released all the minors involved in the rescue to their parents. Kim had turned seventeen just days before the arrest. She was scheduled to be tried as an adult according to the laws of the state of Georgia. She seemed unconcerned about serving time in jail. She needed, however, to return home in time to begin her senior year of school.

My arrest violated my probation, as well as the hundred-foot restriction I was under when I ran to the car. In addition, I was sentenced for time which I had not yet served. I braced myself for the repercussions.

In court, Police Chief Reed Miller stood up and recommended that all thirty-six cases be dead-docketed. We were all free to go. What a mighty God we serve!

I prayed what God imparted to Kim that day would be carried with her throughout her life, encouraging her to serve Him in a great and wonderful way. Imagine my pride when I later saw her picture in *The Advocate* magazine, sitting at the door of that Chamblee clinic.

Too soon, it was time for her to return home.

Two new rescuers arrived to join our efforts in the last month. This month, the wave/ripple brought in only one, an elderly gentleman named John. I affectionately called him the "drip." The first wave of rescuers remained in Fulton County Jail serving their time, while those from later waves were released from other jails.

A SHIFT IN DIRECTION

The demanding schedule and high levels of stress were wearing me out. Another rescue was planned at Surgi Center for the morning. I had to drag myself out of bed. I sat with the other rescuers on the steps of the clinic, then got up to counsel the women as they arrived. The group suggested I go up to the parking lot to meet each woman, giving me more time to talk to the women as they made their way down the sidewalk to the clinic. When we reached the clinic, I would sit on the stairs with our group again. Every time a new car arrived, I made my way up the hill toward the parking lot. I didn't feel well. My legs felt like lead, my chest felt tight, and my throat was sore again.

While speaking with a young lady in her parked car, I was distracted by the sound of persistent honking. This time it was the police, honking and waving at me from the paddy wagon. They took everyone else away and left me alone, even though they could clearly see I was trespassing. I was out by myself *again*. Wow—that was fast!

I collapsed in the parking lot. Several people who were nearby for prayer support took me to the doctor. Seven months of nonstop stress and sixteen-plus-hour days had taken its toll on me. The doctor said the Lord rescued me this time because there was no way I could be this sick in jail. I would have ended up back at Grady Hospital.

Blood tests confirmed the doctor's suspicions. I had a relapse of an old case of mononucleosis. He ordered me to complete bed rest and made it abundantly clear that I was to go to bed immediately. He didn't want me having visitors or talking to anyone—absolutely no activity allowed. If I didn't abide by his orders, he would put me in the hospital. I really couldn't argue with him. I was so weak I could barely lift my head off the pillow.

As I lay in bed recovering, I was encouraged by a flood of get-well cards. Flowers arrived from friends and people from all over the United States I'd never met. I appreciated everyone's concern for me. I felt their prayers and received their encouragement to return to the battle when I was well. I received letters from the missionaries in jail as well—letters bursting with stories about both babies and souls saved in the prisons across Atlanta. A revival was sweeping the jails as the Lord made warriors out of His small army of saints behind those bars.

While confined to my bed, I watched television news reports about rescue activities all over the nation. Pro-lifers were joining in ever-increasing numbers to sit and peacefully pray at abortion clinics. News of over eighty thousand Christians arrested in America reached Europe. Shortly after, Scotland, France, Great Britain, and Holland joined the battle. Soon, Christians in other countries such as Canada, Mexico, and Brazil began rescuing as well.

Countering our progress, I heard rumors that the Chicago Janes were considering organizing again. Active from 1969 to 1973, this group of Chicago women started as an underground abortion referral service run by a university student. Rather than give her own name when contacting a pregnant woman, she would leave a message using the name "Jane."

Trained by illegal abortionists, the Janes realized these abortionists were not doctors as they thought but laymen. If laymen could provide illegal abortions, so could they. The Janes performed dilation and curettage abortions on babies up to fifteen weeks gestation. After fifteen weeks, they induced labor by using an illegal chemical paste that separated the placenta from the wall of the uterus or by piercing the amniotic sac. In four years, it was estimated between eleven to thirteen thousand abortions were performed by nearly 120 women who worked under the constant threat of arrest. Despite their efforts to remain secret, seven women were arrested in 1972 in a Hyde Park high-rise apartment they rented to perform abortions. The charges were dropped when the Supreme Court legalized abortion in 1973. Once again, women were now coming forward, wanting to be trained as Janes.

The effects of rescue reverberated through states, countries, hearts, and homes as many were touched with the need to stand up and be a voice for the voiceless, causing these women to become fearful that abortion would once again become illegal.

Another oppositional group arose at the beginning of the Rescue Movement, filled with pastors in the church who twisted Scripture to defend their attacks on us. Playing directly into Satan's hands, they fell prey to his old, effective strategy of conquering and dividing within—or at least, they tried. No one touched by God through their experiences with rescue could ever be swayed by their opposition. We realized that even those in the church could be bound by darkness. We would never again be concerned about the opinions of men. Although Satan wanted to stir up anger and retaliation in us, instead, we were moved by pity and love.

I listened to pastor after pastor publicly denounce Operation Rescue as violent, rebellious, and ungodly. They distanced themselves from us, ensuring that everyone knew their opposition to our practices. Many encouraged the judges of the land to punish us severely "for bringing shame to the name of Christ." I was concerned for them. We are all free to disagree with brothers and sisters in the Lord, but to come against us publicly, exposing us to ridicule and persecution, is something altogether different.

Leaders in this group accused Operation Rescue of making up the phrase *civil disobedience*, stating we had no respect for the law. What about Martin Luther King Jr.? He was arrested many times for civil disobedience.

He once said, "An individual who breaks a law that conscience tells him is unjust, and who willingly accepts the penalty of imprisonment in order to arouse the conscience of the community over its injustice, is, in reality, expressing the highest respect for the law."

Operation Rescue, however, was not just trying to arouse the conscience of the community. We were trying to save lives!

Some newcomers to the pro-life movement graciously believed these men were naive, confused by the lies swirling about us. The media would show close-up shots of the angry pro-choice crowd beating people and destroying property and then attribute these actions to those who were pro-life. Daily, the media referred to us as violent terrorists. But I did not feel inclined to excuse these pastors, nor did I consider them naive. Before Operation Rescue existed, they gave opinions about the wrongness of pro-life behavior. Our activities simply gave them more fuel for their rhetoric and lack of action.

During my recovery, I became increasingly disturbed that none of our rescuers were able to spend time at the clinics. Many missionaries had already returned home to jobs and personal obligations. The rest were in jail. Children were dying unnoticed, with no one to grieve for them.

As my anxiety increased, I begged the Lord to raise up a full-time sidewalk counselor. Someone who could be out there every day from early in the morning until late in the afternoon, just as I had been. Someone, however, who knew what they were doing. I knew they would be in the wind, rain, and snow in the winter, as well as the heat and humidity in the summer. They would be alone most of the time to be spit on, pushed, cursed at, and lied about. I felt sure the Lord would be able to supernaturally touch someone's heart to take on that dastardly job.

Day after day, I begged the Lord to touch someone's heart and raise them up.

One morning, as I was fervently praying for this much-needed counselor, I said out loud, "Lord, I know You can do it! You can raise up a full-time sidewalk counselor! I know You can!"

Yes, I can. I can raise you *up!*

I gasped. I was so certain the Lord had spoken to me. Instantly, I put my spiritual fingers in my spiritual ears and argued with Him. "No way! Throw me in the deepest, darkest dungeon, and throw away the key. Anything but that! Haven't You been watching? Haven't You noticed how miserably I've been failing at sidewalk counseling? I'm the most unlikely person to do this job!"

As He continued to tug on my heart to convince me I was the one He wanted for the job, I made an outrageous, defiant move. Pushing the sleeves of my nightgown up and crossing my arms over my chest, I turned my body to the wall. "Lord, the doctor said I'm too sick to talk to anybody. I'm not going to discuss this with You any further!" Quickly, I fell sound asleep. There was no clap of thunder or deadly lightning strike in response to my arrogant disrespect of the Almighty.

When I woke up, He was patiently waiting for me to surrender my will once again. Remembering all the other times I had fought Him—and recalling the consequences of my disobedience—I realized I needed to stop my fighting. I was the only one unexplainably released from jail over and over again. I was forced to be on the sidewalks by myself day after long, exhausting day. The Lord used Operation Rescue and The Siege as a vehicle to get me to Atlanta. I now understood that He had brought me here for the ministry of sidewalk counseling.

God used the experiences of my many arrests, physical abuse, and time in jail to change me from a shy, easily frightened introvert into a courageous, usable vessel fitted for this call. Now He asked me to be the answer to my own desperate prayer. I relinquished my will and accepted His invitation to be a full-time sidewalk counselor, as long as He would send me out with new instruction and anointing.

In the weeks that followed, I recalled all the women I ministered to during post-abortion counseling years earlier. I remembered their names and their stories in great detail. I recalled what they said they were thinking and feeling when they found out that they were pregnant and no one would help them. They shared what they thought when they picked up the phone to make the appointment. They told me what they were feeling when driving to the clinics. I especially remembered what they said they were thinking and feeling when walking by the pro-life counselor on the sidewalk.

The Lord explained the things that I should and should not say, the things that I should and should not do—and *why*. No wonder I hadn't been successful. Clearly, I had been saying and doing all the wrong things. The Lord began to break my heart for women who find themselves pregnant and in desperate situations. I recalled the horrible wailing coming from these women during post-abortion counseling. As the regret at what they had done overwhelmed them, they were overtaken with grief over the loss of their children. I remembered many of them getting so emotionally upset they would excuse themselves to vomit, then return to more gut-wrenching wailing. I wanted so very much to prevent other women from experiencing this agony.

As I thought about all the women I had met at these clinics in Atlanta and the reasons they gave for needing an abortion, the Holy Spirit began to teach me. He gave me the convincing arguments needed to defuse every possible reason for choosing an abortion. Without a doubt, I knew I could now reach these abortion-bound women. The Holy Spirit gave me a tremendous sense of confidence.

I now thought about the sidewalks and the clinics in an entirely different light. My heart moved from my desire to minister in jail to an all-consuming desire to minister on the sidewalks. Despite how much I hated those places of child sacrifice, a real urgency to be there rose up inside of me. My heart change could only be due to a supernatural move of God!

The phone rang as I lay in bed, trying to fall asleep. The caller did not identify herself. She took a deep breath, then a torrent of words gushed from her mouth.

"Karen, I heard you are going out tomorrow as a full-time sidewalk counselor, and I just want to let you know that before you and the other missionaries arrived here, there were over seventy local women that were scheduled to cover all the downtown clinics every day, and in two full years we only had eight babies saved."

After filling her lungs with air, she reminded me Atlanta was known across the nation as the City of Blood, and I couldn't sidewalk counsel here because the spiritual stronghold was so great. No matter what I would do, I shouldn't bother going to Midtown Hospital as I wouldn't be able to get any literature to anyone because I only had a couple of seconds to reach them as the cars pulled in.

She sucked in another quick breath. "Don't go to Midtown Hospital." She warned and hung up the phone.

Go to Midtown Hospital and Surgi Center and go now! I felt the urgency from God's Spirit, but I was annoyed—not only at the discouraging telephone call but also at having to get out of bed and go now. Lord, really?

I dragged myself out of bed and got dressed quickly. I didn't want to wake the Duffys and hoped it was okay to borrow their car. Making my way downtown, I pulled into Surgi Center's parking lot and got out of my car. It was exactly midnight. Though the summer night was hot and muggy, I felt cold and started shivering. As I stood in the dark, the full realization of what the Lord had called me to do dawned on me. He had given me a life and death assignment.

Standing there alone, I felt minuscule and utterly incapable of the task set before me. I thought about the phone call that brought me here. "Lord, if seventy women can't do this, *I can't do this!*" I said out loud. My words echoed off the side of the building.

That's right—you can't, but I can!

I looked up over the roof of Surgi Center and noticed the IBM tower in the background. At the top of the building there was beam work that formed the shape of a cross. I remembered these words from Francis Schaeffer in *A Christian Manifesto*: "The hope of all mankind is represented by the cross of Jesus Christ, and through its power all things are possible (Crossway, 2005)." I knew more than anyone that I needed the power of the cross!

I felt overwhelmed with the need to do a personal Jericho march around that horrible place. Slowly, I walked toward the rear of the building. It was completely engulfed in darkness. I circled the structure, then slid down the muddy hill on the other side. I came around the front and once again into the parking lot. Each time I went around, I called out into the dark these words from Zechariah 4:6: "Not by might, nor by power, but by My Spirit says the Lord of hosts."

A righteous anger began to rise in me as I went around and around the building. My heart and mind became determined to stand against this horrible place of child sacrifice! It was needful that I understood I did not have any might or power of my own. But I sure had His Spirit, and I knew He would join me in the fight. Each time I went around, my steps became firmer and my voice louder as I stood on His promises. By the seventh time around, I was swinging my bent arms and clenching my fists. I was literally marching and stomping my feet as I claimed that unholy ground for the Lord and declared victory in the name of Jesus!

Coming to a final stop in the parking lot, I dropped to my knees on the stones. I shouted out, "Lord, You have asked a big thing of me. You have asked me to leave everyone I love and everything I own to serve You. Now I am asking for a big thing in return. Please don't ask me to be out here for two years and only see eight babies saved. I know what I am asking has never been done before, and I know it would take a miracle, but I am asking for nothing short of *one thousand* babies!"

As I stood up to leave, I knew without a doubt that whatever happened in this place, it would be accomplished by His Spirit!

PART TWO

Have I not commanded you? Be strong and of good courage; do not be afraid, nor be dismayed, for the Lord your God is with you wherever you go.

Joshua 1:9

CHAPTER 14

A New Work

My alarm rang at 3:15, signaling the beginning of a new work the Lord was doing in me. At 5:45 my sweet friend Joanna Luttrell arrived to pick me up so we could sidewalk counsel in front of Surgi Center. Joanna had answered the Call to Atlanta weeks earlier, arriving just shortly after the doctor put me on bed rest. What a joy to see my special friend again.

During our ride into town, I shared insights the Lord taught me about sidewalk counseling. When Joanna reached the Fourteenth Street exit off the interstate, I prayed for each piece of the spiritual armor listed in Ephesians 6. I knew we were going into battle. As her car turned onto Spring Street, we immediately saw the spiritual battle portrayed in the natural realm. A line of squad cars lined the street in front of Surgi. We were reminded that "we wrestle not against flesh and blood."

Joanna passed the police and pulled into the AAA parking lot so we wouldn't be accused of trespassing. As we started to get our literature out of the trunk, an officer approached us.

"We heard you missionaries are going to use some new tactics today," he said. "We just want you to know we are ready for you."

I thought he had been given misinformation. He didn't realize it was just me that was changing *my* tactics.

I couldn't help but laugh. "Excuse me . . . new tactics?"

"You do realize the injunction is in effect, and you will be written up."

I stopped laughing.

Shortly after our prayer arrest at Fem Center and just after I was placed on bed rest, an injunction was put on our group. We could not be within fifty feet of the property line of an abortion clinic, even on the sidewalk. The property line, not the front door. This made it impossible to get anywhere near any of the women going in. Of course, this is what the clinic wanted.

The injunction was clearly a violation of our First Amendment rights. The punishment for violating the injunction was a five-hundred-dollar fine and twenty days in jail. The fine and jail time would be multiplied by how many times we had gotten written up when the judge brought us in. One missionary had already been written up for preaching. He had not been trespassing but simply standing on the sidewalk sharing the gospel with another person.

The officer repeated his warning. "You *will* be written up."

In unison, Joanna and I said, "Yes, sir," as he returned to his squad car.

Joanna and I looked at each other, shrugged our shoulders, took the literature out of the trunk, and headed for the sidewalk. We stood on the far side of the driveway, just outside the fifty-foot restriction, as a car approached and turned slowly into the driveway. I knew that when the woman got out of the car and started toward the clinic, I would have to go within the fifty feet to talk to her.

I stood my ground and thought about my conversation with Jay Sekulow days earlier. He was preparing to argue against this injunction before the Supreme Court of Georgia. Jay asked me not to go sidewalk counseling, stating that violating the injunction day after day might hold much more jail time for me than rescuing ever would. It might take a year before he could appear before the court—but the Lord had made it clear that I was to sidewalk counsel *now*. I couldn't agree to stay away. I thanked Jay for his genuine concern for me, but I had to obey the Lord! I had come to fully understand that obedience brings a great spiritual covering, which I desperately needed. I claimed Psalm

20:7 (NIV): "Some trust in chariots and some in horses, but we trust in the name of the Lord our God."

As I looked out at all the squad cars in front of me, discomfort started to nibble at my resolve. I felt a great urge to go back home and hide under the covers. That was when I clearly heard the Lord speak to my spirit: *You just obey Me, and the enemy will not triumph over you!* I received it as both a direct command and an incredible promise. My resolve returned.

I stepped into the fifty-foot perimeter and walked up to the first woman. She returned my smile and reached for my literature. Seeing the police step out of their cars, a frightened look came over her face. Withdrawing her hand, she ran into the clinic.

I was surprised to see all the officers taking my picture, which had never happened before. The clinic personnel came out carrying cameras as well. They started ranting and raving, demanding that we be arrested. An officer told them that as long as we stayed off the property, he couldn't arrest us. He could only write us up for violating the injunction. I asked him why everyone was taking our pictures.

"To prove that you were within the fifty feet," he said.

The clinic personnel went back inside. I was grateful that there were no clinic escorts that day. They must have assumed the police would do their jobs for them and keep us away from the women. We were careful to stay on the sidewalk and not trespass. The police didn't stop us from speaking to anyone, but whenever the women saw the squad cars, they wouldn't come near us.

After a while, one officer asked me where everyone else was.

"Everyone's in jail," I said. "I don't know what you heard about everyone's new tactics, but Joanna and I are it. No other missionaries will be joining us."

He walked away, puzzled. Soon, all the squad cars left. Without the police or clinic escorts, the women stopped, took our literature and spoke with us.

Over the last few months, I had been at Surgi plenty of times without police or escorts. Even then, I had difficulty getting anyone to stop and talk or take my literature. I always felt uncomfortable about the signs I was carrying. I wondered how I would feel if I were the one arriving for an abortion. I couldn't imagine wanting to talk with someone who was carrying a sign of an aborted baby. Even when I changed the signs to beautiful baby pictures, they wouldn't stop. I realized it was because the signs were usually about the baby. Women could not allow themselves to think about or even look at a picture of a baby. If they did, they knew they would not be able to go through with the abortions.

I was determined never to carry a sign while sidewalk counseling again. Signs have shown themselves to be incredibly effective at changing people's minds, and I am sure they have saved many babies. I fully support carrying signs at pickets, demonstrations, and especially at college campuses and greatly admire those who do. When considering the clinics, however, I made up my mind that I would only use them when and where it was impossible to reach the women going in. I wanted to talk to the women, and I knew the signs were keeping them away from me.

That morning—with no police, no escorts, and no signs—nearly every woman accepted our literature, and dozens stopped and let us talk to them. Each one was pleasant. To our great surprise, seven chose life for their children. There were tears of joy and hugs from boyfriends, husbands, and other family members. We were overwhelmed! Joanna took down every name and telephone number so we could keep in touch with them. We knew they might need encouragement to remain pregnant. Many times, there are others at home who pressure these women to go back for their abortions.

When we left that afternoon, we were so excited we could have made it home without the assistance of the car. Even though we grieved for the forty-plus children who died, we praised the Lord for the seven spared. I was so grateful for Joanna's presence and friendship, which began in a holding cell in California. Previously, we had rescued children together through blocking doors to abortion clinics. Today, we rescued children together through sidewalk counseling.

Last night's caller tried to discourage me by sharing that only eight babies had been saved during the past two years. In just a few hours, the Lord gave us seven babies! If I hadn't taken that phone call, I wouldn't have realized what a great miracle had happened in front of our eyes.

"I wonder why the Lord didn't give us eight babies to save today," I told Joanna. That would have been the perfect correlation. Whether seven babies or eight, to God be *all* the glory!

The next day, Joanna and I returned to Surgi. Only three squad cars were there waiting. One officer reminded us he would write us up if we disobeyed the injunction. We told him we understood, then proceeded to walk on the sidewalk inside the fifty-foot boundary. Even though it was our constitutional right to be there, the officer did as promised and wrote us up.

As we had experienced the day before, the women were open to taking our literature or talking to us until they saw the police—then they rushed into the clinic. After more picture taking by both the police and clinic personnel, the squad cars left. With the officers removed and escorts strangely absent, the women now accepted our literature. Nine women allowed us to talk with them. Of those nine, five chose life for their children.

We left that afternoon exhausted from pleading for the lives of the children. The realization that over fifty children had died in the clinic that day weighed heavily on us. We were, however, praising the Lord for the five still alive! I was in shock. I thought maybe yesterday was a fluke and the Lord was just taking pity on us. I'm not sure that I expected Him to do it again today. *Forgive me, Lord, for my lack of faith,* I prayed.

The following day, only one squad car was sent to watch us. After the police left, the women once again were responsive to us. We went home praising the Lord for three more children!

By Thursday, the squad car had backed in across the street to park where the officers could see us. I was so grateful they had moved. Because of all the loose stones on the steep driveway, the women arriving had to look down at the ground and didn't notice the squad car. Four babies were saved that day, with another on Friday—one life so precious to the Lord. Our lengthy list of names and numbers had grown. Joanna and I were beside ourselves. We were shocked, pleased, overwhelmed, elated, amazed, exhausted, and overjoyed.

"Joanna, tell me that this week actually happened, that it's not just my imagination. All those babies were saved, right?"

"Yes, they were!"

"No one is going to believe it, you know." I sighed. "I'm not sure that I even do. After all those months out there by myself. Maybe it's just you!"

"Now stop that! You did most of the counseling, you know."

"I know, but . . ."

"But nothing!" She scolded me. "Stop letting the devil make you doubt! You said getting rid of the signs would make a difference, and it did!"

Joanna reminded me she had come to Atlanta to rescue, and soon she would return to rescue with the other missionaries who had been released from jail. In her usual motherly way, she reassured me she would help me sidewalk counsel tomorrow. My heart sank. I didn't feel ready to be alone on the sidewalk again. I would miss my friend and the courage that seemed to emanate from her very being.

On Saturday morning, Joanna joined me as promised. Saturday had always been the clinic's busiest day. Today it was triple parked. Five escorts came to the sidewalk, standing in our way and shoving us aside to keep us away from the women. I lost count of how many women went in. It was well over seventy. It was difficult trying to reach the women, with so many arriving at one time and the escorts working hard to block us. We saw the officers across the street laughing as they watched the escorts pushing us, impeding our access to the sidewalk.

A NEW WORK

We knew it would do no good to protest. We had become accustomed to the double standard.

Despite their behavior, four children were spared a horrible death that day. The week ended with an unbelievable number of children saved—twenty total! We gave the Lord all the glory.

Over the weekend, Joanna and I reached out to call the women who had chosen life for their babies and follow up with them. Late Sunday afternoon, Joanna called me to share incredible news—one mother we met on the first day saw her doctor and found out she was carrying twins!

"Karen, there *were* eight babies saved the first day," she said, reminding me of the discouraging phone call I received the night before we began to sidewalk counsel. "God really *did* in one day what took two years before. There were actually twenty-one babies saved last week!"

I hung up the phone and let her words sink past my unbelief. I slowly accepted that I had been a part of the miraculous display of the Lord's power. I was overwhelmed so many children who were once scheduled for death were still alive. I was amazed to think that the King had graciously let me be a part of what He had done. Even words of praise were difficult to find. I sat in silent awe of Him.

Our group numbers continued to dwindle. Since there were now so few missionaries, often they would all be arrested during a rescue and removed before the women even arrived. Getting access to counsel the women at a rescue became impossible, so they decided to do a "Krypto Rescue"—one where rescuers sit with their backs to each other in a circle, putting heavy-duty krypton bicycle locks on their necks and interlocking them to each other. The locks were impossible to cut by normal means and would require firefighters to cut them off. Not wanting to keep the firemen from other emergencies, the rescuers sometimes agreed to unlock them if the police agreed to keep the clinic closed until the sidewalk counselors had time to talk with the women.

Joanna had had a complicated operation on her neck a couple of years earlier. I begged her not to join this rescue, but she insisted.

Seven of our missionaries, as well as a few prayer supporters, arrived early in the morning at a private doctor's office in DeKalb County. Krypto rescues were done by the missionaries in previous waves, but none had been done at a private doctor's office before. I was shocked to find out about the obstetricians and gynecologists who did abortions in their offices, trying to avoid the stigma of being called abortionists.

As five rescuers sat, another rescuer locked them all together. He then left, taking the key with him. I went back in to check on everyone, especially Joanna. Any little bit of movement would pull on each other's necks and could cause injuries. I continued to go in and out while waiting for the police who had been called and would be arriving soon.

While outside, I watched for the women who would be arriving for their appointments. I also kept my eye on the sky, which was growing darker and darker. I wondered how long the rain would hold off.

Several squad cars arrived. One officer asked me who I was and what I was doing there. I explained our mission and told him I wanted to stand outside to counsel the women arriving for their abortions.

As two cars drove into the parking lot, the officer nodded in their direction and said, "Go do your thing."

I walked toward the first car. The passenger rolled her window down, took the literature I held out to her, and asked me what was going on. I explained who we were and why we were there and assured her we cared a great deal about her.

The gentleman driving the car reached over to touch her hand and said to her, "See, I'm not the only one that doesn't want you to do this."

She jerked her hand away from his, rolled the window up, and wouldn't let me say anything more to her. I was grateful that she at least had the literature. I prayed she would read it.

I walked toward the second car just as two more cars rolled in. As the fire trucks arrived, they eased into the driveway to block the entrance, preventing any other cars from entering the parking lot. A few cars pulled up, then drove away when they couldn't get in. I prayed they wouldn't return. Several firefighters approached the back door.

The fire chief nodded to me. "I can't wait to see this!" he said as he walked by.

The passenger of the second car refused to roll the window down. The driver opened his window long enough to make sure I could hear him cussing at me.

The third car had two people in the front seat and three in the back. A man sitting in the back rolled his window down. Pointing to my literature, he asked me for some of that "stuff."

As he began looking at it, he said, "Man, this ain't right!" He pushed on the back of the seat in front of him and said, "Hey! You can't do this. It just ain't right!"

The woman screamed at him and told me to get away from her car. He rolled the window up at her command. I could still hear their angry voices.

As I was approaching the fourth and final car, the two people in it got out. The young man rushed to the passenger side and put his arm around his girlfriend. They turned their confused faces toward me. He asked me if I would answer a question for them. They had gone to an abortion clinic last week, and the clinic told them it wasn't really a baby.

"She just wants to know if it has fingers yet," he said.

She looked at me and told me she was only twelve weeks pregnant. I was infuriated but resisted the anger I felt at the clinic for lying to this young couple. I showed them my plastic model of a ten-to-twelve-week old fetus sucking its thumb.

The woman grabbed her stomach, bent over, and let out a horrible sound. "It has fingers!" Standing upright, she turned to him and smiled. "It has fingers!"

"You want to keep it?" he asked, smiling back.

"Well, of course. It has fingers!"

Completely ignoring me, they got back into the car.

While I talked with this couple, the man in the second car kept getting in and out, cussing and yelling at me.

"Leave them alone and mind your own #%&@# business, bitch!" He threw a rock at me.

I rubbed the stinging place on my arm. "God bless you, sir," I said. I felt that now familiar ache in my heart—not for me but for him, knowing how he had been captured by darkness.

I realized there had been a time when my heart would have been offended or hurt by someone treating me this way. Now my heart was miraculously changed by His Spirit. This change came suddenly, powerfully on the sidewalk at my first rescue. As the power of God entered my soul that day, so did the character of Christ that can but only love those who persecute me.

This change did not come naturally! It was His Spirit in me that enabled me to love my enemies and have their best interests in mind. Ever since that first rescue, I would look at those who meant me harm with my heart breaking for them, leaving me yearning for their deliverance. That was God at work, not me! Those who opposed me simply could not touch me, for I held an ever-abiding knowledge of God's will for my life. It overshadowed me with confidence, love, and peace that truly passes all understanding. It mattered not what source or vehicle Satan used to deliver his fiery darts. They fell to the ground, unable to perform their intended destruction.

I went back to check on Joanna again, passing the chief and two firemen who were making their way out of the doorway.

"Your friend asked me to tell you she is okay. She sure is a brave little woman," the chief said. "I've got to say that this all reminds me of the civil rights movement." He had been arrested many times himself during those years.

"That's great, especially since you are white and could have said it wasn't your battle."

"It's no different from y'all. You could easily say it's not your battle because they're not your children, but it's just the right thing to do. It's always right to stand up for innocent people, especially when they are as helpless as a baby in the womb. Y'all keep right on doing what you're doing." He pointed up to the sky. "You don't worry about anyone else but Him. You know He's in agreement with you!"

A loud clap of thunder filled the air.

"See?" he said, laughing. "He's not only agreeing, but He's also sending sound effects to accompany y'all."

The chief turned to go inside as the rain began to fall.

The man from the first car walked over to ask the fireman if they could get out of the parking lot—the same man who didn't want his girlfriend to have the abortion.

He smiled at me. "She decided to have the baby."

His girlfriend rolled down her window, reached out, and squeezed my hand. "Please tell the others inside that I said, 'Thank you so much.' If this hadn't happened here today, I would have just done it. It gave me time to think and read your literature."

"Yes! That's why they did it!"

Later that evening, as I sat and watched the news about the Krypto Rescue on Channel 11, I prayed for the rescuers in jail. I thanked the Lord that they all made it safely through without damage to their necks—and for the two children saved by His glory and grace.

CHAPTER 15

Pressing On

I returned to Surgi Center by myself, as Joanna was re-arrested and sent to Fulton County Jail. The escorts, however, increased in number, taunting me incessantly every day. Sometimes there were as many as eight at a time. It's amazing how grown people can be such bullies. With twisted faces and clenched fists, they called me profane names and spewed out the evil acts they wanted to do to me.

Raymond and Doris were two escorts who loved to mock my Jesus and me as they hissed, spit, laughed, and made lewd comments. They sandwiched me in between the two of them, getting as close as they could, making the hot weather even more unbearable. They were especially furious about the Krypto Rescue we'd recently held.

"We're going to squash you like bugs," they said.

I fixed my mind on the children saved during the rescue. "Only if God says so!"

I marveled at how the escorts' words had so little effect on me. I gave credit completely to the promise I'd claimed, found in Ezekiel 3:8–9: "Behold, I have made your face strong against their faces, and your forehead strong against their foreheads. Like adamant stone, harder than flint, I have made your forehead; do not be afraid of them, nor be dismayed at their looks, though they are a rebellious house."

One morning, I arrived at Surgi at five thirty. Though it was dark outside, the heat and humidity already made me uncomfortable. I was grateful the escorts hadn't arrived yet. As I was busy getting literature from my trunk, I noticed that a large black car had already arrived and was parked at the farthest corner of the lot, as though trying to hide in the darkness. Though I was no longer involved with blocking entrances to clinics, I was still a missionary willing to help to spare a mother and baby from abortion, no matter the cost to me. I didn't mind getting arrested for trespassing if it could lead to saving a child's life. I walked into the clinic parking lot and approached the car.

The heavily tinted windows made it impossible to see who was inside. It could be someone trying to entrap me for trespassing, or it could be someone who wanted to do me harm. Even so, I tapped on the passenger's window. I was relieved when a sweet young girl rolled the window down. She looked to be in her late teens, as did the driver. She seemed apprehensive and frightened. It wasn't because of me, or she would have never rolled the window down.

I smiled at her and said, "Good morning, honey."

Before I could say another word, the driver leaned over. "She's scared to death of the abortion. Tell her there's nothing to be afraid of here."

The young girl turned to me with a furrowed brow, expecting me to alleviate her fears. Looking into her beautiful brown eyes, I told her I cared about her and, therefore, had to tell her the truth.

"Yes, you are right to be afraid of this place."

I handed her a copy of *The Abortion Injury Report* and pointed to the picture of an ambulance parked at the side door of Surgi Center. I explained that the ambulance was taking Catherine Pierce to Crawford Long Hospital, where she later died after the abortion performed there at Surgi Center.

Suddenly, a powerful woman's voice came out of the darkness of the back seat. Each word was spoken slowly and deliberately. "Put . . . the . . . car . . . in . . . reverse . . . we're . . . out . . . of . . . here!"

The driver obeyed her orders, and the car moved backward. I didn't want them to go to another clinic instead.

"Wait! Read the rest of the paper!"

The American Rights Coalition published this report that had saved many lives of those who came to Surgi Center seeking an abortion. The car stopped.

"This paper was written to educate and protect women regarding the dangers of abortion and includes many other articles," I said. "It explains how most all abortion clinics are seldom if ever inspected and are unsanitary and dangerous. The 'doctors' are many times unskilled, resulting in severe damages and many deaths."

The voice from the back seat spoke again. "Turn the light on!"

As the interior light came on, I saw a woman's huge hand embellished with many large rings and long red fingernails reach forward. Her hand motioned toward the paper. I remained silent, even though I could have still talked to the young girl. We both held our breath. She stared straight ahead, sitting up as stiff as a board. The presence of the woman in the back seat was in control of everyone, including me. When I saw a tear escape the young girl's eye, I gently patted her forearm, hoping I would not be detected.

The back door of the car slowly opened. With the door and tinted window obscuring my view of her, I could only see the woman's feet. Her large, red-shoed foot crushed the stones with great force as she got out of the car one foot at a time. The car rocked as she pulled on the doorframe to assist her large body through the opening. Standing to her nearly six-foot height, she curled her finger toward me, beckoning me near.

More afraid of her than any clinic escort, Satan worshipper, police officer, or judge, I reluctantly moved toward her. She grabbed me by the back of the head with one of her large hands while clutching my back with the other hand. Before I could resist, she pushed my head into her massive bosom, nearly suffocating me.

"Honey, you just saved my baby's life!" she bellowed. She continued to hold me in her vise-like grip, rocking me back and forth.

With my arms flailing, I was almost out of breath but managed to mumble, "And your grandbaby's life."

Unable to hear my muffled voice with my face still pushed into her grandiose chest, she released me.

"What did you say, honey?"

"And your grandbaby's life. Your grandbaby's life was also saved." Timidly, I added, "Grandma?"

Her eyes bulged. I thought for sure she was one of those women who never wanted to be called Grandma. She reached for me again, but this time I dodged her powerful grasp. Her daughter had stepped out of the car, so she grabbed her instead.

"Honey, I never really thought about the baby—your baby—my grandchild." She began to cry, to wail, to scream. Her loud voice echoed off the side of the building. She tossed her daughter around like a rag doll, begging for forgiveness.

The car moaned under her weight as she got back in. Her daughter got in the back seat with her, under siege of her mother's passionate hug. The young girl gave me a tearful, shy smile. Rolling the window down, her mother reached out for my hand. Her gentle touch surprised me.

"God bless you, honey. I'll take real good care of both of them," she said.

The driver mouthed *thank you* to me, and they pulled away.

The morning sun lightened the sky to a pale pink. Traffic rapidly increased, and noises filled the air as the hustle and bustle of city life began. In my usual preparation for the day, I started walking up and down in front of the clinic singing, "Jesus, Jesus, Jesus, there's just something about that name." Then the escorts arrived. Five—no, *six* today. *Lord, give me strength, patience, and endurance,* I prayed.

As the day dragged on, car after car pulled into the parking lot, sometimes arriving five at a time. Many of the occupants were friendly; most were not. Many took my literature; most did not. Today's clients seemed extraordinarily arrogant. They walked tall and confident. One even skipped in.

The temperature climbed rapidly. The scorching sun burned the exposed skin on the back of my neck. Because I was alone without other counselors, I drank only a little water, or else I would have to go across the street to use the restroom. I didn't want to miss even one car arriving. Today, like many other days, I had a headache from the heat, the lack of water, and squinting in the bright sunlight, despite my sunglasses. I continually waved my skirt to cool off my legs that were burning from the heat coming off the hot pavement. The effort proved futile.

I was getting cranky. My patience was wearing thin with the escorts as they pushed and blocked. I was grateful three of them had already left. An officer drove by and honked his horn. He used his finger to make a check mark in the air, indicating that he was writing me up on the injunction. I resisted sticking my tongue out at him. I wondered how many violations I had now and when they would order me to court.

Another car drove by and the driver threw the remains of their lunch at me, cussing at me, telling me to get a job and mind my own #%&@# business. Following closely behind that vehicle was another car with a mom and dad and their teenage daughter. My heart sank when I saw them getting out of the car, because parents accompanying daughters are the most difficult ones to counsel. The parents got on either side of her, the father closest to me. Before I could even say anything, the father cussed at me and told me to stay away from her. The young girl looked confused and was crying. When I started to say something, her father put his finger in my face and threatened to punch me if I said anything to her.

"God bless you, sir," I said.

Fifteen minutes later, another family arrived. This father also threatened to hit me.

"I'm so sorry, honey," I said to the teenage girl, who was sobbing.

Her mother became angry at her for crying and jerked on her arm, pulling her toward the clinic. It was very apparent that these young women had lost *their* choice, as their moms and dads were the ones exercising their own choosing in the matter.

An hour later, the same scenario repeated itself—only this time, the father pushed me. As I fell into the street, a car nearly hit me.

The police watching from across the street did nothing. I begged the Lord to show me how to deal with parents bringing their daughters for abortions. I felt so sorry for these young women. I had learned that the younger they were, the more they were against the abortions. They had no idea what was involved in raising a child; they just knew they wanted their babies. I knew their mothers assumed they would be the ones to raise the babies, and they weren't about to take on that responsibility. Mothers would shout out to me that they had already put in their eighteen years, and they weren't going to do it again. Many times, young women are brought in by both their mothers and their grandmothers. It was so sad to watch three generations come to take the life of the fourth.

Soon after I had been pushed into the street, three women arrived together and asked for my literature over the loud protests of Raymond and Doris. As they walked toward the clinic, one stopped to read the literature. The others stopped as well and started reading their copies. Doris yelled out that it was all lies, but they ignored her.

One kept reading, shaking her head. She looked at her friends. "Do you think that it's true, that it's really a baby?"

They nodded yes. She told her friends she didn't want to do it then.

To my surprise, another one responded, "Me either."

They asked me if they could keep the literature and give it to a friend who was also pregnant and thinking about having an abortion. As they walked toward their car, I tried to ask them for their names and numbers.

"Blah, blah, blah," Doris yelled out.

One woman turned around and came back to thank me. She said her two friends were the ones coming for the abortions. She had tried to talk them out of it, but they wouldn't listen to her. She felt sure with this literature, they could persuade their other friend to have her baby as well. She then turned her attention to Doris and frowned. "You need to behave!"

Doris just laughed.

The merciless sun continued its relentless torture into late afternoon. The escorts and the police had left hours earlier. They knew that no one else would be arriving and that all the women were already inside. I always stayed until the end of the day when the women were all leaving. I wanted to make sure they each received post-abortion literature as they left with their empty wombs. It's funny how most everyone would take the post-abortion literature when I told them it was for encouragement after an abortion. Nearly all of them were crying—whole families were crying. There was no determination or arrogance then. My heart ached for them. I knew that regret and remorse would now take up residence in hearts and steal their joy, just like the abortions stole the lives of their children.

As the last woman approached me, I handed her a tissue as well. Unable to look at me because of her shame, she bowed her head low.

"I shouldn't have done it," she said.

I knew my hug, no matter how warm and sincere, was doing little to help. When I encouraged her to look for the gospel tract inside the literature, she quickened her steps away. I prayed she would go to the cross for her healing.

I dragged my weary body to the car, thanking the Lord for the three children spared. As best as I could, I surrendered to Him all the others—so many others—who lost their lives there today. I reached for the key to start the engine and jumped when someone knocked on my window.

"Hey! Don't leave yet!"

Rolling the window down, I turned to look at a young couple standing next to the car with their arms around each other. The man stretched his arms out to me, so I stepped out of the car to receive his hug. He explained they had changed their minds after reading the literature. I asked why they took so long to leave.

"The clinic wouldn't give my money back until the close of the entire day," he said, "and I wasn't going anywhere without it."

I smiled as I watched them drive away. I wondered when I had handed the literature to them. I didn't remember them at all. I climbed back into my car, praising the Lord that there were actually four babies saved that day.

My sidewalk counseling activities were not limited to Surgi Center alone. I would also counsel outside smaller abortion clinics nearby. During this time, I encountered women with tender hearts who responded to me and chose life for their children, along with those who were hard-hearted and refused to listen, leaving the clinics with empty wombs.

One day, I heard some commotion as I parked along the street near a smaller clinic. An officer ran up to me, begging me for my help.

"You have to do something. Look!"

On the driveway, a man on his knees had his arms wrapped tightly around his wife's legs. She stood there like a statue with her large, protruding abdomen. "Please don't kill Timmy." The husband begged, his voice urgent and loud.

The officer was noticeably upset. I saw him brush a tear aside. "She stated she didn't want to be pregnant anymore," he said.

The officer had overheard the husband remind his wife they had waited nine years to get pregnant—and how excited they both were when it finally happened. They'd already wallpapered the nursery and bought all the baby furniture.

"They named their little boy Timmy." The officer wiped away another tear. "Do something!"

I reminded him I would have to trespass.

He didn't hesitate. "Go!"

As I approached the couple, the husband entreated me with his eyes. He turned back to his wife, pleading repeatedly, "Honey, please don't kill Timmy, please don't kill Timmy." His voice was strained and filled with pain.

I thought I was hardened to most everything I see, but this scene tore at my heart. As I stepped in front of the pregnant woman, I saw it. The look. The blank, trance-like look that says, "It doesn't matter what you say or do, I don't want to be pregnant anymore!" No matter what I said, there was no response. At one point, I clapped my hands loudly in her face. For a split second, she focused on me, and then her eyes went dead again.

The clinic personnel came out of the building and yelled at the officer. They had called him to protect their client from her husband's harassment. The officer ignored them, in agony over what he was witnessing. The clinic personnel took matters into their own hands, prying the husband's hands from his wife's legs. He crawled after her, grasping her ankle, increasing the intensity of his pleas as he begged for Timmy's life.

As his wife was escorted to the door, the clinic personnel reminded the husband it was *her* body and *her* choice. Still on his knees, he pounded his fists on the ground, uttering a horrific, mournful sound of agony. A searing hot pain shot through my chest to my stomach. I wanted to scream, "Someone call the police!" but I already knew there was nothing an officer could do. She had her *rights*!

Besides, an officer was already there. He stood back, shaking his head, holding his hand on his chest as if to calm the pain he was feeling. Here was a woman, determined to do what she wanted to do, causing crushing pain for everyone else in her life. I never got used to this blatant display of selfishness and cruelty.

I sat beside the husband in silence. He was on the ground, rocking back and forth. His whole body shook with deep, sorrowful sobs.

When he was able, he spoke just above a whisper. "Thanks for trying. She only had three more weeks to go." He was quiet for a moment, then began wailing again. "I can't even bury my little boy!"

My own tears flowed in such abundance they left my face and streamed down my neck. My spirit was greatly disturbed. I felt unbearable anguish at not being able to help him and little Timmy. I thought about taking the officer's handcuffs and running inside to handcuff myself to her or to the surgical table. If I did, they would do the abortion anyway or call another officer to take me away. There wasn't anything I could do by myself.

The officer helped this defeated husband to stand. He stumbled to his car. He slumped over the steering wheel and sobbed some more. I stood there and touched his shaking shoulder. Lifting his head and staring straight ahead, he put the car in gear and slowly pulled away.

When we could no longer see him, I looked at the officer. "Thanks for caring," I said.

He nodded silently and turned to leave.

I wasn't able to learn the names of that man and his wife that day but never, ever will I forget the name Timmy.

CHAPTER 16

Climbing the Learning Curve

On Saturday, I arrived at Surgi and found the parking lot full of cars triple parked, again. The sweltering heatwave persisted, effectively sapping strength from my weary body. I drew in my breath deeply, feeling as though I was drinking in the thick, humid air. I forced my mind toward encouragement, thanking the Lord that despite all the opposition from the escorts, He had miraculously saved so many children that week. I marveled at how the Lord makes a way during seemingly impossible circumstances.

Every day I learned new ways to reach abortion-bound women. When presented with a different scenario, I learned what to say, what to do—and what not to say, what not to do. I drew on past failures and experiences, as well as the pointed instructions the Lord gave me while I was in bed recovering from mononucleosis.

I learned that if I want to save the child, I needed to concentrate on the woman and her needs. She was the one I was talking to, not the baby. She was the one making the decision, not the baby. If I didn't win her over, there was no chance to save the child. She may have already spent days—perhaps weeks—contemplating this decision for abortion. If she walked into an abortion clinic, she had decided for herself over the baby. A plea for the baby would only incite her to anger and close the door of opportunity for me to talk to her further, and she would refuse the literature I offered.

Women who have had abortions have told me that once they decided to abort, they could not allow themselves to think about, talk about, or look at anything to do with a baby. They would put their defenses up and get angry, running from anyone who even said the word "baby." It's no wonder they ran from the signs, which almost always showed a picture of, or talked about, a baby. Only occasionally would they leave. Instead of running away, they usually would run into the clinic, where they mistakenly thought they were safe.

Although there are exceptions to the rule, I learned that most women choose abortion for selfish reasons. If a woman was thinking only about herself and then decided to leave the abortion clinic, it usually wasn't for the baby's sake. It would be because I had convinced her that to do so was in *her* best interests. Thinking about the baby would usually be secondary to her own welfare. If she was thinking about the baby over herself, she wouldn't be at an abortion clinic in the first place—unless she was being forced by someone, completely uneducated about abortion, or overwhelmed by difficult circumstances.

Arrogant, prideful women arrived at Surgi every day. Many of them would try to mask their self-love—but on that Saturday, I came face to face with a self-centered, belligerent woman. I could read her body language loud and clear. Whereas most women would arrive in baggy sweatpants and T-shirts, this woman approached the sidewalk as if she were walking down the runway at a fashion show. Her fashionable and perfectly coordinated attire was accompanied by a carefully chosen jewel-studded designer tote, resting just so on her slender shoulder. When I held out the literature to her, she lowered her eyes while keeping her head lifted high.

As she approached, I greeted her cheerfully. "Good morning, I'm just here to let you know that I care about you, making sure that you have all the facts about abortion while making your choice."

"I've already made my choice, not that it's any of your business. Out of my way."

She pushed me aside. Her long legs moved her along the sidewalk much too fast. In moments, she would reach the clinic door. Quickening my own steps, I came up alongside her and once again encouraged her to take the literature. Raymond followed closely at my heels, tapping on both of my shoulders repeatedly. He blew my hair up on the back of my head with his foul breath. I tried to ignore what was meant to aggravate and distract me.

The woman hesitated briefly to look at him. I knew it would be unproductive to mention the baby, so instead I showed her the article about Catherine Pierce. Doris ran up in front of me and grabbed the material out of my hand, sandwiching me between herself and Raymond. As he tapped on my shoulders from behind, she tapped on both sides of my ears.

"Blah, blah, blah."

We moved alongside the pregnant woman as one noisy, throbbing entity. We were rapidly approaching the end of the sidewalk, where she would turn into the clinic.

"Women have lost their bowels and now have bags on their sides," I said.

She stopped dead in her tracks—so suddenly that my tormentors and I passed her by and had to back up our steps. She demanded I repeat what I had said, while Doris continued to chant, "Blah, blah, blah."

Infuriated, she placed her hands on her hips, squinted her eyes, and leaned down into Doris's face.

"Shut up, or I'll shut you up!" she threatened.

Too bad I can't get away with that, I thought.

Doris slinked off like a wounded animal. I saw her glance across the street toward the police—but they were only there to protect her from me. I had mixed emotions. On one hand, I was glad Doris had shut up, but I also felt desperately sorry for her. She was a wounded person who looked as if she was about to cry. Raymond went over to Doris and began patting her on the top of her head.

The fashion model yelled to get my attention. She wanted answers. I explained that many women had their uteruses perforated by sharp abortion instruments. When the suction machine was turned on, the bowels were sometimes vacuumed out along with the baby, often causing them to lose their uteruses and leaving them unable to have any more children.

She seemed unconcerned about the possibility of becoming sterile. Instead, she asked, "What did you say about a bag?"

"Oh, yes. If the woman survives, she may have to wear a colostomy bag for the rest of her life."

She sucked in her breath and flipped back her hair. "Humph! I'm a fashion model. I can't have a bag on my side. I'm out of here!"

I followed quickly after her as she walked to her car. "What are you going to do?"

"Well, have the baby. It had better be a girl. Then we can be mother and daughter models!"

Somehow, I knew that was exactly what would happen.

I turned back toward the sidewalk and saw that Doris had recovered from her shock. She was headed straight for me. I was so weary of her. I asked the Lord for an extra measure of endurance to put up with her constant interference.

There was one detail I couldn't help but notice about Doris, since her face was usually just inches from mine. She had incredibly beautiful blue eyes. Many times when I prayed for her, I imagined her countenance completely changed and light coming into those eyes. I prayed she would come to know the Lord. I wasn't sure how pure my prayer for her was, however. Did I want her saved for her sake or for mine? I begged the Lord to make my heart right.

Needing a break, I walked toward the office building across the street to make a phone call. I leaned my head against the wall next to the telephone, closing my eyes, and letting out a long sigh. I became aware of someone standing close by and recognized Alfred, the building's guard.

"They're in rare form today, aren't they?" he said.

"You mean Raymond and Doris? Yeah, they sure are pretty annoying. At least it's only the two of them. There are usually so many more escorts on Saturdays."

"I don't know how you put up with them. I would have punched them out a long time ago."

"As much as I would like to, I can't do that."

"Yeah, the cops would haul you off in no time. That's just what they're waiting for."

"Well, yes, but they're not the only ones watching," I said. "The Lord's watching too. He expects better behavior from me than He does from them."

"God's not the only one watching. We all watch you. Everyone from the lobby to the top floor. You're everyone's entertainment every day." He chuckled. "You should hear the cheering going on when they see you walking a girl back to her car."

I was shocked. I was always so busy trying to reach the women and deal with the escorts every day, I had no idea I was being watched from across the street. Tears stung my eyes. I suddenly didn't feel so all alone. For a moment, I thought I glimpsed the "great cloud of witnesses" from the book of Hebrews, cheering me on as well.

One executive entered the otherwise empty lobby. Alfred called him over and introduced us. The executive shook my hand. He assured me a large number of people deeply respected me. They were proud of me for the work I was doing.

"I hope you're encouraged to know that many people are praying for you every day."

Stunned, I forgot about the telephone call and started back across the street. *I'm so glad I resisted punching Doris several times this morning. I almost pushed her back yesterday.* I thanked the Lord for the extra incentive to behave myself and watch my testimony—and for the tremendous encouragement of knowing others were covering me in prayer. I no longer felt so alone.

I stepped back onto the sidewalk and into my war zone. Immediately, Doris was back in my face.

A car with three women in it pulled in from the side entrance of AAA Parking. One of the tires dropped hard into a deep rut. Getting out, the driver began cursing and throwing a fit over possible damage to her car.

Great! She's already mad, and now she's headed straight for me.

She marched up to me, ready for a fight. I started separating out a piece of literature from the stack in my hands. As I did, my laminated copy of "David" dropped from my hand and landed at her feet. David was a large, late-term aborted baby who was decapitated, with one arm torn from his body. She picked up the picture, examined it carefully and handed it back to me.

"So? I don't want the kid!" she said.

Clearly, a plea for the baby wasn't going to work with this woman either.

She stood in front of me with one hand on her hip and held a cigarette in the other, leaning forward to intimidate me. "So what kind of crap are you going to try to feed me? I suppose you are going to call me selfish and self-centered just because I want to get rid of it. Well, I *am* selfish and self-centered, and I'm damn proud of it! I've worked hard to take control of my life. I'll take control of everyone else's life if I want to, and I'm sure not about to let no damn kid control *mine*."

I glanced at Doris. Even she was a little taken aback. She stood with her mouth open, staring at the woman. I couldn't help laughing out loud. I prayed a quick prayer to recall the things the Lord had taught me, so I would know how to respond. It was evident that she was putting herself first, so I chose to throw her off and agree with her.

"Honey, you need to think about yourself!"

She looked shocked. I had her attention.

"Honey, please take the time to think about yourself and protect yourself."

"What do you mean?"

I took out the article on Catherine Pierce and said I was concerned she was going into the clinic. I talked about the other areas of concern mentioned in the article.

She relaxed her stance and put her cigarette out.

"Please think about yourself. I don't want to see you be the next one the ambulance takes away from here."

I let her know she was running a risk to herself, no matter which clinic she went to. I shared all the statistics cleverly kept away from the public's knowledge. She could go to the courthouse and look up all the abortion-related injuries and deaths in Atlanta. I suspected she might have already had one abortion, or several. I told her how each additional abortion may endanger her life further, asking which one would be one too many.

She let out a sigh. She asked if I knew someone who might want "the kid"—a mixed-race child. I assured her I knew of several couples who would gladly receive and love her precious child.

"Okay, I'll have it, but they gotta pay for the attorney and everything!"

She walked over to my car so I could write down her name and number.

"I'm so proud of your willingness to make someone else happy by giving them your child as a gift," I said.

"I told you, I don't care about nobody else, especially the kid!" She turned and walked away.

I reminded myself that I could not change anyone's heart. A woman with a self-centered state of mind chooses life for her child only if she believes it's what is best for herself. If I had been carrying a sign with a baby's image, it would not have had any effect on her at all. Still, I wholeheartedly agree that signs can be very effective. I believe that society needs to *see* what it is they cry out for so vehemently. Most still believe the lie that the baby is a blob of tissue. The rest refuse to believe that abortions are done through all nine months of pregnancy. They voice their disgust at pro-lifers for holding those horrible signs where everyone can see. If the signs showing abortions are so terrible that they can't stand to look at them, then maybe we shouldn't be performing abortions on helpless little children. I only put down my signs while sidewalk counseling. I found that they chased women away from me, and I was losing the opportunity to counsel them.

I applaud those who faithfully hold their signs in all other settings that not only educate but turn the hearts of our nation to the truth.

I yearned for the shade that did not exist. Perspiration drenched my face. As I leaned down to pick up some literature I had dropped, my sunglasses slipped off. The tops of my feet were blackened by the persistent, pounding sun. I tried to stretch the muscles in my lower back and legs, which were screaming for relief after my standing on the pavement, hour after hour. I begged the Lord to give me one more baby before I left for the day. *Just one more, Lord. Please.*

Standing up from my stretching endeavor, I noticed a man wearing a dress shirt, dress pants, and a loosened tie arrive with his girlfriend. When I saw her walking, my heart broke. Neither was dressed for an appointment that day. She wore a beautiful flowered dress, a reflection of her gentle, sweet countenance. I knew she would suffer terribly from the regret abortion brings.

The man held his hand up to the escorts, signaling them to stay away. He then motioned to me with the other hand to come near. "She wants to read what you have."

It seemed this couple was still in the decision-making process. With that in mind—and sensing her gentle spirit—I knew that this time, with this woman, making a plea for the baby was the right thing to do. When I encouraged her to protect her emotional health and her tender mother's heart, she started to cry. When I described how I imagined she would look with her sweet little one in her arms, her shoulders shook. I assured her she would experience great joy in motherhood, no matter what her current circumstances presented. She nodded and turned her tearful face toward the man. With one hand still stretched out toward the escorts, he drew her close with his other arm and turned her back toward the car.

"Thank you so much," she said.

"You're going to have your baby?"

She nodded. "Yes!" After putting her safely in the car, the man walked back to me. Without saying a word, he gave me a hug, then returned to his car. She waved to me as they pulled away.

I thanked the Lord for answering my prayer—one last baby was saved that day. I was learning from Him. Psalm 32:8 (ESV) says, "I will instruct you and teach you in the way you should go; I will counsel you with my eye on you." Faithfully, He was helping me.

I got in my car to leave, struggling to keep from falling asleep behind the wheel as I made my way home. The ten-hour day at Surgi Center left my head pounding and my heart thumping strangely. I felt nearly burned to a crisp, exhausted clear through to my bones—and it was only my third week as a full-time sidewalk counselor.

CHAPTER 17

Blessed Assistance

As the weeks went by, the injunction against our group received more national coverage. Now others were learning we could not be within fifty feet of the property line of an abortion clinic. Some of the local residents were stunned. Over twenty people stood across the street from Fem Center to protest and pray on Saturday mornings. When they showed up, I chuckled to see they were not violating the injunction from where they stood, but I was still greatly encouraged by each one. I asked them to pray that the Lord would raise up someone to sidewalk counsel with me at Surgi Center and Midtown Hospital. I simply needed help.

That afternoon, I arrived home late to the ringing of the phone. Sue Yingst, who worked at the Operation Rescue office, was calling to ask if she could join me at Surgi Center every morning before going to the office. Sue had answered the call to be a missionary in Atlanta months earlier, and we were surprised to learn we were from the same town in California. She promised to meet me at 5:30 on Monday morning. *Wow, that was fast—what an answer to prayer, Lord!*

The Lord was so faithful to answer prayers for me quickly, no matter my need. When I had needed transportation, Joanna gave me rides to Surgi Center, joining me to sidewalk counsel. One day, I learned she was going out of town for three days, leaving me without transportation. We stood on the sidewalk and asked the Lord to meet my need. The next day, there was a knock at the Duffys' door. Tom Haddock, a man I had met at a rally months before, was standing at the door holding up a set of car keys. He and his wife Lucy wanted to make sure I could get to the clinics every day. They gave me a car, paid for the insurance, and provided a card to purchase gas. An envelope on the front seat contained a note from them, thanking me for all I was doing. I praised the Lord for this sweet, generous couple He had raised up for me.

Others blessed me as well. Correspondence from people I didn't even know had increased, containing checks with their letters. Most were from single women and widows that were small in amount but growing in number. The checks arrived so frequently that the Duffy children started referring to the mail truck as "Karen's Manna Mobile." I felt the Lord's generosity to me through these gifts, as He had already arranged to meet nearly all my needs.

Monday morning, I approached Surgi Center and saw Sue standing under a streetlight, looking like an angel. I gave her a hug and let her know how glad I was to see her. We started our morning reading of Psalm 91 and prayed together. Sue confided her fears to me. "I think I'm more scared of sidewalk counseling than I was of rescuing," she said.

"Remember, courage is not the absence of fear."

I encouraged Sue with the guidance I received from the Holy Spirit when I was sick. Lessons He had taught me—don't carry signs, don't bring crowds of people, don't preach, never shout at anyone, go out in a spirit of love and not condemnation. With Sue's gentle spirit, she didn't need correction for inappropriate behavior, nor did she have a bad attitude.

"Just make sure you speak the truth in love," I said.

"Whoa, I am more of an introvert than you are. I won't be talking to anybody—no way! Maybe I can hand out literature or something, but I can never, ever speak to anyone. Actually, I may not be able to do much more than just be here."

To alleviate her anxiety, I assured Sue her presence there was an incredible blessing to me. I appreciated her very much.

I discovered that for whatever reason, it seemed most everyone would arrive with the same prevailing spirit on the same day. There would be days when everyone came reasonably open to me; other days, they would be closed down and refused to talk. Some days they all arrived with heavy spirits; other days, they were laughing and joking. Most days, they seemed relatively kind and friendly.

Today, however, Sue was to be blessed with a first-day baptism from angry, unreasonable, violent clients as they cussed and shoved. Two women threatened to mace Sue. Others tore up her literature and threw it on the ground. They went in and out of the parking lot, trying to run us over with their cars. They threw food at us, threatening to get their guns out of their cars to shoot us—and these were the pregnant women making the threats!

The clinic escorts were far worse. They realized the officers parked across the street enjoyed watching the commotion, empowering them to act up. I feared we might get hurt. I assured Sue this was the enemy kicking up a fuss to discourage and scare her, trying to keep her from coming back tomorrow. I reminded her that his roar might be loud, but the Lord had already removed his teeth, and she needed to hold her ground! For two and a half hours, she did just that. She stood in the same spot—never moving, barely breathing. She just smiled. Every time I needed it, I would look at her and be encouraged by her smile. I groaned within when she left for work.

At 5:30 a.m. the next day, Sue returned. And the next day, and the day after that. Sue returned every day and smiled for two and a half hours. On Saturdays, she smiled all day. I watched as Sue gained more and more courage, undeterred by the behavior of the escorts—eventually approaching and speaking with the women. She turned into quite an effective sidewalk counselor.

Every day, I grew more amazed at the number of children saved, despite the opposition from the escorts. I laughed whenever the Lord caused something to distract them so I could reach a girl. I marveled at how He would give me the exact words to say that would sway a heart. Sometimes I would say things that surprised even me, knowing it came directly from the Holy Spirit.

Such was the case one morning when a teenager walked by with her furious mother, who told me to mind my own business.

"Honey, just do the opposite of what they tell you to do," I said to the young girl. I walked away wondering why I'd said such a thing.

An hour later she walked out, skipping with her now jubilant mother, who told me how excited she was about having a grandchild.

"What changed your mind?" I asked the girl.

"I did the opposite of what they told me to do, like you said. When they told me to look away from the ultrasound, I looked at it instead, and I saw my baby sucking its thumb. I knew I couldn't do it then."

The next girl who arrived said she needed the abortion because she was overwhelmed with her college courses. She couldn't deal with a baby right now. I thought it strange when she added, "Right now, I'm studying the life of President Lincoln."

"Lincoln said, 'Freedom to choose doesn't make it right to choose wrong.'"

She stopped dead in her tracks. Instead of turning around to walk back to me, she retraced her steps backward and stood in front of me. She looked at me with a puzzled look and kept repeating, "'Freedom to choose doesn't make it right to choose wrong... freedom to choose doesn't make it right to choose wrong.' Abortion is wrong. I choose to have my baby." She ran back to her car and to her waiting boyfriend.

I stood there, completely puzzled. I told Sue that I simply did not know that quote from Lincoln. That evening, while looking for something in a stack of papers on my desk, I found that very quote. I must have read it at some point, and the Holy Spirit brought it to my memory at just the right time. *Thank You, Lord!*

Joanna joined us on days she wasn't rescuing or in jail or visiting and mentoring someone she led to the Lord in jail. When she was with me, she stayed all day. We spent long, exhausting hours together. Joanna's passion and love for the Lord—and for the moms and babies—is evident to all who meet her.

One day, I saw Joanna literally on her knees on the sidewalk, begging for the life of a child. The woman broke down and chose life.

Another day, I poured my heart out to a woman and then discovered she didn't understand a word I said. She didn't speak English. Joanna walked up and without missing a beat, encouraged her to choose life in fluent Spanish. I was shocked. I asked how she learned to speak Spanish.

"Living in California," she said.

I lived in California for twenty-one years, but I never learned to speak Spanish. In turn, when she was talking to someone and was stumped, she'd just look at me, and I would have the right thing to say. With the Lord's help, we spent every day tag-teaming.

Too soon, Joanna would be leaving again, going home for several weeks. We stood on the sidewalk and asked the Lord to provide another sidewalk counselor for me. Now hungry, we walked into McDonald's and noticed a man standing in line in front of us. Noticing Joanna's pro-life T-shirt, he began talking with us. His name was Peter. He agreed to attend a pro-life rally that night and would bring his wife, Ann. At the rally, Ann told me she wanted to sidewalk counsel with me on Monday. Ann promised to be with me all day for several weeks—but after that, she could only come in the mornings before going back to work. Ann had plans to return to work the same day Joanna was coming back to Atlanta. Lord, You are so awesome!

I taught Ann my woman-centered approach to sidewalk counseling. She learned quickly. When Sue joined us again, the two of them hit it off immediately. As the reality of what was happening at Surgi dawned on her more fully, Ann experienced severe grieving and started crying every day. Ann cried; Sue smiled.

Seeing the vast numbers of cars at Surgi made it worse for Ann. I suggested she go with Sue to Midtown for the mornings, giving her a break from Surgi for a couple of hours. Midtown's parking lot didn't fill up until late afternoon, and Ann would be back at her own job by then. Observing the layout at Midtown, we realized we wouldn't have an opportunity to speak to the women. Our only option was to get their cars to stop as they pulled into the driveway. Without signs alerting them to who we were, nearly every car stopped, and the drivers accepted our literature before heading into the back parking lot. So began our morning ritual—Ann and Sue going to Midtown together, while I stayed behind at Surgi by myself. Ann would rejoin me for a short time when Sue left for work. What a tremendous encouragement they were to me.

There were many abortion clinics in downtown Atlanta, but the Lord singled out these three on my heart—Surgi Center, Midtown Hospital, and Feminist Women's Clinic. With the burden increasing every day to cover these clinics, I felt led to do a three-day fast and pray for more counselors.

The morning after I completed the fast, I received a call from Madia Bowman. She had been part of the group of local counselors that were active at the downtown clinics before I came to Atlanta. Ever since her group stopped counseling, she had been praying fervently, asking the Lord to raise up a full-time sidewalk counselor. When she heard about me, she knew I was the answer to her prayer. She homeschooled her five children and couldn't go out every day but wanted to join me several mornings a week. When I hung up the phone, it rang again. This time it was Pam North, another member of the former counseling group. She was also a homeschool mom who wanted to help as much as her schedule allowed. She asked if she could bring her friend along as well.

What a joy it was to meet these incredible ladies. They were all committed to the Lord and filled with love for each other, the moms, and the babies. Soon, all the downtown clinics were covered every morning. As the schedules of the clinics began to change, I was able to divide up time at each of the clinics in the afternoons by myself.

Lord, thank You for being a God Who hears prayer and answers prayer!

A new problem soon surfaced: we were continually running out of literature. Christian Action Council had been graciously providing the brochures for us, but it became quite costly for them. They introduced other possible handouts to me, but it frustrated me that each one seemed to conflict with my method of sidewalk counseling. They suggested I write my own brochure, which they would print for me. Perimeter Church also agreed to make copies for us. Soon we were provided thousands of copies each month of the literature I had prepared.

The first day I brought our new literature to Surgi, it seemed to be quite effective as six babies were saved that day. I didn't know just how effective it was until the next day, however. By 10:00 a.m., the clinic had put up an easel in the lobby with a big sign that read, "No Pro-Life Literature Allowed." They took our literature away from the women who walked into the clinic, leaving them with no choice at all.

It was clear the escorts had been given instructions to beef up their efforts as well. I was getting frustrated that I couldn't get more literature to the pregnant women. At noontime, I stopped a gentleman walking by, humming to himself on his way to lunch. I held out a large stack of my new brochures and asked him if he would please take them inside and put them down on a table somewhere. He agreed, without even asking me why I didn't do it myself. I watched as he walked up the steps of Surgi, opened the glass doors, and placed the literature in front of the sign on the lip of the easel that prohibited pro-life literature. He walked back out, still humming as he nodded to me, and continued walking down the sidewalk.

I did my best to contain both laughter and praise for the Lord so I wouldn't alert the escorts outside to what had happened. The easel was positioned away from the view of the personnel inside the clinic. I stood there and watched woman after woman get up and take the brochures off the easel.

Shortly afterward, one woman left, then another one, and then a third. When I stopped and questioned them, they each said they couldn't go through with their abortions after reading the brochure. It was still in their hands. Before the day was over, two more women left. One had a brochure in her hand; the other woman's brochure was sticking out of her purse.

I laughed all the way home at the Lord's great sense of humor, as well as how He always turns the enemy's plans inside out. The previous week, the clinic had put up a sign inside which read, "Catholics for Choice," along with a not-so-Catholic brochure attached. One girl ran out of the clinic with a look of terror on her face. When I stopped her, she said she couldn't have the abortion and had to get out of there *fast*.

"There's a sign in there that says, 'Catholics for Choice.' When I saw it, I remembered *I* was Catholic," she said. "As a Catholic, I can't do that."

To God be the glory!

Sue continued to sidewalk counsel at the clinic every morning before she left for her office position with Operation Rescue later in the day. She shared with her coworkers the amazing miracles the Lord was doing and how so many babies were being saved. The director of Operation Rescue Atlanta heard these reports and asked if I would give a training seminar. Many attended the seminar, resulting in two more women joining our efforts at the clinics.

I was incredibly blessed by these women. I believed that the Lord had hand-picked each one to assist me, bringing their differing gifts and talents. They paired up perfectly and were faithful to keep their commitment to the Lord and me. I watched with great joy as they experienced firsthand a mother choosing life because of something the Lord encouraged them to say or do. Tears of joy for children saved mingled with tears of sorrow for those who are lost. We all shared in the exultation and sorrow that only a fellow sidewalk counselor would know. The Lord used these mutual experiences to bind our hearts together in a most beautiful way.

We were all grateful for each other and also for Steve Mercer, another gift from God. He stopped by Surgi Center every morning on his way to work at IBM to bring us hot tea and bagels. Steve offered the escorts bagels, but they rejected them. They called him our Bagel Buddy. That was, until he started bringing muffins. Then they called him the Muffin Man.

Everyone insisted that the Muffin Man was sweet on me. Well, he may have been, but I made it abundantly clear to him that the Lord was my husband, and I was keeping it that way, thank you very much!

CHAPTER 18

An Interlude of Peace

Drawing in breaths of cool, fresh air, I looked around and praised the Lord for His beautiful handiwork. Before me stretched the emerald-green water of Hartwell Lake. The red clay shoreline and towering pines were reflected so beautifully in the calm water. The sky was clear and blue. Except for an occasional bird and the lapping of the water against the dock, all was quiet and so very peaceful. I came here to Holt and Linda's "Praise Place" for a few days of quietness and, hopefully, some rest.

As I sat in the slightly chilly morning air, I gathered a cotton shawl around me. The hours I had spent in full-time ministry, sometimes up to twenty hours a day, had threatened to steal my health. Many days I would leave home in the dark and return home in the dark, getting only a few hours of sleep. My days and nights ran together, but I didn't know what else to do. How could I say no to the genuine pleas for help I received on a daily basis?

Every time I was able to hold one of the many babies rescued from a cruel death was worth all my time, effort, and loss of sleep. As I looked into each precious little face and felt each tiny little hand grasp my pinky, I was grateful for the privilege of serving the Lord in this way. I knew I was doing exactly what He wanted me to do. I also knew that rest and relaxation was something Jesus also felt the need to take. Now I was here, following His example.

I heard Linda's voice call out, beckoning me to breakfast. I made my way back up the hill to her cabin, overwhelmed with gratitude for this gift she had showered on me, determined to spoil me for the next few days. As we sat together on the back porch, I devoured the delicious breakfast Linda had made and basked in her friendship. I loved to listen to her talk with her delightful Southern accent. Linda began to ask me questions about Steve. She loved Steve. Everyone loved Steve.

Steve was kindhearted, gracious, dependable, and obviously in love with me. He was constantly concerned about the pressures I was under and would encourage me to take time out of my busy schedule so he could minister to me. Whenever possible—and only when I knew for sure that the clinics were covered—Steve would pick me up on a Saturday morning for a drive to the mountains. He carried a pillow and an afghan in the car for me because he knew that within minutes I would nod off like a child. After a good sleep, I would wake up to a day of hiking and soaking in nature. At the end of the trail, we would enjoy the lunch he'd prepared. Between the beauty of God's creation and Steve's tender care, stress and anxiety would melt off me. He would return me home in the evening, refreshed and encouraged.

Steve had asked if I would date him, which I was reluctant to do. I didn't want anything or anyone distracting me from the commitment I'd made to be completely available for the Lord. Steve understood. He felt the Lord had commissioned him, however, to be my encourager. He asked if I would at least agree to that. I reluctantly agreed to let him be my encourager but nothing more.

"Okay for now," he said.

Steve smiled. I didn't.

I was serious about my commitment to the Lord. I had fallen in love with Him and had invited Him to be my husband. One day, I was walking and humming the famous hymn "In the Garden," which I had sung hundreds of times before. It was as if the words I had memorized long ago suddenly became alive to me:

And He walks with me.

And He talks with me,

And He tells me I am His own.
And the joy we share as we tarry there,
None other has ever known.

What? I stopped dead in my tracks. Those were *my* words, *my* thoughts, *my* sentiments. I wanted to tell the author of that hymn, "How dare you! He is mine! He is the lover of *my* soul!"

Then I realized how foolish I was being. To think that the Great I Am, Who is literal Love, would not be able to love all of us without taking anything away from His love for me was absurd. The Lord made me feel so very special. I felt like every flower that bloomed, bloomed for me. I believed that every sunrise and sunset, He had orchestrated just for me. He was entirely mine. He walked with me, talked with me, laughed and cried with me. I had His hand to hold, His shoulder to cry on, His counsel to guide me, and His love to comfort me. I was full and complete in Christ.

Poor Steve. He didn't stand a chance!

Linda and I washed the dishes, then read the Word together. She wanted to know if she had missed out on anything when she and her family were in Florida on vacation. Immediately, my mind turned to a recent encounter I had with Frances, the inmate I had met in Key Road Prison, who had given me so much trouble before she accepted Christ. I couldn't wait to tell her the good news!

"I was sitting in the lobby of Fulton County Jail, waiting to visit Joanna, when I noticed pretty sandaled feet standing in front of me, and I heard a voice call out, 'Church lady!' At first, I didn't recognize the woman standing in front of me, but when I did, I gasped out loud. It was my Frances! I jumped up and gave her a big hug. We both laughed and cried."

Frances stood before me, a completely changed woman. It was no wonder I didn't recognize her at first glance. She looked very feminine in a lovely dress and matching sandals. Her hair had grown out, and she was wearing lipstick and tiny pearl earrings. Frances got very quiet and took my hands in hers as tears flowed down her radiant face.

"The change on the outside ain't nothin' like the change on the inside, Ms. Karen," she said.

"Linda, you should have been there. She had so much love inside for Jesus that sometimes she felt like bursting. She was so beautiful. I'm so glad the Lord gave me that opportunity to see her."

Linda sat shaking her head and smiling through glistening eyes. "Karen, I could listen to you for hours. I'm so encouraged whenever I hear stories about how the Lord changes lives. What a sweet gift from God to let you see her again. How wonderful to see both your hard work and the Lord's transforming power standing right in front of you!"

The sun was warming up the day, so Linda suggested we make our way down to the water to float on the rafts. We carried plastic containers overflowing with freshly cut fruit and glasses of cold sweet tea. I climbed down the ladder and onto my raft. The water felt much too cold to get into yet. The gentle motion of rocking on the water nearly put me to sleep. Although I greatly needed sleep, I needed Linda's fellowship more.

"So often I think about how all of you missionaries have changed my life," Linda said. "I was so upset when I first came home and found nineteen of you in my house. I wondered why the Lord would do such a terrible thing to me just before Christmas. I was so angry at Holt! I did my best to find host families for all of you."

"I know, you got rid of me fast."

"I'm so sorry about that. I guess I was in shock. I'm glad we decided to keep four of the men with us. Their example of godliness and love for the Lord put me to shame. I didn't realize how self-absorbed and selfish I was. I did a lot of repenting, and hopefully, a lot of changing through their example. Now I wonder why the Lord would do such an incredible thing for me as to send all of you to *my* house when He could have chosen someone else to bless!"

I was glad the Lord had sent me to Linda's house. If Linda hadn't taken me in, I may not have met the Duffy family, and that would have truly been a great loss for me. Linda was a tremendous blessing to me, especially when she joined me to sidewalk counsel with our ministry, Women 4 Women. After all, we were a group of women who cared for other women during a difficult time in their lives. "Speaking the truth in love" was our motto.

We marveled at how the Lord had led us each step of the way in this ministry to women, even when He interrupted our plans that seemed headed in the right direction. The Lord showed me that my plans to open a crisis pregnancy center down the street from Surgi Center was my dream, not the dream or plans He had for me. I would have had to do it all in the flesh. I learned if the Lord is not in something, it usually does not flourish. He might choose to bless the effort, but there is a huge difference between the Lord blessing our work and the Holy Spirit inhabiting our efforts. The results and success are evident when He inhabits a ministry or calling.

It was clear to me now that had I gone ahead with my own plans, it would have taken me away from God's calling on my life to sidewalk counseling. Already the Lord had saved over eight hundred babies—and perhaps many more we never learned about. Linda was excitedly preparing for the Celebrate One Thousand banquet, our upcoming gala once we reached the milestone of one thousand babies saved.

"Karen, who do you think will get the number one thousand baby?" Linda asked. "Probably you. You're the one who's out there the most."

"I don't know. I think it's funny how everyone is trying for it. I'd love to see it be Madia. She is so faithful to sidewalk counseling. She never let her own pregnancies stop her from going out. Remember how she stood out on the sidewalk while she was in labor? She refused to go to the hospital until she had fulfilled every minute she had committed to for counseling that day. I think it would be great if she were the one to receive that honor. Besides, she's the one who prayed me here to Atlanta."

Feeling the plastic under my body getting hotter, I rolled off the raft and into the water. The temperature was a bit cold and caused me to shiver. Though water remained on my list of fears, I still delighted in the feel of the water as I swam. I was not a powerful swimmer, so I asked Linda to keep an eye on me as I headed for the center of the lake. Turning onto my back, I looked up at the beautiful blue sky, enjoying the sensation of weightlessness, grateful for this time of rest and refreshment. Soon, my fears of being in water resurfaced. I hated having my ears in water. The sound was terrifying to me. I was afraid of swimming alongside snakes and snapping turtles, and never opened my eyes underwater. Sufficiently scared, I decided it was time to go back.

After we made our way back to the dock, Linda ordered me to stay and rest as she prepared an early dinner for us. Lying on the lounge chair with the sun warming my back, I felt myself falling into a blissful, deep slumber. It seemed just moments had passed when I felt Linda gently shaking my shoulder, letting me know dinner was ready. I was amazed to find I was now in the shade.

Linda was a most excellent cook, and I savored every bite of the dinner she had prepared. She agreed to let me help with the dishes before taking our peach cobbler out onto the porch. As darkness settled into the quiet cove, I rocked my chair gently. The tree frogs and crickets announced their presence. My soul was at peace.

Linda went inside to answer the phone. When she returned to the porch, she said that Holt and the children would be there for a couple of hours before we left tomorrow. "Do you mind? He's bringing Rescue too."

I thought it was hilarious they named their new dog "Rescue." I guess our missionaries made an impression on their whole family!

"He can be a real pain while you're swimming because as a Labrador, he won't stay out of the water. He really thinks he's a rescuer. He keeps dragging everyone back to shore. Unfortunately, he does a lot of scratching in the process."

"Oh, don't worry about that. Swimming is not something I have to do. I really have a fear of water. Especially water I can't see through like rivers, lakes, and especially the ocean."

"Really? You always seem so brave."

"How funny. I forget you didn't know me back when. I used to be the world's biggest scaredy-cat. The Lord has worked so many fears out of me."

"Really! What was your greatest fear?"

"Dogs! I was scared of dogs!"

"Oh no! Do you want me to tell Holt to leave Rescue at home?"

"No. It is one fear the Lord used Operation Rescue to help me overcome." I settled back in my chair as I began to tell Linda how God released me from my fear. "It was during a rescue in San Diego . . ."

Like the first rescue I took part in, it started pouring as soon as the police began to inflict pain on the people who were being arrested. Once again, we felt the rain was the Lord showing His approval of us after many years of a severe drought.

The usual vicious crowd was there, as well as ACT UP, a violent homosexual group who yelled, "Racist, sexist, anti-gay—Operation Rescue, go away!" along with other slogans I never want to repeat. I was with a large group of rescuers on one side of the abortion clinic.

One pastor near me stood up to pray. "Look at that!" he yelled, pointing to the gutter in front of us.

I strained to look over the crowd. Then I saw hundreds of the plastic fetal models given to us that morning. They were floating by in the rainwater that was rushing into the sewer. Apparently, they had been dropped by those already arrested at the front door.

Another voice yelled, "They've got dogs! They're going to turn the dogs on us!"

I saw the dogs, right in front of us. Ever since I was a very young child, I had a reoccurring nightmare with a dog attacking me. In my dream, it had my arm in its mouth. Its top fangs had gone through the bottom of my arm; its bottom fangs had gone through the top of my arm. No matter how I screamed, no one ever came to help me. Until that day, I was still having that dream occasionally. Dogs were my greatest fear.

A noisy panic rose from the crowd of rescuers. With my heart in my throat, I sat there waiting to see what was going to happen next. I thought about the nunchakus and how the Lord required me to face that fear. I remembered how He helped me to do it, but He didn't prevent the pain. I still had the brace on my arm that day in San Diego. I wondered if the Lord would require the same thing of me about the dogs. I wondered how great the pain would be.

"Oh, no!" I gasped.

"Don't worry, it will be okay. They won't attack," said my friend, who sat next to me.

"How do you know?"

"I know attack dogs. I train them."

We watched as two officers slammed a frail, elderly man down on his face on the pavement. One officer twisted his hand behind him and leaned heavily on his fragile back with one knee while shoving his other knee into his ribs. Another officer, with his knee on his head, pulled on his nose and yelled, "Get up!"

"Never!" the elderly man said.

"How can he get up with you on him?" someone yelled from the crowd.

"Stop it! He's just an old man! Come pick on me, you bullies!" another person added.

"Get up, or I'll tell the dog to attack!" said the officer, holding the dog by its restraints.

"Never!" The elderly man refused to back down.

The officer continued to entice the dog forward in a menacing manner. It was as if he wanted to anger and encourage the dog to attack when he gave the command. The dog was making a terrible sound—dreadful and frightening. It howled as it lunged toward the elderly man, held back by its restraint. Saliva poured from his mouth as it bared his scary, powerful teeth.

Another officer, restraining another attack dog, waited behind them. The officer commanded the elderly man to get up, threatening to release the dog if he didn't comply.

"Never!"

The officers started hurting the elderly man again. Some twisted his nose and scraped his face against the pavement, while two more jabbed him in the ribs with their knees.

I prayed for the man while shaking inside, watching the dog. I looked to my friend for encouragement.

With her eyes still on the dog, she said, "The dog will *not* attack the old man—but I'm not sure what he'll do to the officers holding him down."

"Yeah, but . . ."

"Trust me, well-trained dogs will not attack passive, helpless people. Just relax!"

Just relax? Yeah, right! I thought. I told her the reoccurring nightmare I'd had since childhood about being attacked by a dog, expecting some gentle, compassionate understanding.

"Get over it!" she yelled.

I jumped. "Alrighty then!"

I figured since I didn't die from the nunchakus, I wouldn't die from a dog bite either. Even if it did attack, although my friend said it wouldn't, I decided I had to put my fear of dogs to rest. *Well, that was easy*, I thought as I sat there and considered what just happened. I simply obeyed her command, and the fear was gone! I also learned right there and then that I just needed to shout at the bogeyman, no matter what form he took, and he would run. *Resist Satan, and he will flee from you.*

The officers continued to command the elderly man to get up, and he continued to refuse to comply. With one quick motion, the officer released the dog, who lunged forward and growled into the faces of the officers holding the elderly man down. The officers jumped up and backed away. The dog started whimpering and leaned down to the elderly man and licked his tears away. Everyone jumped up and started cheering and laughing, clapping and praising the Lord. The police realized it was no use to continue, so they turned around and put the dogs in their vehicles.

"... and that's how I overcame my fear of dogs!" I said to Linda, who was overcome by this story of God's faithfulness.

As the evening came to a close, I looked at the moon reflecting beautifully on the calm water. I have always felt like the moon was God's eye keeping watch over me. And so He was.

CHAPTER 19

Miraculous Changes

I closed the door quietly so as not to wake Melissa and the children. Dan had already left for work. I stepped out into the darkness, bracing myself against the cold. It was December 1991 and my third winter in Atlanta. I sat in my car waiting for it to warm up a bit as I watched the massive pine trees bend and sway from the force of the howling wind.

The moon was hanging brightly in the blackness, calling out to me. I loved to look at the moon—the warm golden moon of harvest and the white, cold moon of winter. The moon made me think of the Creator, the One Who only needs to speak and all things become new. As I pulled away from the house, I asked my Creator God to create an atmosphere of acceptance and openness toward me today. Not only from the men and women I would meet, but from the escorts, the clinic personnel, and the abortionists. I also asked Him to create afresh and anew the love I needed for them as well. I needed this every day. As I drove along the interstate, the moon appeared to follow me. I thanked Him for His watchful eye, attending me wherever I went.

I turned onto Spring Street and saw the all-too-familiar clinic sign. My chest tightened. I became aware of that silent inner sigh, *Here we go again, Lord*. My car slid as I pulled into the driveway, tires spinning on the thick layer of ice on the steep hill. My eyes quickly scanned the parking lot next to the clinic for any cars that may have already arrived, but it was empty.

Pulling forward a bit, then putting the car into reverse, I turned the wheel to maneuver past a familiar large stone. My back tire dropped hard into a deep hole as my car came to a stop in my AAA parking spot, opposite the side of the clinic. *I could do this in my sleep*, I thought. Although it was always an effort to park here, I could see both the parking lot and most of the sidewalk in front of the clinic. That way, should I need to return to the car during the day to thaw out a bit, I could keep an eye on everyone—especially the clinic escorts who liked to donate potatoes by placing them in the tailpipe of my car.

I turned off the headlights, plunging the parking lot into darkness. I placed earmuffs over my hat, tucked in my scarf, rebuttoned my coat, and put on the gloves I had laid in front of the heater vent. Rejecting the idea of staying in the car the entire day, I opened the door, stepped out, and immediately slid on the ice. I grabbed the door handle to stop my fall. Bracing myself against the side of the car, I managed to slam the door closed. The sound echoed against the building. Repulsed by the frigid air, my lungs joined in with an equally echoing cough.

I smiled when I heard the lonely cough. In the past, I would have been scared to death to hear the sound of my own cough coming back at me in the darkness. Now I was amazed at how completely safe I felt. It simply never occurred to me to be afraid. Since my husband was the Creator of the Universe, the Great I Am Himself, how could I be afraid of anything?

And then, of course, there were my angels. It is said we all have a guardian angel. I have two. I have never seen them, but I knew they were there with me, always. I chatted with them from time to time, and I gave them secret names. Some days, I knew they were completely exhausted from keeping me safe all day. I apologized to them often.

Turning to walk down the dark, empty sidewalk, I assured myself that they indeed were with me now.

I began slowly walking up and down in front of the clinic, worshipping the Lord while asking for that day's protection, grace, and courage. As always, I sang, "Jesus, Jesus, Jesus, there's just something about that name." As the name of Jesus reverberated against the building, I grew bolder and bolder. I knew the power of that name strengthened me, but I also knew the power of that name weakened the forces of evil there.

I often imagined invisible evil forces stationed on the roof, hunched over, drooling, snorting, and spitting out curses at me. I would look up, yell Scripture at them, and *feel* them shrink back from God's Word. *Thank You, Lord, for the sensitivity to the spiritual world You gave me.* This was truly a battle of good against evil there at the very altar of Baal.

I temporarily ceased from my singing to the Lord and my shouting at the demons on the roof. All I could hear was the sound of the ice quietly cracking beneath my feet as it yielded to my every step. I whispered out into the dark, "Thank You, Lord, for the tread on these new boots and for my sister Donna who sent them to me."

Many of my counselors were out sick or had left town for the holidays, leaving me there by myself. I wished I could call Joanna, but unfortunately, she'd returned to California that past July. Her time committed to Atlanta as a missionary had ended. I missed her terribly but was glad she experienced some changes that had taken place there.

We now had two gracious and professional police officers who sat across the street to watch us. They observed that our counselors never harassed the women going in for their abortions. They realized we were not there to condemn them or pass judgment on them but rather to offer them love and compassion. They saw that the women stopped voluntarily to talk to us and accepted our literature. These new officers started getting excited when they saw women turn around and leave, refusing to go into the clinic. They would turn on their sirens with a *whoop-whoop* sound and give us a thumbs-up sign out their windows every time someone chose life and walked back to their cars.

Other policemen followed Steve's example and were bringing us cold tea during hot days and hot tea during cold days. Their wives collected baby clothes and baby furniture for me. I never got used to seeing squad cars pulling into the parking lot at Surgi and the officers who took baby cribs out and put them into my car.

Previously, the officers had written me up for injunction violations every day, six days a week, for the first eight months of the order. Then the Lord began to sway the hearts of the police on my behalf. They refused to write me up no matter how much the clinic personnel screamed at them. The police told me that one hundred and forty-five of my recorded violations had mysteriously disappeared. It seemed that they could only find sixty-three of them. Even that would hold a stiff fine and almost three and a half years in jail. If the lost violations were added, it would have been over eleven years of jail time. Jay Sekulow was right when he said that violating the injunction every day held the potential for much more jail time than rescuing ever would.

A week before I was to report to the criminal court for sentencing on the violations, the Supreme Court of Georgia gave their decision regarding the injunction Jay had argued. They upheld the injunction but modified the language. We could be within the fifty feet as long as there were no more than twenty of us at a time. All the pictures they took of me showed I was either alone or with only one or two other ladies every time. I never had to appear, never paid a fine, and never served a day for the injunction. Every single day for a full year, I kept on obeying and trusting, not knowing what the outcome would be. The Lord kept His promise, and the enemy did not triumph over me. More importantly, four hundred and twenty-eight babies were saved during that twelve-month period.

As I would tell my pregnant moms, "You can't go wrong by doing right—and it's always right to obey God." To God be the glory!

During that time, Margie Pitts Hames would come to Surgi Center at least once a week to tell me they were going to "fry" me for violating the injunction.

I would respond, "Only if God says so, Margie."

She was hardly convinced. "You just wait and see."

Margie was a powerful attorney in Atlanta. On January 22, 1973, the Supreme Court ruled on *Roe v. Wade,* allowing abortion on demand. That same afternoon, Margie won her argument for *Doe v. Bolton*, which ushered in the right for abortions throughout all nine months of pregnancy.

When she would visit me at the clinics, she would threaten, "I know people in high places, Black." She assured me she had the police officers, the mayor, the DA, the law, and the Supreme Court of America on her side.

I, however, had the Great I Am, my constant companion, to defend me. I became burdened for Margie and prayed for her relentlessly. I genuinely desired God's best for her, knowing what amazing things such a gifted and determined person could do for the Lord.

Then Margie reminded me that I still needed to go to court for the previous twelve arrests for rescue. She said I would go to Hardwick Prison, pay a huge fine, and be banished from Atlanta.

On the day of my appearance in court, the judge inquired why there were so many officers in the courtroom.

One of them yelled from the back, "Because we love her!"

The judge called me forward to stand before him. "Ms. Black, what if I told you that you couldn't go out to the clinics tomorrow? What would you do?"

"Your Honor, I don't want to be belligerent or disrespectful, but the Lord told me He wants me out there, and I have to obey Him."

"I could take your license away from you," the judge said.

"Well, I'm sure someone will give me a ride down there, Your Honor."

"You could lose your job."

"Oh, I gave up my job a long time ago, Your Honor. I live by faith, and I never go without a thing."

"You could go to jail for a very long time!"

"That's okay, Your Honor. I have been there lots of times before. I'll just have a jail ministry then."

Genuinely agitated and exasperated, the judge let out a loud moan and began rubbing his forehead. He put his glasses on and opened my file. I assumed it was very full, as they referred to me as a repeat offender. I didn't know until sometime later that several of my moms had mailed letters to him pleading on my behalf. They begged him to please not take me off the sidewalks or send me to jail. One woman wrote if I had not been there that day, she would have made the biggest mistake of her life. I was told that the letters in my file contained pictures of their babies, but I didn't know that at the time. The judge closed the file, took off his glasses, and looked up at me.

"Okay. No jail time, no fine. So that your present *ministry* can continue, I'm not restricting you from any of the clinics," he concluded.

I praised the Lord that in this strong city called Atlanta, the Lord showed His marvelous kindness to me. Psalm 31:19 and 21 says, "Oh, how great is Your goodness which You have laid up for those who fear You, which You have prepared for those who trust in You in the presence of the sons of men! Blessed be the Lord, for He has shown me His marvelous kindness in a strong city!" He swayed the hearts of those in high places to do whatsoever He willed on my behalf.

The judge agreed with the prosecutor to give me some measure of punishment, so he sentenced me to one hundred and sixty days of community service. Assigned to a recycling center, I worked eight to ten hours on Saturdays, sorting trash into glass, plastic, and cans. I would go home with every muscle aching and nerves jarred from the deafening sounds of the can and glass crushing machines and covered in sour milk and sticky soda.

I was right where the Lord wanted me to be. People on probation ran the entire place, and they all wanted to know why I was there. After I spoke with them, many girls canceled their scheduled abortions. One man returned to say he had talked his niece out of an abortion using the literature I distributed. Young men changed their minds completely about abortion, as well as sex outside of marriage. Each week, I was met by many asking for more pro-life and abstinence literature. The Lord helped me to win their respect. At lunchtime, the supervisor made everyone hush so I could share the gospel. Two men and one woman trusted Christ during the time I served there!

MIRACULOUS CHANGES

Suddenly, the streetlight flickered and made a snapping sound, jarring me from my mental wanderings. Stomping my feet, hoping to warm them up a bit, I saw women were arriving along with Stacy, one of the clinic workers. The director of Surgi had recently ordered Stacy to come outside whenever possible. She wanted her out front with us when the escorts couldn't be there. Raymond had stopped coming to the clinics a year ago. Doris, however, never went away.

Stacy was receptive to the love we extended to her. She began to help us. She would come out of the clinic to tell us the number of patients scheduled for the day and what time the last one was supposed to arrive. She snuck literature in for us. We called her our "Rahab." Stacy wanted to know who that was, so we gave her a Bible to read Rahab's story. A few days later, I saw her standing under the abortion clinic sign, reading the Bible. I wished I had a camera. What a picture!

The director sent out other clinic personnel to be escorts as well. This gave us the chance to befriend them and share Christ every day. Over time, three of them trusted Christ and left the clinic. As one left, she gave us the thumbs-up sign, telling us to keep up the good work. Another pulled a girl aside and encouraged her to have her baby—and she quit the next day.

The greatest victory yet was to be with Patricia. She arrived every morning walking through the back parking lot and would head straight for me. The other counselors all groaned when they saw her, knowing what was about to happen. Patricia carried a canvas bag containing many heavy objects she used to hit me. I referred to it as her "bag of bricks."

She would swing the bag at me and say, "Damn you to hell!"

Every single day I braced myself against the bag, which caused huge bruises on my arms, legs, and back. I asked the Lord to give me the strength every morning to just say, "God bless you." As the bruises increased, I somehow kept my commitment to say these words (between clenched teeth).

Then things began to change. Not in Patricia. She was as mean as ever. The change was in me. A supernatural grieving for her came over me. I thought about her, I prayed for her, I begged the Lord to deliver her of her anger and whatever abuse she had suffered that made her so mean. I wept for her.

One morning, I could tell Patricia had added extra items to her "bag of bricks." The hatred in her eyes and the force with which she hit me were particularly brutal.

When she said, "Damn you to hell!" it was with more fury than I had ever heard before.

Supernaturally, I felt her excruciating inner pain. A horrific mourning for her came over me. I fell to my knees and began sobbing uncontrollably. She turned around with a look of glee on her face, thinking I was crying from the physical pain she had inflicted.

"I'm so sorry, Patricia," I managed to say. "Please let the Lord love you."

Her face dropped. She started toward me but then stopped herself. Patricia turned toward the clinic and looked back at me. I saw her tears.

That night, unknown to me until later, Patricia went to a church near her home and trusted Christ. The next day when I saw her approaching, I braced myself for her abuse. Instead, she dropped her "bag of bricks" at my feet and gave me a long, sincere hug, thanking me for caring about her.

Shortly afterward, she quit her job at the clinic and started working in an obstetrician's office. She came by to tell us it was so rewarding to see the women leave every day, still pregnant. There were times I had thought there was no hope for Patricia, but the Lord proved me wrong once again. I was amazed at His wonder-working power—mostly for what He had done in *my* heart!

Sue was particularly excited about Patricia and the other clinic workers who had quit. She had been there from the beginning and knew how difficult they were making our lives every day. After Patricia's change of heart, Sue reminded me how I told each of our counselors they couldn't come out to sidewalk counsel if they didn't think they could love the women, the clinic personnel, the escorts, and the abortionists.

"I was shocked at how adamant you were," she said. "I thought you were going to chase away the counselors before they ever started."

"We simply couldn't risk any nonsense or poor testimonies," I said. "I knew we had to have the best counselors. Their love for the Lord and others shines through, and everyone sees it!"

Sue was the counselor who caused the escorts' hearts to soften toward us. On one freezing day in winter, one escort stood without any gloves on. Sue took off her mittens and handed them to the escort.

Taking the mittens, her face softened. "Thank you," she said. The escort's attitude toward us began changing from that day on.

Not everyone was at peace with us, however. Many displayed their hatred daily, further angered by our lawsuit. Jay had previously asked those of us who were arrested while praying if he could represent us in a lawsuit against the City of Atlanta for unlawful arrest and imprisonment. He wanted the city to stop violating our First Amendment rights. We agreed to the lawsuit only because we felt it would mean less harassment for the missionaries who would follow after us.

Imagine both my surprise and concern when the front page of the *Atlanta Journal* reported on our lawsuit under the title, "Karen Black versus the City of Atlanta."

Yikes! I didn't expect that. I was reminded frequently by the clinic escorts we would surely lose the case. When they heard I had also been asked to be part of a lawsuit against the City of Los Angeles, they laughed even harder. They believed we were too few and too stupid to take on the police in these powerful cities.

They're right, I thought. *We will win only if God says so!*

And He did.

As the streetlight went out in response to the early morning's faint light, my solitary shadow vanished from the sidewalk.

People ran past me, rushing to get in, out of the cold. It was a challenge to get anyone to stop and talk to me. Most of the women refused the literature I offered them that morning, but many of the men received the "For Men Only" brochures. I asked each of them to share the other brochure with the women, which I had carefully tucked behind theirs.

One woman did stop, however, saying it was her friend who was in the clinic for an abortion. "What can I say to get her to leave?" she asked.

I gave her some suggestions and handed her my plastic baby model to show her friend. As I watched her enter the clinic, I prayed the baby model would make a difference and that I'd get it back—because I usually didn't.

I walked back to my car to warm up. My body, stiff from the cold, sank into the equally cold car seat. My hand shook as I reached for the key to start the engine. I pulled my gloves off and placed them near the heater vent, keeping the glove liners on. As my body thawed out, I started to relax. Denying my body the sleep it craved, I sat up and reached for my thermos, savoring the last drop of its hot and delicious contents. I pulled on my now warm gloves, knowing they would stay that way for a mere thirty seconds.

I gathered the courage to step outside into the painfully frigid wind once again and received an instant reward. The young woman who had taken my fetal model held it up for me to see as she ran toward me with her equally happy friend in tow. Thank You, Lord!

Only six more hours to go.

CHAPTER 20

Lessons Learned

I heard a strange shuffling sound before I turned and saw her. A thin pink thread clung to her tangled mess of unkempt hair, matted and filled with lint. She was bent over, hugging herself in a futile attempt to keep warm. The wind wafted up behind her, carrying her pungent body odor to me. Her T-shirt and sweatpants, torn at both shoulders and knees, were covered with filth and food. She looked the size of a child as even I, at just over five feet, was taller than she.

My heart broke as I saw a cold, pitiful woman approaching me. The sound was coming from her rubber flip-flops, nearly flattened from use. I wondered why she was tiptoeing on the balls of her feet. As she got closer, I saw the heels of her sandals were both completely torn away as she desperately tried to keep her bare and purple feet off the cold pavement. I looked down into her dirty face as she came to a stop in front of me. Her toothless mouth was framed by her aged, deeply furrowed face.

"Good morning," I said, smiling at her.

She stared back at me. I asked if I could help her. She continued to stare. I asked if she needed something to eat. She shook her head no.

I realized she was staring at the scarf around my neck. I asked if she would like it. She nodded yes. I took the scarf off and put it on her head, covering her freezing ears, and tied it around her neck. She then stared at my mittens. I asked if she would like them as well. She nodded. I pulled them onto her cold, purple hands. She was now staring at my coat. *I'll be naked by the time she's done with me*, I thought. I took off my coat and placed it on her small, frail body. I zipped it up and tucked the scarf in. I could see her respond to the warmth from my body heat lingering inside the coat.

I, however, was feeling anything but warmth at that moment as a gust of frigid air caused a violent shiver to go through me. Hoping this would be the end of the shedding of my clothes, I asked her again if I could get her something to eat. She shook her head and began staring at my shoes—a brand-new pair of sneakers I had just bought the day before. I didn't feel the need for boots anymore, as there were now only patches of snow and ice on the sidewalk. Her continual staring was uncomfortable. I walked away. She followed me, glaring at my feet. I couldn't get away from her. *These are my brand-new sneakers! Besides, I'm not going to stand out here on the sidewalk without any shoes on. How embarrassing*! Her eyes never left my feet.

I looked at her purple feet and half-shoes. I knew her feet had to be the coldest part of her body. I tried to ignore that she was constantly trying to balance herself on the balls of her feet. She followed me, making that strange sound as she shuffled along in her half-shoes.

Finally, with a sigh and a silent grumble, I sat down with her on the frosty grass. I removed the dirty, inadequate flip-flops from her feet. Reluctantly, I pulled off my sneakers and began to place them on her cold, calloused feet. She pushed my hand away and shook her head, staring again at my feet.

"I know, you need shoes," I said. "These are brand new. I just got them yesterday." I had bought a pair of sneakers and one pair of white socks. The shoes and socks didn't take my very last penny, however. Seventeen cents remained after the purchase.

Again, I tried to put my sneakers on her—and again, she pushed my hand away, shook her head, and stared at my feet. *My socks! She wants my socks!*

Now annoyed, I put the shoes on her and said, "Enough is enough! You can have my shoes but not my socks!"

Helping her to a standing position, I asked her one final time if I could take her somewhere or get some food for her. She looked right through me with horrible disappointment in her eyes. They pierced my very soul. I ignored the pain and guilt I felt as she turned and walked away. I turned and walked in the opposite direction, trying to shed the rapidly increasing uneasy feeling in the pit of my stomach.

I remembered I had left my hat in the car. I told myself that it would help her stay warm. It would make me feel better to give it to her. But it was too late. She was gone.

Moments before she'd appeared on the sidewalk, I'd felt the Lord tell me to stay the full amount of time I had committed to be at Midtown Hospital that day. Not one minute less. Only fifteen more minutes remained, but it started to feel more like an hour. I figured the Lord wanted me to stay to the last minute so I could talk to someone who had not yet arrived.

I glanced at the cars waiting for the light to change and saw the drivers looking at me. Now I was the one hugging myself to stay warm as the wind and cold cut through my thin blouse. With no hat, coat, scarf, gloves, or shoes, I must have looked like a fool standing there in the cold in my stocking feet. I picked up my sidewalk counseling brochures and walked back and forth in front of Midtown. I felt my socks stick to the patches of ice.

Turning back down the sidewalk, I saw small pieces of lint and strings from my socks stuck in the ice. The light turned red again, and more cars stopped. More people sat in their cars, staring. I berated myself for being embarrassed. I realized I didn't want to be mistaken for a homeless person. I thought about the old woman and couldn't believe that I was more concerned about appearances than her desperate helplessness.

When the time was up and no one had arrived, I started across the street to my car. My spirit was heavy. I was ashamed of myself.

Making my way down Ponce De Leon, I scanned the road, hoping to see her to give her my socks. I couldn't find her. I realized it was an opportunity lost.

My shoeless foot felt strange on the brake and gas pedals as I drove home. I kept thinking of verses about giving to the needy. "Give to the one who begs from you" (Matthew 5:42), and "If a brother or sister is naked and destitute of daily food, and one of you says to them, 'Depart in peace, be warmed and filled,' but you do not give them the things which are needed for the body, what does it profit?" (James 2:15–16).

I did give to her when she begged of me. I did offer her food, I did cover her body, but I didn't give her my *all*. I didn't give her the very thing I knew I needed to give her when I first looked at her feet. I put my own needs before hers. I was more concerned about what I would look like and wondered when I would have enough money to buy another pair of sneakers or new socks. In addition to my selfishness and pride, I was faithless.

After all the Lord had done for me, how could I ever doubt His ability to care for all my needs? Had He not already provided so beautifully, so thoroughly? Other people faithfully responded to the Lord and were meeting my needs, *all* my needs. Yet I had not met the most pressing need she presented to me. Had the Lord not given His *all* for me? I had asked Him to make me broken bread and poured-out wine, but I had fallen short. Instead, I felt Him reassuring me He remembered I was made of dust.

Nevertheless, I wanted to be like Him. I wanted to give my all in service to Him as I served others.

Arriving at home, I noticed a package addressed to me propped up against the front door. I was excited to see that the package was from my longtime and cherished friend, Jackie. Two weeks earlier, she had called and said she'd sent a package to me via UPS. She refused to tell me what was in the package.

"It's a surprise. Just let me know when it comes," she said.

I went inside and put on Melissa's sweater, which I'd found hanging on the back of the kitchen chair. I made a cup of tea to help warm myself. I knew the package would contain a letter, and I wanted to sit down and take the time to savor Jackie's correspondence along with the hot tea.

When I opened the package, I couldn't believe what I had found. Nestled between carefully placed tissue paper was a beautiful scarf with matching hat and gloves. Further examination of the box revealed two more sets of matching scarfs, hats, and gloves. Knowing me as she did, Jackie had sent my favorite colors. Finding these items in Southern California must have been a task for her—a real labor of love.

I carried my generous gifts to my room. Hanging on my bedroom door was a beautiful long, heavily insulated coat with a note pinned to the left shoulder that read, "To keep you warm, Karen." Then on my bed, I saw a large shoe box. Taped to the top of the box was another note in different handwriting that said, "For Karen Black." Inside was a pair of high-quality sneakers with thick, comfortable soles and three pairs of warm, padded white socks.

Tears stung my eyes as I felt a wave of shame and regret come over me. I dropped to the floor next to my bed. I sat there shaking my head with tears streaming down my face. Once again, I confessed my selfish, doubting heart. I realized afresh I could never out-give God, even when I give what I think is my all, for He can always replace my meager offerings. And when I do fail to give my all, He loves and provides for me anyway. He is faithful to His Word: "If we are faithless, He remains faithful" (2 Timothy 2:13).

I called Jackie to tell her about the events of the day, letting her know her package had arrived.

She laughed. "I sent that over two weeks ago. I wonder where the Lord has been hiding it all this time, making sure that you didn't get it until today to drive this lesson home so clearly."

"Yes, I gave away one scarf and one set of gloves. He gave me back three. He even multiplied the hat I didn't give away," I said.

The coat I gave away couldn't begin to compare to the one I received. The expensive sneakers were not at all like the ones I bought at the discount store. Even the socks were of a much better quality. "He gave me back three pairs even when I selfishly clung to my one."

I felt bad because I received nicer things than the poor homeless lady. I knew the Lord didn't want me to live with guilt. He gave me yet another lesson about His great faithfulness and love for me. The knowledge of His forgiveness, unsurpassable love, and provision filled me to overflowing. I would never forget this lesson.

When Melissa came home, I asked her to please call her friends and ask for donations of coats, hats, scarfs, and mittens for me to take with me sidewalk counseling. I told her shoes and socks were a must. At four thirty the next morning, I left the house and found two fully stuffed shopping bags waiting by the door with a note that said, "More to come."

Thank you, Melissa—and thank You, Lord!

Stepping over both drunks and rats, I made my way up a narrow, dark stairwell. The hot air intensified the smell of alcohol, vomit, and cat feces. Following closely were my two "assistants." I smiled at their eagerness, always quick to lend me a helping hand upon my arrival on Saturday afternoons. *Thank You, Lord, for giving me favor with all the gang members here in the housing projects.*

I delivered a highchair, a stroller, and a large box of clothes to one of my young mothers. I only had time for a hug and a short prayer, as I had many more deliveries to make. Thanking her for graciously giving back three large boxes of clothes her child had grown out of, I left and made my way back down the stairs.

Another one of my manly friends opened the door and took my burden from me. "Ya ought not to be carryin' nothin' so heavy, Biscol," he said.

I was confused the first time they called me "Biscol." I soon learned it was an acronym for "Baby Saving Church Lady" (BSCL) and their nickname for me.

I started to open the door to the car when I heard another young man say, "Let me get that fer ya, Ms. Biscol."

I backed away and let him open the door for me. Soon, I was surrounded by many admirers, each dressed in their *colors* (and I don't mean their tattoos), with both knives and chains at their sides. I received their hugs and kisses on both cheeks.

Standing at the front of the usual crowd was my favorite giant. Very tall and quite large, he would hold out his massive hand to me every Saturday, expecting me to give him another stack of gospel tracts. He would then walk up to everyone on the sidewalk and parking lot and encourage them to take one.

"Ms. Biscol says you need Jesus!" he would tell them.

Sometimes his encouragement was a bit rough, but everyone always consented and took a tract.

The first day I went to this particularly dangerous part of the city, I didn't give a thought to where I was going and the possibility of anything bad happening. I just knew that I had baby clothes to deliver to a young woman who had left the clinic. Locating the address, I parked my car, then took out a box of baby items and my purse. I locked the car door, accidentally leaving my keys in the ignition.

Immediately, some scary-looking, mean-faced gang members surrounded me, staring. I walked up to the one who looked like he might be their leader.

I smiled. "I bet you guys would all know how to break into my car—if you don't mind doing so, I'd appreciate it."

I heard someone chuckle. I told them I was there to bring some baby clothes to a pregnant woman, and I needed their help to get my keys out of the car. Not knowing if the car would still be there when I came back, I turned and opened the door to the apartment building. I made my way up the foul-smelling, dark stairway.

The apartment felt as hot as an oven. Dark, heavy curtains covered the windows. Despite the darkness, I could see the nicotine-stained walls. A cloud of dust and smoke hung in the air. The television was blasting as the pregnant girl's three brothers were passed out on the couch and floor. The girl's mother looked up at me from her small chair and smiled warmly. Through the thin walls, I could hear children crying and people screaming and cussing in other apartments.

The young and vulnerable face of the pregnant girl I'd first met at Surgi now smiled at me and eagerly reached for the box of baby items I had brought for her. I watched her pull out each beautiful matching outfit, carefully washed and folded. A dread came over me as I realized how truly pathetic my offering was—how were these baby clothes going to help her raise this child?

What have I done? I had encouraged her to bring her child into this awful, drug-infested, violent environment. But what was the alternative? Using more violence by killing the child through an abortion was not the answer either. Right then and there, I begged the Lord to help me make a real, substantial difference in these women's lives to help them prepare for motherhood.

Promising to keep in touch, I said goodbye and made my way back down the crowded stairs, accidentally stepping on someone's hand. He never noticed. I opened the door and sucked in the fresh air, noticing that all the *gentlemen* were still standing by my car.

As I approached, their snarls changed to smiles. They backed away from the car so I could see that they had washed it. One of them was finishing up the windows. They handed me the keys and thanked me for helping babies.

Breathing a sigh of relief, I thanked them and reached for my car door—but then I turned around, gave each of them a hug, and said, "God bless you."

They laughed and hugged me back. "God bless you too."

So started the relationships I quickly came to treasure.

As the months went by, I returned to the housing projects and learned all their real names, as well as their street names. Not one had a father involved in their life. Their mothers would invite me in for sweet tea. I listened for hours to these mothers' painful, tearful stories. Each of these young men would meet me on delivery days, eager to help me carry cribs and baby items to needy young women. I wondered how many had fathered these children.

Many times, we held hands in the parking lot together to pray. My heart broke at the depth of despair they lived with daily, experiencing things most of us would never encounter in our entire lives. Many trusted Christ. Most did not, but I gave them verses from the Word to memorize every week, and I trusted the Lord would help them recall the verses when His Spirit called to them. My little group of helpers often changed, as some died from stabbings, shootings, and overdoses. Others would take their places in our circle of prayer. My heart was both broken and warmed by each of them.

On this day, I was encouraged, knowing that I would help a young pregnant woman move out of this place. She wanted to give her child a better life than she had known. She had voiced a sincere desire to get her bachelor's degree in computer science. The public assistance for her education, although appreciated, would not cover all her expenses, especially after the baby was born.

Her aunt lived in a much safer place across town and had agreed to let her live with her, but couldn't babysit because of her own job. I secured a group of people who would cover her childcare costs as long as she maintained at least a B average. She would use MARTA, Atlanta's public transportation system, to get back and forth to school. Although she would receive food stamps until she earned her degree, the goal was to help her become completely free of the welfare system as soon as possible. I assigned a personal life coach to her to help keep her on task. It was going to take all she had to complete the four years ahead of her. I felt with the help offered her, and hard work on her part, she would see her dream come true.

The Lord had raised up so many people to help me and my organization, Women 4 Women. He sent a variety of people to help the mothers—those who were wealthy, poor, young, and old.

One homebound, discouraged widow in poor health was making quilts every day, thinking she was no longer of any value to society. When she learned about Women 4 Women, she sent some baby quilts to me, and I took them to the clinics. One pregnant woman who was uncertain about her decision saw me hold up one quilt with a cute teddy bear on the front. Seeing the quilt touched her heart, and excitedly, she chose life for her child.

Later, I brought her baby, wrapped in the same quilt, to that sweet widow. I explained that her quilt had helped save the child's life. She shared the story with many of her friends. Soon, other widows joined her efforts to make quilts for us and became our small band of widows who had found a renewed purpose in life.

I learned how important it was to send each of our turnarounds home with a baby gift, realizing they may return home to friends and family who might continue to encourage them to have an abortion. I knew a sweet, tiny set of baby booties or a cute baby outfit would touch their hearts. I wanted their decision for life fortified with excitement about the baby. Their faces would light up as they hugged the baby items we gave them. It helped them to stand up against those negative voices.

Another group of women met monthly to fill baby gift bags with tiny, adorable outfits. Their efforts had a profound effect on a young woman named Carol, who had been taken to Surgi for an abortion against her will. Her mother and father, who had been divorced for years, came together to take their daughter to Atlanta for the abortion. After the mother forced her daughter inside, the father stopped and talked to me. He agreed that the abortion would be wrong, so he went in and brought her out. Her mother was furious, screaming and cussing at him. I could hear her mom yelling as their car pulled out of the driveway.

The mom continued to yell until she was hoarse. Carol tried to get her mom to look at the cute baby clothes we had given to her, but her mom refused.

"I don't want to look at any of that junk those stupid people gave you!"

After many attempts, her mom relented and took the bag. Taking out the first little shirt with a cute giraffe on the front, she softened.

"Yeah, that's sweet. It's tiny, but you know it's going to be big for a newborn." Her mom explained how little the baby would be.

Carol realized the fight had gone out of her mom when she said, "I wonder if it will be a girl or a boy. I think a girl would be nice."

Several months had passed, and Carol was still pregnant and happy. I was glad she told me about her mom's change of heart.

"It always goes that way. She just didn't know that when you were at Surgi," I said.

"But that's not all. My mom insisted we stop on the way home and go shopping for the baby. They bought baby furniture with all the money they had brought for the abortion."

"That's so special, Carol. Many grandmothers end up doing that."

"That's still not all. My mom and dad have been talking and meeting to discuss how to help the baby and me, and *now they are getting remarried!*"

Carol said her mom's heart began to change with the bag of baby clothes. Now, as I met with the women who prepared the baby gift bags, I wanted each faithful one to know what amazing things the Lord can do with their efforts. Men were also joining our team, as well as whole families.

Homeless people came to help too. Even *they* desired to stop children from dying. Especially a homeless couple named Darlene and Frank, whom I first met in front of Midtown Hospital. Darlene, who was so very pregnant, first appeared in front of me on the sidewalk, trying to pull her coat closed over her large abdomen.

I stopped her and offered her my literature. When she realized I thought she was there for an abortion, she was horrified. She screamed that no matter how difficult her life was, she could never do such a thing!

Then her husband walked up next to her. He was wrapped in a large blanket and wanted to know about Midtown Hospital. I explained it was an abortion clinic. Many of the women going in there were in tough situations and felt they had no other choice.

He looked at me, raised his eyebrow, and nodded at his wife. "Can't get much worse than our situation. We would never consider such a thing!" He shared their story about experiencing sudden, unexpected homelessness.

When he saw a woman refuse the literature and walk past him to go into the clinic, he took the brochure from me and followed her inside. Within minutes, he came back out with her. He assured her it was going to be okay. Crying, she hugged him and Darlene and left. Frank took ten more brochures and went back inside. I warned him he could be arrested.

He turned and looked at me as if I didn't understand. "Babies are dying in there!"

Fifteen minutes later, he came out. He had talked out loud to all of them at once, encouraging them to leave. Some of them were angry, some of them were crying.

Mission accomplished, he and Darlene had to go. He had a job interview. As they walked away, I told him I would try to get a coat for him.

"Come back on Monday if you can," I said.

He was an incredibly tall, large man. Long ago, I had stopped wondering about the "how" of getting things for others. I just relied on the "Who."

I learned that lesson the first time I promised something to a turnaround, nearly a year ago. Her name was Denise, and she was the last one to arrive at Surgi Center that day. I stopped her and shared both the literature and my concern for her. She was having an abortion because she didn't have a crib for her baby. I tried to hide my disbelief that a child would die because of a lack of furniture. She would not consider my suggestion of using a basket or a dresser drawer until the baby got bigger.

"My baby gets the best, or it gets nothing!"

I was desperate to save her child.

"I can get that for you."

"You can?"

"Sure! I'll get you a crib, a changing table, a dresser, and anything else you need. How about a stroller and a bouncy seat? I'll get all the crib bedding and a carousel for the crib and bumper pads. You do what I can't do—you be pregnant, and I'll get all the things you need."

"Can you get all white furniture?"

"Sure!"

"Okay, I'll keep the baby then."

Shocked at the ease of her new decision, I took down her name and number and told her I would call her soon. I got in my car to leave, wondering how I was going to do what I had promised her. I was a full-time missionary. I didn't own a thing, didn't have a job, and had no means of my own to purchase all the things I told her I would get for her.

I was reminded that Mom always said, "The consequences of our obedience are God's problem."

I was at the clinic in obedience. I said what I needed to say to encourage her to change her mind—now He had to do the rest.

As I arrived home and pulled into the driveway, I could see that He had gone ahead of me once again. There on the front lawn was a white crib, changing table, and dresser. I also saw a stroller and a bouncy seat. Melissa stood in the middle of the pile with her hands on her hips and a confused look on her face.

"Where did this all come from?" she asked. "Did you ask someone for all this for one of your mothers?"

"Yes."

"Who?"

"God."

"Yeah, but who delivered it?"

I didn't know, but God did. I told Melissa about Denise's specific requests. She laughed and then cried. Then I noticed the beautiful bedding and bumper pads covered in pink daisies and a matching carousel. Denise was having a girl! I figured the Lord knew how to put in proper orders, so surely there was no doubt. Everything seemed to be brand new, including a swing I had not promised.

I told Melissa my need to find an enormous winter coat for Frank, the homeless man. She asked if I thought it too would show up on the lawn in the morning. Instead, I counted on her to make some calls and have it ready by Monday. She did, and I brought the coat to Midtown and gave it to Frank. I also shared the name and phone number of an employer offering him a job with transportation. He started work the very next day.

The lives of Frank, Darlene, and Denise turned around in incredible ways. Frank and Darlene had a boy, and yes, Denise had her girl! The Lord continued to touch their hearts through the generous outpouring of love from the Body of Christ.

In the end, no matter how many people I questioned, I never found out *how* the baby furniture arrived on the front lawn that day—but I did know by *Whom*.

CHAPTER 21

Christians Aren't Perfect

The sudden appearance of sleet driven by a powerful wind caught me by surprise. My umbrella got caught by the wind and jerked out of my hand, half flying, half tumbling up the hill. I hurried toward my car to get another umbrella from the trunk. The wind increased, and the sleet turned to hail, blowing sideways. I held my literature to the side of my face, attempting to shield my cheek from the painful pelting ice. As suddenly as it began, the hail stopped, and a heavy rain began.

My second umbrella turned inside out several times as I made my way toward a young woman rushing into Surgi Center. I used this opportunity to get close to her as I held my umbrella over her head. I handed her literature, assuring her I was there to help her and encouraged her to choose life for her child. She thanked me for the brochure—as well as my umbrella, and promptly took it from my hand. She left me standing alone in the rain as she hurried into the clinic. *What?* That wasn't exactly what I had in mind in *sharing* my umbrella.

A line of cars began pulling into the parking lot at a steady pace, so getting into my car and out of the rain for even a moment was out of the question. I was so grateful Steve had given me a raincoat the day before. I had forgotten, however, to snap the hood on. I left it at home on the kitchen table, along with my lunch. As the downpour turned into a deluge, freezing rain poured down my back. Chills ran through my entire body.

The rainwater rushed rapidly down the hill, gushing over my feet on the sidewalk. The gutter was so full it spilled into the middle of the first lane of traffic. As some people drove by, they slowed down to avoid hitting the deep puddle. Others would speed up and get as close to me as possible, opening their windows and sharing their morning obscenities with me. Waves of water went over my head, hitting me with such force I would stumble to stay on my feet. Now my ears were full of rain as well.

Scripture says that we are to give thanks in *all* things. I had learned long ago to do just that. I marvel at how the Lord uses difficult situations to protect me from something worse.

With my teeth chattering, I said, "Thank You for this torrent of rain, Lord."

Because the rain was coming down so heavily, the women stayed in their cars, waiting until the rain decreased. This gave me an opportunity to get the literature to them while they were sitting there. They barely cracked their windows open, so I was not able to talk to them. I'm sure I looked a sight walking from car to car in the pouring rain, taking literature from the plastic baggy I found in my car. I slid and fell twice on the wet, muddy grass. Before I finished with the long line of cars, two of the first cars pulled away. Were they turnarounds? I didn't know. I wouldn't count them unless I knew for sure.

Stacy told me how many women were scheduled this early part of the morning, so I counted them as they arrived. I knew I would have some time before the next wave showed up. I grabbed a pair of dry socks from the bag of items for the homeless in the trunk. McDonald's had the strongest and hottest hand dryers in town, so I made my way there, heading directly to the ladies' room. I knew I looked a mess, with soaking wet hair, mascara on my face, and mud on my clothes. I ignored the stares and continued toward the restroom, my water-filled sneakers making a squishing sound with every step. I turned on both dryers, holding a shoe up to each one.

With the sound of flushing toilets, two stall doors opened and each young lady made their way to the sinks. I moved both shoes to one dryer. I noticed that one of them looked pensive and worried as she stared at me.

Her friend asked, "What happened to you? How did you get so wet?"

As I explained my situation, I couldn't help noticing the sideways glance she gave to her friend.

I turned toward the one I felt was pregnant. "Don't go to Fem Center, honey. Let me and my ministry, Women 4 Women, help you instead."

Her eyes opened wide. Without saying a word, she let me continue. I explained all the ways we could help her. I assured her she would be blessed with this child, no matter how difficult her situation was.

Her friend had stepped back behind her, holding her hands in a praying position and squeezing her eyes tightly closed. She mouthed a silent prayer.

The pregnant girl let out her breath with a loud sigh. "How did you know?"

I ignored her question, encouraging her to choose life for herself and her baby. With tears flowing, she agreed. Her friend jumped up and down, hugging her first and then me. The pregnant girl eagerly reached into her purse for a pen and paper. She wrote down her name and number and, with one more hug for me, turned and walked out the door.

Before they left, I learned they had been on their way to Fem Center, next to the McDonald's. I hadn't made plans to go there that day. The Lord reminded me to thank Him for *all* things. If I hadn't been so wet, I wouldn't have gone to McDonald's to dry my shoes, and I would never have met them.

I walked out with my now dry shoes and socks. The smell of food reminded me I was starving, but I didn't have any money with me.

With a sigh and a shrug, I made my way back to Surgi, breathing a prayer for some money. Right on cue, the second wave of cars started

to arrive. This group of women was somehow different. They refused my offers of literature, giving me looks filled with contempt. It felt as if a strange evil spirit had arrived with them. Then I realized why. The parking lot was filling up with cars with the all-too-familiar bumper stickers on them: "Christians Aren't Perfect, Just Forgiven," "God Is My Co-pilot," and "I Love Jesus."

I had grown accustomed to seeing these bumper stickers, as well as well-worn Bibles in the back windows of cars, every single day—but never this many at one time, on one day. I felt attacked. It was as if Satan had gathered them all together for a grand display of his power because he knew how much it bothered me. Many times, it was the fear of God that caused women to listen and choose life for their children. This didn't happen with those claiming to be Christians. Their fear of God had been replaced with an arrogant confidence in their "buddy" Jesus.

I sat down on a rock as another car arrived, pulling up next to me to park.

Before I could stand up, an older woman jumped out and pointed her finger in my face. "You're right. You're one hundred percent right! It's a baby, it's perfectly formed, it feels pain, and yes, it's murder—but ain't it wonderful God forgives everything!"

I watched her as she walked away. When I stood up, I could see a church bulletin lying on the front seat of her car. Written on the front were directions to Surgi Center from Tennessee. I often saw this on Monday mornings. *God help us!* I sat down on the rock again and thought how the Lord must be grieving—not only at the loss of His little creations but also about the behavior of those who claimed to be His children. I thought about the picture of the church this was sending to the lost world. I was angry, frustrated, and bewildered because I didn't know what to do about it.

Daily I comforted myself with the thought that these people were probably not born-again Christians. Anyone can call themself a Christian, after all. The Lord always gets a bad rap when Christians claim His name in conjunction with their ungodly behavior.

I remembered the women I counseled in the past following their abortions, particularly the pastors' wives. Repeatedly, they said the reason for their abortion was so they could remain free to serve the Lord. My stomach turned every time someone used that excuse. When I considered their profession of Christ, I concluded that while they may be believers, they had best not call themselves followers. To follow Christ means to follow what He says *to do,* not what He says *not to do!*

My daily disappointment and grief intensified as yet another car arrived with its distinctive Christian bumper sticker. As I approached the car, I noticed the T-shirt worn by the young teenage girl had the name of her Christian school written on the front. It appeared that her father was accompanying her. He looked like a preacher. She gave me a weak smile as he swiftly escorted her by me, nudging me away with his shoulder.

"Shame on you!" he said, as he rushed her to the door.

The sun came out, and with the help of a steady breeze, the leaves had dried. I looked down at some leaves that had attached themselves to my shoelaces. I reached down and pulled them off. I was famished. I asked again for the Lord to give me some money for food.

Before long, I saw the 'preacher' father walking back toward his car. I held out the literature to him, but he refused. I shared my concern for his daughter. He swung around angrily to face me.

"My daughter attends a Christian school! Do you understand how important it is for her to sit under the instruction of the Word of God every day? She can't attend a Christian school and remain pregnant. The Lord understands."

Anger rose in me.

"No, He doesn't!" I saw that he had a small book in the pocket of his dress shirt. "You have a New Testament in your pocket!"

"Yes, I'm a preacher, and I'm going to be witnessing while I'm in there." He opened the trunk of his car and took out a fist full of gospel tracts and started back toward the clinic entrance.

Inside, I shook.

"I am standing out here praying that the women sitting inside will think on the holiness of a God they will have to give an account to someday about their abortions. I'm praying the fear of God will cause them to leave—and you stand here saying that you are going in there to 'witness' to them. Your presence in there as your daughter waits for an abortion will only put a stamp of approval on what they are doing. It will chase away any doubts they might have!"

He stomped back up to me and leaned in to my face. "What do *you* know about God? You're a *nobody*! You're just a woman! *I am a man of God!*" He turned back toward the clinic and yelled over his shoulder, "Shame on you!"

"No! *Shame on you!*" I yelled back.

He brushed me off with a condescending wave of his hand. "You're just a woman. A nobody woman."

Tears stung my eyes. With frustration overwhelming me, I kicked the telephone pole. *Lord, I can't believe how many preachers bring their wives and daughters here for abortions. How is this possible? What do I do? But he's right, Lord. I am nobody to them. Why don't You send some preachers out here? Why don't You send Billy Graham himself out here?*

Deep within my spirit, I felt the Lord respond. *No, I don't need Billy Graham. I have chosen you! I'm going to make you a Billy Graham, and I'm going to tell the world!*

With another frustrated kick to the telephone pole, I said, "Yeah, right!"

A young lady who was leaving the clinic approached me, letting me know she was choosing life for her twins. I quickly wiped away my tears and tried to focus on her, not the jumble of emotions I was experiencing. I was frustrated and so very hungry. With my stomach growling, I reminded the Lord of my need for some money.

Another leaf had gotten stuck on the top of my shoe, flapping in the breeze. I shook my foot to dislodge the distraction while continuing to talk with her. She noticed my frustration and looked down at my foot.

"Look!" she said. "There's a twenty-dollar bill stuck to your shoe."

The Lord had answered my prayer for money, and there I was trying to kick away His provision!

I decided I would go and buy myself a sandwich, knowing the last woman had been seen that morning and the others wouldn't be arriving for another hour. With food and a cup of hot tea in my stomach, I settled down a bit.

The rain started to fall again. As much as I wanted to go straight home, I knew I had to return to the clinic. The arrival of cars was sporadic, allowing me more time to stay in my car. I kept the heater on to dry my wet feet. I looked at the preacher's car and prayed one of his tracts would indeed reach someone with the gospel.

As more cars arrived, I got out to meet them, glad it was just sprinkling now. A man driving by yelled for me to "mind your own business and get a job." His unfinished lunch landed on the front of my right arm. As if the Lord Himself loudly protested the food that was thrown at me, a clap of thunder rumbled, releasing a sudden downpour of rain. I thanked the Lord for washing the food off me so quickly—but again, I was totally drenched.

It was now late afternoon. As the Christians exited the clinic, I saw the preacher's sweet daughter. Walking slowly, she seemed to be in a lot of pain. Blood ran down her leg. She was sobbing.

Her father yelled at her to "Stand up and act like a lady!"

I wanted to show him just how unladylike *I* could be and go over and punch him out. Instead, I said, "God bless you, honey" to his daughter and handed her the post-abortion brochure.

Surprisingly, he let her keep it.

I stood in the pouring rain watching the preacher pull out of the parking lot. His car was followed by the many others with Christian bumper stickers. I thought about all the women who repeatedly said their pastors told them that "under the circumstances" their abortions would be okay, that God would forgive them. Many of them showed me verses their pastors had written down for them, reassuring them God understood. They carried their Bibles into the clinic for comfort.

I heard many pastors wonder why the Lord didn't seem to answer their prayers for their churches. I wondered if any of them had ever read Isaiah 1:15–17: "When you spread out your hands, I will hide My eyes from you; Even though you make many prayers, I will not hear. Put away the evil of your doings from before My eyes. Your hands are full of blood. Cease to do evil, learn to do good, seek justice, rebuke the oppressor, *defend the fatherless*, plead for the widow." Could it be their sins regarding abortion—through commission or omission—were why their prayers were left unanswered and their ministries ineffective?

I heard many women say to me, "If my pastor thought abortion was as bad as you think it is, he would preach against it, but he never does."

How many pastors know how their silence on the subject is translated as permission by thousands upon thousands of church-going women?

As the last young girl walked by, her mother pushed my hand and brochure out of the way. "Honey, my pastor said that it's covered by the blood, and nothing can separate me from the love of God. The Holy Spirit will give me peace."

Yes—but only after He brings her through the painful process of revealing the full awfulness of what she has done. Only after this gut-wrenching realization will she be able to repent. Only then will she be forgiven, and only then will she be restored to find the peace she mistakenly thought was so easily achieved.

Instead of driving directly out of the parking lot, this mother pulled up alongside me, rolled down her window, and shouted through the rain, "Believe me, I know Him!"

Either she was wrong, or the Word of God was wrong. First John 2:4 says: "He who says, 'I know Him,' and does not keep His commandments, is a liar and the truth is not in him."

Every day I saw and heard things which the average Christian, or even active pro-lifer, would never experience unless they went to abortion clinics. Only then would they fully understand these are places of child sacrifice.

Often, I stood out on the sidewalk overwhelmed with what I experienced, unable to share it with anyone. *How could this be happening? How did we get to the place where no one is affected, driving by knowing that innocent children are systematically killed here every day?*

Francis Schaeffer said, "Every abortion clinic should have a sign over the door saying, 'Open by Permission of the Church'" (*The Christian Manifesto*, Crossway, 2005).

What happened to our sense of responsibility, to our sense of decency? Was there no one left who cared? Were we that skilled at stifling the Holy Spirit of God?

As long, hard days turned into longer, harder weeks and months, I slowly began to harbor anger toward the church in general—and the church of Atlanta in particular. As each day went by, I thought about my children, missing them so much I thought my heart would break. I would go to church and see happy, laughing families going out together for lunch, enjoying each other's company. *Maybe if you all did your part about abortion here in your own city, the Lord wouldn't have had to send a missionary. Maybe then I could go home to my own children.*

I listened to dads at church talking about their children's ball games—and then I thought of the men who would play catch in the parking lot at Surgi with each other, while their children were being killed inside. "My child has a ball game" was an excuse often used by churchgoers who couldn't attend the Saturday prayer vigils at Fem Center.

I was so grateful for Perimeter Church and my pastor, Randy Pope, and his firm stand on abortion. I admired how he tenderly considered the feelings of the women when he addressed the subject. Many of the women thought there was something wrong with them for feeling terrible about their abortions, when the world told them they had done nothing wrong. Randy's words of truth about the horrors of abortion, given with much grace and love, legitimized their feelings and opened them up to repentance and restoration.

So often I am scolded by Christians who say the Great Commission is more important than the battle against abortion. Yes, Jesus came to die and paid a horrible price so we could have eternal life. The gospel of Christ truly is the power of God to salvation. It is literally the most important message we are called to share—but the gospel is exactly why He says we are not to stand back and let the innocent die. Living out the dictates of the Great Commission should be the natural outflow of our lives wherever we go, in whatever we say or do. Should I not at least incorporate the abortion battle somewhere into this calling?

Given my temperament and my personality, I would rather disappear into the background, vaporized on the very spot rather than be called upon by God to voice the uncomfortable, unpopular, pointed things of the Lord. I would rather love people and make them feel good about themselves. But my heart burns inside me, compelling me toward the words of Isaiah 58:1. "Lift up your voice . . . tell My people their transgressions . . . and their sins."

CHAPTER 22

I Don't Think So!

Still reeling from my experience with the pastor the day before, I stood in front of Surgi asking the Lord to help me, to show me how to handle the next pastor I knew would be coming.

Ann raised her voice to shake me out of my mental wandering. "Didn't you say there was a pastor down here yesterday?"

"Yes, and I'm telling you, if one more shows up here, I'm going to lose it!"

"Look!" Ann said, nodding her head down toward the sidewalk.

Even though it was still dark out, I could clearly read the plate on the front of a black car which had pulled up alongside the sidewalk. The word "Clergy" was written in large, bold, black letters, set against a white background. I was instantly angered.

"That does it! I've had it! He's the fourteenth pastor!"

I stormed down the hill toward his car—arms swinging, feet stomping. Before I could reach the car, a woman jumped out of the backseat and ran to the front door. I pounded on the driver's heavily tinted window. It rolled down.

"Is this your car?" I asked.

"Yes."

I pointed to the front of the car. "It says 'Clergy' on the front."

With a big smile, the man told me his name and the name of the local church he pastored.

"What are you doing here?" I yelled, startling him. I pointed toward the front door of Surgi. "Who was that woman?" My voice was agitated as I screeched at him.

"I don't know," he stammered.

"You bring a woman for an abortion, and you don't even know who she is?"

A young teenage boy was sitting in the front seat. "That's his wife," he said.

I pointed to the parking lot behind me. "Pull in there!" I yelled, exasperated.

The car moved forward and turned into the driveway. I stomped back up the hill, arms swinging again. As I passed Ann, she raised her eyebrows, with her eyes wide open.

"*Karen* . . ."

I passed her by and headed toward his car. He had backed his car into the corner as far as it could go. I was determined to give him a full-fledged sermon, but instead, I started crying. By the time I reached his car, I was sobbing and visibly shaking. I pounded on his window again. He opened it and started to give me some excuse. With clenched fists, I began blubbering out all my accumulated anger and disappointment I had been feeling toward the church and especially toward pastors.

"No wonder we can't get anywhere in this battle," I choked out. "We can't get you pastors to come down here to help us! We can't get you to care about these women and their children! We can't get you to preach that sin is sin and abortion is murder! No wonder God doesn't use you. You won't have power here because you have taken part in evil yourself!"

He opened his mouth to say something, but I didn't let him talk.

I took a deep breath and yelled, "I'm not going to argue with you!" With my hand shaking terribly, I pointed down toward the clinic. "Get out of this car right now and go down to get your wife out of there! If you don't, I'm going across the street and calling LOVE 86 Christian Radio. I'll give them your name and the name of your church. I'm going to tell them your wife is here having an abortion!"

He jumped out of the car like his seat was on fire! He ran down the hill, sliding on the stones. Quickly, he reappeared with his wife in tow. She slid into the back seat on the other side of the car, away from me. He took his seat behind the wheel.

"And don't think you can just go to another clinic somewhere in town, because we're everywhere!" I threatened. How I wished that were true. I pointed to Ann, who stood nearby, eyes bulging. "She's going to follow you!"

I told Ann to get in her van. She looked at me like I was nuts, but she did it anyway.

As his car pulled away, I yelled, "And furthermore, I'm going to your church in three months, and she had better look pregnant!"

Then they were gone.

Silence now filled the dark parking lot. Somehow, I thought I could still hear my words hanging in the air. My legs turned to rubber. I sat down right in the middle of the parking lot.

I always instruct my sidewalk counselors that no matter what, they should always—always—extend understanding, grace, and mercy to everyone down there and never yell at anyone. I had not extended this consideration to him. I rebuked myself for my behavior, but then I thought, *No! He has no business calling himself 'clergy' and bringing his wife for an abortion!*

I did, however, feel the need to confess I had let a root of bitterness toward the church of Atlanta creep into my heart. I wanted nothing more to do with the bitterness. I wanted nothing to stand in the way of the Holy Spirit moving freely in my heart, especially for the individuals in the Body of Christ who had so graciously welcomed me there.

Ann returned sometime later, having watched them get onto the freeway. "Karen, when I saw how upset you were, I thought you were going to get arrested for attempted murder! Are you actually going to go to their church in three months?"

"No. I was so upset, I'd already forgotten his name and the name of his church before I even followed him to the parking lot—but I wasn't going to let him know that."

"Well, I'm glad you chased him out of here. It worked, and the baby is safe."

The Lord had answered my prayer, showing me there is only one way to deal with pastors at the clinics, but it left me horribly disheartened. Why did I have to battle them in the first place?

More weary than usual, I returned home that evening feeling terribly sad about pastors. In all fairness to our shepherds, those of us who sit in our pews every Sunday have the same Word of God to read and the same Spirit of God to show us the way toward righteousness.

Our pastors can't take all the blame. God help us all!

Later in the afternoon, I was more disturbed than usual by the arrival of the medical disposal truck. I watched this truck back up to the side door of Surgi every week. One time, I stood on the hill behind the alley and took a picture of the driver. The muscles in his arms and neck bulged as he struggled to carry a large, heavy box filled with the bodies of dead babies. I counted five boxes that day.

Today was more disturbing because of an item a pro-lifer had found after digging through Surgi's dumpster. I was horrified to see an attractive, well-prepared brochure outlining a reimbursement plan for the clinic's harvested fetal organs. Carefully listed in alphabetical order were such organs as the brains, eyes, intact spinal cords, livers, and pancreases, to name a few. Alongside each organ was the accompanying payment, which increased in value with every additional week of gestation. Apparently, the clinics were making more from the sale of fetal organs than they were already making from the abortions. I had known for years that this practice existed but to actually see it in writing startled me. My heart sank as I thought about these children whose lives were not worth anything to anyone, but their bodies sure were!

A clinic escort ripped the brochure from my hand and ran away with it—but not before its contents were indelibly etched in my mind, causing me to wonder about so many things:

I wondered if the mothers were aware that after they paid for their abortions, the clinic was going to profit even more from the sale of their children's bodies.

I wondered how so-called blobs of tissue managed to have brains and intact spinal cords.

I wondered how a woman could simply walk into a building and pay to have her child killed.

I wondered how I could let these mothers go by me and walk in each day.

I wondered how we, as a society, had let this happen.

I wondered what I could do about it.

I wondered if the driver knew what he was transporting. As his truck pulled out past me, he gave me a friendly finger greeting. *Yeah, he knows! I wondered how much he was paid.*

I wondered how the Lord could bear to see this every day, at every clinic, in every city, in every state, in every country in the world.

I could barely breathe.

Exhausted from the long hours I had spent shivering in the cold, as well as the emotional energy expended, I drove home, trying not to wonder anymore. As disturbing thoughts tried to invade my mind, I made every effort to cast them from me, replacing them with thoughts that would lift my spirit and lighten my burdened soul.

Purposefully, I began to praise the Lord and quote Scripture to remind me of all things good and pleasant—but I felt a severe rebuke coming from the Holy Spirit of God. I realized the Lord had not brought me this far to ignore what I saw and experienced. Would He actually want me to stand outside an abortion clinic and not feel the evil or not grieve about the horrifying things taking place inside? Was this not what my life and ministry were about? Why would He allow me to run away mentally and emotionally from what He had called me to do? Yet there I was, trying desperately to run away from the things I felt powerless to change.

I thought about how the spirit of murder had grown incredibly powerful, systematically feeding on children. I thought about the contrast of how the Lord *gave* His blood, but the spirit of murder takes the blood of children, growing more arrogant and defiant, drunk with power. I thought about how small and insignificant I felt, trying to fight a battle that had enlarged to such enormous proportions that it was now incomprehensible. This was only 1992. I shuddered to think what it would be like in another twenty years.

While I didn't have the words to adequately describe the horror of abortion, I did feel the ever-present, utter awfulness of it residing deeply in the pit of my stomach. It gnawed relentlessly at the center of my being. My mind struggled to find ways to prevent the silent screams of the innocent, helpless child undergoing barbaric pain as its life was ending. My heart broke for the woman who, when she realizes what she has done, will experience constant, never-ending cries of despair and a lifetime of regret.

The horrific grieving which never left me was for the Lord Himself. My mind could not comprehend His vastness—the grand scale of all He is, all He creates. If all that He did was huge in breadth and height, how utterly vast in scope and measure must be the indescribable pain He experienced at every single abortion. It was impossible to imagine what He must feel as His beautiful gift was thrown back into His face, bloodied and rejected.

Every day I stood on the sidewalk and said repeatedly, "I'm so sorry, Lord. I'm so very, very sorry Lord." I knew that because His great love never lessened and His Holiness never decreased, surely He never got used to these daily tragedies and, therefore, neither should I. I repented of my desire to be rid of this heavy burden, because I knew to do so would put me at risk of indifference. My ministry and effectiveness could be lost forever.

As the day came to a close, I ran to my High Tower, the One Who understood and grieved the most. The previous clinging, heavy dread evaporated in His embrace. I knew He would be faithful to help me endure in the midst of all that I experienced every day. I knew it wasn't just about sparing moms and babies from abortion. As the Potter, He wanted to use the pressure of my calling to mold me to be more conformed to His image. A settling came into my soul as I prayed. I believed the knowledge that three children were spared from death today would somehow ease His pain and suffering, as well as my own.

CHAPTER 23

Death Threats and the Mafia

It was 5:00 a.m. and still dark when I pulled into the driveway at Surgi. A man stood under the streetlight in a tan raincoat, holding an umbrella in the light rain. I made a mental note of him, parked the car, and then turned to look back in his direction. He was gone.

I found Sue and Ann sitting in Sue's car, waiting for a fresh supply of literature I brought with me. They left for Midtown Hospital, leaving me alone at Surgi as planned.

Alone on the sidewalk, I heard a man's voice behind me say, "You need to stop doing this."

Tired, discouraged, and wishing I could quit, I laughed at this thought. "Great! I was hoping someone would tell me I could stop and go home," I said.

"You don't understand," the man said. "You need to stop doing this right now!"

I laughed again and turned to look at him. Nothing about the man made me fearful. He was very attractive, of average build and height, with sandy colored hair and a soft voice. People were always stopping on the sidewalk to talk to me—to encourage me or to cuss me out. I didn't pay any attention to this man. I thought he was perhaps a businessman on his way to work who stopped to give me his opinion, something which happened on a regular basis.

"You *will* stop doing this or *else*." He nodded his head toward Surgi. "You're costing them a lot of money."

"Really?" I said. I never thought about the money they might be losing because of all the canceled abortions. I thought how awful it was for others to make money off the death of a child. "Well, good!"

He shook his head. Slowly, articulately, he said, "You . . . are . . . going . . . to . . . die!"

I shrugged, still too stupid to understand what was happening. "Only if God says so!"

"Look, I know who you live with, and I know the names of their children. Dan and Melissa Duffy. Their children are Meghan Leah and Brian James."

My heart leaped in my chest. I didn't know Meghan and Brian's middle names, but he did. He accurately told me what time I left the house every morning, which route I took to get to the clinics, which clinic I went to first, and on which days.

"You stop, or we'll stop you!" He nodded his head toward Surgi again. "They won't be blamed. It won't happen here. It will look like an accident, but you *will* die if you come back out here tomorrow!"

He now had my attention. An incredible rage welled up inside me. Here I had given up everything to follow the call of my Lord and Savior, the Creator of the Universe, the Maker of all things—including him— and I was to disobey the Great I Am, to obey some mere human being? *How dare you!* I was ticked! The brief moment of fear had vanished, completely taken over by an overwhelming sense of indignation.

"Do you know what they do in there?" I asked.

"Yes."

"No, you don't!"

"Abortions," he said.

"But do you know what really happens to the baby during an abortion?"

"Yeah, yeah. It's just a blob of tissue."

I had expected him to respond with this usual, uneducated way of thinking. Shaking with anger, I reached into my pocket and took out my laminated picture of David. The man looked at the picture, sucked his breath in, and began to choke on his saliva. At that very moment, a car pulled into the driveway. I went over to offer them literature and spoke to them briefly. When I turned around, he was gone.

The reality of what had just transpired began to dawn on me. It took me awhile, but after all, it's not every day that one receives a direct death threat. Then I got *really* mad! I rapidly paced back and forth on the sidewalk, kicking stones and yelling, "Just who do they think they are?" I turned in the direction where he had been standing and yelled out into the dark and the rain, "Besides, you can't threaten me with heaven, you dummy!"

I was convinced that no one could continue in this battle unless they were willing to lay down their lives—not only jeopardizing their families, careers, possessions, comfort, or safety. They must be ready to die in the place of one of these children, or *something* would stop them. I remembered Sue and Ann and wondered if their lives were in danger as well. Even though the threat came directly to me, they were with me almost every day.

I had calmed down considerably by the time they arrived back at Surgi at our agreed upon time. I shared the events of the morning with them. They looked at each other and just shrugged.

"He threatened you, not us," Sue said. "Besides, like you always say, '*Only if God says so!*'"

They were totally unconcerned about the threat, changing the subject to share their excitement about a woman who let them talk to her. She chose life for her child. I still felt Ann needed to share the threat with her husband. I told her I would understand if he said he didn't want her coming out anymore.

A squad car pulled up, and an officer got out. I had only seen him a handful of times.

"So did anything unusual happen today?" he asked.

"Well, it's not too unusual for someone to say they're going to kill Karen, but I think this is a serious threat this time." Sue explained what had happened.

"That sounds like an official death threat, maybe even mafia. We can't protect you from the mafia! You can't come out here anymore."

"You tell God that," I said. "I'm much more concerned about what *He* thinks than anybody else."

I remembered hearing rumors that the mafia was involved in the abortion issue because of the money to be made. My mind began to wander. I could stay home, hide under my bed out of fear, and die anyway on my appointed day as the Lord comes for me. How awful that would be, to meet the Lord in a state of fear, after all He had done to prove He is right by my side wherever I go, whatever I do. *I want to die in the line of duty, thank you very much.*

I became aware that the officer was still looking at me.

He sighed. "You're going to come back out here tomorrow, aren't you?"

"Yes, sir. Besides, I'll be killed only . . ."

Sue and Ann joined me in unison.

"*. . . if God says so!*"

Driving home later that day, I knew I had to tell Dan and Melissa. After all, their children had been named. I felt they would be disturbed to know their family was being watched because of me.

After sharing the news, I said, "I understand if you want me to move out."

Dan laughed. "Are you kidding? You have more angels around you than anyone we know. We want you right here!"

"Costing them a lot of money?" Melissa said. "Way to go!"

Only the Duffys, I thought as I walked into my room. I realized the rubber would meet the road the next morning when I left for downtown in the dark, all alone. I remembered the portion of Scripture the Lord led me to just weeks earlier, during a day of prayer and fasting. In the next few days, two other individuals had shared this verse with me. I needed to read it again.

I reached for my Bible and opened to Job 5. It reads:

> He frustrates the devices of the crafty so that their hands cannot carry out their plans. He catches the wise in their own craftiness, and the counsel of the cunning comes

quickly upon them. They meet with darkness in the daytime, and grope at noontime as in the night. But He saves the needy from the sword, from the mouth of the mighty, and from their hand. (Job 5:12–15)

As my eyes fell on Job 5:26—"You shall come to the grave full of age"—I felt sure the Lord would deliver me. Forty-four years old is not yet full of age.

I then turned to Psalm 68, where I had left off the night before during my evening study. A supernatural calm came over me as I read the second half of Psalm 68:20: "And to God, the Lord belong escapes from death." I took a deep breath and fell sound asleep.

The following afternoon, I returned home from the clinic and wondered why the Duffys were standing on the front porch. It looked like they were all waiting for me.

As I walked to the front door, they cheered. "She's still alive! She's still alive!"

Until that moment, I had completely forgotten about the death threat. I suddenly realized it never came to my mind in the morning, all day on the sidewalk, or my drive home. Apparently, Sue and Ann must not have mentioned it either. I laughed out loud when I thought about how the Lord had not only protected my body but my mind as well. I was still alive and so were seven more babies today!

There was no need to fear tomorrow.

My friend Debbie Gibson came from California for a week to learn how to sidewalk counsel. Debbie and her husband had a strong desire to adopt a baby. She would often call me to pray for a baby to become available for them, asking me to add their names to the list I kept of couples waiting to adopt. As with other potential adoptive parents, they discovered that infants were not readily available for placement. She had considered the statistics which revealed that 1.2 million babies were aborted every year—and 1.2 million couples were waiting to adopt. I suggested her future child might be one who was saved through sidewalk counseling.

Our first morning together started immediately. As she blinked away the sleep from her eyes at 3:15, I laughingly told her it was to prepare for the 3:00 a.m. feedings she could expect when she got her baby.

Debbie was an excellent student. She listened and watched and asked many questions. She was undeterred by difficult, sometimes angry pregnant women, and equally undisturbed with the always difficult, always angry clinic escorts. She cried when children were lost; she laughed and rejoiced when they were saved. I so enjoyed spending time with Debbie. We talked about friends back in California. I felt a sweet, however short, connection with home.

Debbie's last day on the sidewalk was one that would show her firsthand the Lord's ability to keep us safe.

A couple arrived, took our literature, and listened intently as I spoke to them. The woman asked about the picture of David I held in my hands. Due to the gruesomeness of the picture, I always took time to explain the image before showing it, preparing the viewer. Without warning, she took it from my hand. As soon as she looked at it, she started screaming and buried her head in her husband's chest.

Her husband rushed her down the sidewalk toward the clinic, screaming and cussing at me over his shoulder. As they neared the front door, he came halfway back and told me he would be right out to get his gun from of his car and blow me away. He started for the clinic, then turned again, making sure I understood he would return to kill me! I'd had a lot of angry men threaten to kill me out there before, but I felt sure this one would try.

Debbie's eyes were wide open in shock. "Karen, he means it. You better leave!"

Before I could reply, I suddenly felt my bladder fill in a strange way. My need to use the restroom was both urgent and painful. I told Debbie I would be right back. I turned to cross the street and walked into the office building directly across from Surgi.

I was shocked to see the floor of the usually clean restroom covered with toilet tissue and other questionable substances floating in a couple of inches of water. The concern for my bladder overcame my concern for my shoes, so I walked on my heels to an empty stall.

When I tried to open the door of the stall to leave, it refused to open. I shook the door. I pushed hard against it. I yelled for help repeatedly. The door wouldn't budge, and no one ever came. Never had I been in that restroom before without several women coming and going. It was a very busy building. Today, of all days, no one came.

I waited a little longer. I was concerned that Debbie was across the street by herself—the angry man might try to hurt her instead. She was probably worried about me taking so long. I tried opening the door again and pounded on it, but it would not open. I continued to yell for help. I refused to crawl through the dirty water under the door, so I just stood there waiting for someone to come in.

Standing with my hands on my hips and staring at the stubborn door, I watched it slowly open by itself. As I exited the building, I saw the angry man's car leaving Surgi.

I crossed the street and stood next to Debbie, whose hand was on her chest.

"Thank You, Lord!" she said.

Excitedly, she told me while I was gone, she was begging the Lord to keep me in the restroom. The man who threatened to kill me had left the parking lot just moments before she saw me exit the building. "Karen, he just missed seeing you!"

Debbie explained that as soon as I went across the street and walked into the building, the man came out of the clinic. He went to his car and got his gun, then waved it around, pacing back and forth as he looked for me. While he kept waiting, Debbie kept praying the Lord would keep me safe across the street. She was confident the man would indeed shoot me if he could.

"Now, can we *please* leave?"

We walked to my car. Debbie wondered how I knew to stay away for so long, so I shared what had happened. When I told her how the door had finally opened by itself, she laughed.

"The Lord was answering my prayers!" she said. "When I begged Him to keep you over there, He probably had an angel leaning on the outside of the door and another one keeping everyone else out. When He knew it was safe, the angel opened the door for you. You're right—He's always present and never fails to look out for you."

Although Debbie had been scared for me, she was glad she had this experience. She would never forget how God was able to protect those who serve Him. She knew He would do the same for her back home.

The following day, I drove Debbie to the airport. "It usually takes nine months to have a baby," she said. "I wonder how long I'll have to wait for mine."

I prayed it would be soon. And it was. One year after her visit to Atlanta, Debbie met a pregnant woman while sidewalk counseling in California. The woman not only chose life for her baby but chose Debbie to be her baby's adoptive mom.

Though the enemy tried his best to deter us, his threats were falling flat. No threat, intimidation, slander, or abuse could stop us from doing the work God called us to do. As the weeks and months went by, we were rapidly closing in on the goal of saving one thousand babies in two years. Each of us was trying hard to be the one who would reach the magic number. I never saw our counselors so eager to approach someone on the sidewalk. They were in great competition with each other.

Finally, on Tuesday morning, August 18, Madia encouraged a sweet young woman to choose life for her little one, and she became our number "One Thousand." Though she was the one thousandth mother, it was actually the one thousand and third baby, since three sets of twins were born during that time. I was not there with Madia that day but was so glad it was her. Usually, Madia was not able to get the names or telephone numbers of a turnaround mother, but this one freely volunteered her information. She never would have believed we could have reached one thousand turnarounds had she not sidewalk counseled for the last two years.

We invited this young pregnant woman to be our guest of honor, along with her entire family, to the Celebrate One Thousand banquet in October. Linda worked hard to make the evening special with entertainment and a delicious dinner. A four-by-twelve-foot poster filled with pictures of babies hung under the Celebrate One Thousand banner. Linda had enlisted many women and children to cut out pictures, pictures, and more pictures of babies from magazines. The goal was to glue pictures of one thousand babies onto the poster. After weeks of hard work, the poster was completely covered, yet they had only been able to fit the pictures of seven hundred babies on it.

I stood in silence with our counselors looking at the poster, overwhelmed by the massive sea of beautiful little faces pictured there. There were tears as the memories of the last two years flooded our thoughts. No one spoke. Then simultaneously, as if on cue, we all said quietly, "To God be the glory." No one knew better than us it would have never happened except for the power and presence of God Himself!

It always amazed me how He never forgot to answer my prayers. I remembered that lonely night two years earlier at Surgi Center when I was on my knees in the dark, begging Him to give me one thousand babies. So much had happened since that night. He remained faithful to me through it all.

I drove home that night to the home of my new host family: Jack and Lisa Alexander and their three young sons. They were a family from my church whose house I agreed to take care of while they were in Europe. The Duffys hadn't wanted me to leave, afraid I wouldn't come back to them. They were right. I felt it would be good to give Brian back his bedroom, which I had been using for the last two years.

I agreed to stay on with the Alexanders after they returned home. Brian got his room back, and I got a lovely basement apartment.

The evening Jack and Lisa returned from Europe, they spoke with me. "Karen, we can't go down to the clinics like you do, but we would like to do our part. If you ever have a woman who feels she must have an abortion because she can't pay her medical bills, please tell her we will do that for her." I wrote their numbers down on a piece of paper and put it in the pocket of the coat I would wear the next morning.

At 6:15 the next morning, a small truck pulled into Surgi. A woman stepped out, refused my literature, and walked into the clinic. Her husband got out from the passenger side, walked to the back of the truck, and sat down on the bumper. He covered his face with his hands and wept openly. Tears streamed down his face.

My heart was breaking as I walked over to him.

He looked up at me. "I've tried everything to save my little boy. I need a miracle!"

I asked him why his wife felt she needed to have an abortion. He explained he had just changed jobs and his health insurance would not cover her pregnancy, because she was already in her fifth month. She didn't want to have the abortion but didn't feel she could take one more year of financial stress.

"Would she have the baby if someone promised to pay all her medical bills?" I asked.

"Ma'am, miracles like that don't happen anymore. If there was really someone who would do that, then I would know for sure there really is a God."

I took the paper out of my pocket. "Here's your miracle! These people will do it."

He couldn't believe it. To convince him, I took him across the street and placed a call. Lisa answered the phone, prayed with him, and assured him they would help them.

He ran back toward the clinic, jumping up and down, yelling, "There really is a God . . . there really is a God!"

The man ran into Surgi Center. When he came back out, he was carrying his wife. They were laughing and crying. They both hugged and kissed me. He swung me around and around the parking lot. When they left to go home to have their baby, they kept honking their horn all the way up the hill. He stuck his hand out the window, waving the piece of paper with the Alexanders' names and numbers on it. She looked backward, throwing me kisses. I waved back.

I marveled at how the Lord would use each of us if we would only make ourselves available. As a missionary, I could never have afforded to pay someone's medical expenses—yet He touched the hearts of those who could do what I couldn't. Indeed, so much could be accomplished if the church would just be the church and freely give their individual gifts and talents for kingdom work.

CHAPTER 24

Heavy Hearts

It was a horribly hot afternoon in July 1992. The air was heavy, but my heart was heavier still. Though I was back on the dock at Linda's Praise Place, I found praise eluding me.

Sitting with his back to me and feet hanging off the side of the dock, my son Jeromy struggled to attach a worm to a fishhook. I watched with an aching heart. The cost of his determination left blood soaking through many layers of gauze wrapped around what used to be his fingers.

Jeromy's fingers had been caught in a one-hundred-ton metal press, leaving three of them amputated, and his pinky twisted and broken.

He dropped a line into the water. Watching him gaze off into the distance, I saw his shoulders drop.

"Mom, I wish Dad was here. I wish I could talk to him, see him." Now an adult himself who experienced a lifetime of mostly silence and indifference from his father, he still hung on to hope.

"I know, honey" was my usual response to his impossible request.

The wind suddenly picked up and blew hot air at us. As if carried on the very wind itself, memories swept across my mind with unwelcomed force, sending me back to another July many years earlier. Gone! Forever gone! Gone was my friend, lover, and childhood sweetheart. Gone was the father of my children, my comfort, and my so special husband.

I cried out, "Lord, Lord! How can this be?" With my heart ripped open and bleeding, I begged God for help and release from the pain. I rocked back and forth on my knees, grasping my stomach that felt as if it contained the agony of hell itself.

Ours had been a sweet, serene home, filled with the laughter of our children: Jeromy, age nine, and Kimberly, soon to be five. Happy and well-adjusted, they brought great joy to our home. My husband was a father and a provider who made us proud—kind, considerate, and dependable, able to repair and build anything with great skill and expertise. Suddenly, without warning, he was gone.

I had met him at age fourteen, married him at age nineteen, and lost him after fourteen years of marriage. I had spent half of my life with this man. *How does one function when half of you is missing?* I wondered.

I was worn out from the lack of sleep and hearing my children constantly beg for their father, filling me with frustration because I seemed unable to comfort them.

One night I awoke to Jeromy standing over me, shaking and crying.

"Mommy, please give me a picture of Daddy. I'm scared because I can't remember what he looks like."

Jeromy started sleeping with his father's picture and the baseball mitt his dad had given him. He didn't feel safe anymore, and neither did I.

Both Jeromy and Kimberly refused to go outside that entire summer. They didn't have a daddy to play with. They insisted everyone stared at them and called me a "Bible thumper." It was their dad, after all, who didn't want to be married to a religious fanatic. Apparently, he had told the neighbors that as well. I wondered how they could let their children throw eggs at us when we left for church on Sundays. Scrubbing dried up eggs off the driveway and garage door became a regular Sunday afternoon chore for me.

Slowly, in time, both children refused to believe me when I tried to convince them that their father loved them. They no longer wanted to visit him or speak to him on the phone. Over the years, Kim, who found her comfort in me, fared much better than her brother. Jeromy was left with a broken heart that would not heal. He became bitter. He had been profoundly affected by the loss of his father. Truly, abandonment is the cruelest of all human experiences.

Jeromy's bitterness for his father grew into bitterness for me and, most horribly, for God. My love for the Lord was the reason he'd lost his dad. I don't think Jeromy believed his father had professed Christ and that together we had planned to raise our children for the Lord, long before we ever married. My husband later confessed he had lied to me, telling me what I wanted to hear. He said he would have done anything to marry me.

During those years, Jeromy spent short periods of time with his dad—times that would end in additional abandonment. At sixteen, he turned from his peers at church and toward new friends who led him into drugs and much confusion. By the time I left for Atlanta, Jeromy had made his way out of that difficult season of life, but his heart was still so far away from the Lord.

When he learned a beautiful young woman in California was carrying his child, he wondered how he would care for them. The mother of this young woman had visited me in Atlanta and expressed her desire to move there. We agreed it was best for Jeromy to go ahead and secure a job, preparing for their arrival.

No one expected this job would lead to a terrible accident.

On the morning of the accident, I was already feeling a bit overwhelmed by all the sudden changes that were taking place with my children in the last few months. Jeromy was staying with the Duffys, near his new job. I was living with the Alexander family, and Kim was staying with me. I had just recently learned that she was pregnant as well. Kim was getting married the very next day.

An early telephone call woke us up from a sound sleep. Jeromy had been in an accident and had been flown by helicopter to the hospital.

When we arrived at the hospital, the doctor told me to prepare myself because the injury was severe. We couldn't see him until he was bandaged up.

When we were finally allowed to see him, Jeromy said, "Mom, do you think they'll give me back my money for the tux?"

He was supposed to walk his sister down the aisle. Kim was beside herself, crying. She didn't think she could get married the next day. Jeromy insisted it was "just a little scratch" and that she should go forward with the wedding.

The doctors said they were very sorry, but there was no way to reconstruct his fingers. They had been totally crushed and would have to be amputated. The massive number of bandages on his hand could not contain the blood that was steadily streaming from his elevated hand into a metal bowl.

My heart was breaking. A nurse escorted me to the room where Jeromy would stay after the surgery. All alone in this quiet place, I forced myself to find something to praise the Lord for in a desperate attempt to pull myself from despair. I thanked Him that Jeromy did not bleed to death, that he did not lose his whole hand, that he still had his thumb and partial use of his pinky. Soon Melissa and Linda burst into the room, then hugged and comforted me. I felt great relief as they prayed for my broken heart.

I celebrated Kim's wedding the next day with a heavy heart. She left immediately after the wedding for the hospital to see her brother before leaving on her honeymoon. He was barely aware of her presence because of heavy sedation. Their father had made the trip to attend Kim's wedding and visited Jeromy before returning home. I wasn't sure how aware Jeromy was of him either.

For the next ten days, I would take the early morning shift at Surgi and then go to the hospital later when I knew Jeromy would be awake. On one of those days, Jeromy was experiencing horrible pain.

"Mom, I'm so glad you do what you do. They put me to sleep to amputate my fingers, but they don't put the babies to sleep. They tear apart their whole bodies!" His voice grew more intense. "Don't ever stop doing what you're doing!"

The next morning, as I was standing on the sidewalk in front of Surgi, I saw a young man turning to walk inside the clinic. I couldn't help but notice he was missing an arm and immediately thought about Jeromy's situation. Forgetting all about offering him the literature, I rudely blurted out, "How did you lose your arm?"

"Oh, it was a motorcycle accident years ago."

I mentioned Jeromy's accident and the terrible pain he was in. The young man touched the place where his arm was missing.

"I forgot how painful it was to lose my arm."

I showed him the picture of David with his severed arm and explained his child would lose its arms without any anesthesia.

He grabbed hold of his side, where his arm used to be. "No! I can't let that happen to him. The pain will be horrible!"

He ran into Surgi Center and within seconds came back out with his girlfriend. She was smiling, grateful, and very pregnant. They both hugged and thanked me, then turned to leave. The young man stopped and came back to me. "Do you think you would have asked me about how I lost my arm if your son hadn't just lost his fingers?"

"No. I know I wouldn't have."

"Go and tell him that his experience saved our child's life today!"

I nearly flew to the hospital to tell Jeromy. He was grateful, as was I, that something good had come out of something so terrible.

Now here we were at the Praise Place. Weeks had passed since the accident. Jeromy would be leaving soon for California, as the mother of his baby would not be moving to Atlanta after all. He wanted to be near her and the baby when he was born.

Jeromy seldom complained about his pain anymore. He seemed to have a heightened concern for others who were struggling with difficulties, but I knew he was angry. After seeking counsel from a pastor in California, Jeromy was told he should go on ahead to Georgia and help his pregnant sister move as well. Jeromy didn't feel it was the right thing to do. He didn't want to leave the mother of his child, even if for a short time. When assured that she and her family would be moving to Georgia shortly, he agreed, but very reluctantly.

"I told you I shouldn't have left, Mom." He felt like he had only come to Georgia to lose his fingers—and he blamed me, for I was the one who had encouraged the move.

So many hurtful things had happened in the last few months. I felt overwhelmed and discouraged, always on the verge of tears. In addition, I had prayed for the Lord to let me see abortion the way that He saw it, and He had answered my prayer. I woke up every morning crying. I cried throughout each day, and I went to bed crying every night. I seemed unable to stop.

One day, several months earlier, Joanna was in Atlanta for a short visit and accompanied me to Surgi. I felt a strange sorrow come over me. I felt the Lord ask me if I was willing to give my grandchildren back to Him. Immediately, the tears began to flow.

Joanna lost her patience with me. "What are you blubbering about now?"

"The Lord just asked me to give my grandchildren to Him."

Joanna threw her hands up into the air. "You don't have any grandchildren!"

"I know, but that's what He said."

Later that afternoon, Jeromy called to tell me his girlfriend was pregnant with my first grandchild. After the call, I sat down on the bottom step leading to my basement apartment and started to cry again.

Within seconds, I heard the voice of Dr. James Dobson come over the radio. "Christian parents need to stop blaming themselves for their adult children's decisions." Still, it wasn't how I wanted to receive my first grandchild.

Disappointed but determined to praise the Lord, I assured both Jeromy and the mother of his child they were both greatly loved. I was so grateful, knowing all too well how available abortion could be for her.

She was an exceptional young woman in many ways, and it comforted me to know she would be a dedicated mother to my grandson.

I was entirely unprepared to have my sweet Kimberly tell me the same thing just one month later.

"Don't blame yourself, Mom. Don't tell yourself you should have been home taking care of me all this time. It still would have happened. You are not to blame. I chose to do wrong."

Disappointment and failure flooded my soul. I hurt for Kim, knowing she felt the same thing.

Kim gave me her news very late that night. I hadn't had time to fully absorb this information before it was time to get up to go to Surgi early the next morning. Standing on the sidewalk in the dark by myself, I felt so lonely, fighting still more tears. My head was spinning. I didn't know how I was going to help Kim with the baby.

I saw a mother and a father walking toward me on the sidewalk. A sweet young girl was with them, crying. As the mother approached, she put her arm out and pointed at me.

Before I could say anything, she spoke up in her own defense. "You don't have any idea what it's like to have a child in a crisis pregnancy!"

That was exactly the last thing I needed to hear. I couldn't hold back my tears as a stream of words came flooding out. "You're right, I don't know what it's like to have *a* child in a crisis pregnancy—but I know what it's like having *two* children in crisis pregnancies at the same time, and I don't have a husband, and I'm a missionary, and I don't have any money, and I don't know what I'm going to do . . ."

Feeling my pain, the mother came over to me, put her arms around me and patted me on my back. "It's okay, honey. It's okay. These things have a way of working out. It's okay. It will be all right!"

"You're right!" I said. "These things do work out. You arrived in a Mercedes. I assume you don't have any financial difficulties. You and your husband were holding hands. There is love here. If I can do this alone, you can do this together!"

The mother looked at her husband. "She's right. We can do this."

They called their daughter back, and the mother burst into tears. I was warmed by the sight of the three of them embracing each other. I watched hope and joy blossom. The parents promised love and support as excitement grew about their grandchild. They waved to me as they pulled away.

I realized I now knew how to reach the parents who were bringing their daughters for abortions. From that day forward, I ignored the young pregnant daughters arriving. Instead, I concentrated on the mothers/grandmothers. I now knew the pain, disappointment, fear, and uncertainty they were facing. While sharing my own experiences, I was able to reach out and comfort their mother's hearts, while at the same time encouraging their grandmother's hearts to come to life. I knew the Lord didn't want my children to get pregnant outside of marriage to give me an object lesson for sidewalk counseling, but their experiences were not wasted. Again, He was faithful to teach me how to reach out in love to troubled hearts. To God be the glory!

As the weeks went by, I began to beat myself up. I felt I had completely failed as a mother. Isn't that what all good mothers do, after all? We wear our badges of failure so well. I felt so much guilt for leaving my youngest child to go and serve the Lord. Regret and confusion flooded my already burdened soul. Telling myself that Kim was now nineteen and Jeromy was twenty-three didn't help much. I still felt responsible.

One morning, I woke up and started to laugh out loud at the incredible way the Lord lifted my burden. I am not someone who ordinarily has dreams from the Lord, but while I was sleeping, I experienced a dream that was truly a direct gift from God. It was short, clear, and unforgettable.

In the dream, I was sitting on the couch in my parents' living room. Jeromy, Kim, and I were having a family meeting, discussing some of the problems they were facing. Jeromy had apparently gotten into some trouble relating to drugs, and his girlfriend was pregnant. I was saying I couldn't believe that Kim was pregnant as well.

"I stayed here at home in California with the two of you, making sure you were cared for and had all the direction you would need to make wise decisions. Then you went and got in trouble and pregnant anyway, *and I missed out on Atlanta!*"

Through the dream, I realized the Lord was telling me that Kim was right. My children would have done exactly what they did, even if I had been right there with them. My heart was filled with gratitude to the Lord for a dream which sent a clear and loving reminder to me: I was right where He wanted me to be, doing exactly what He wanted me to do.

It is a dream I would never forget!

CHAPTER 25

Open Doors

For a long time, I skillfully ignored the voice of the Lord when He wanted me to join Him in a new work. Now He had invited me to teach others those lessons on sidewalk counseling that He had taught me. Of course, that would mean interacting with more people than I, as a little introvert, would ever be comfortable doing.

I had already written a sidewalk counseling training seminar and had given the presentation several times to a handful of local people, which went quite well. Still, being so shy, I was not eager to do what He requested.

The times I spent arguing with the Lord and resisting His will were less often and of shorter duration now. Reluctantly, I told the Lord I would obey Him but had no idea where to find all the people He wanted me to teach. I sensed in my spirit He would open the doors, if I was willing to walk through them. I groaned. *Yes, Sir.*

News regarding the effectiveness of my woman-centered counseling in Atlanta began to spread. I received invitations to present my seminar to sidewalk counseling ministries in neighboring states. People told me they felt the Lord would use me to speak all over the nation and possibly around the world. I didn't want to think about it.

Before long, I was contacted by a woman involved with *Family News in Focus*, who asked me to record a shortened version of my "Equipping for Life" training method for their radio program. The thought of being on the radio struck terror in my heart, but she said

I could stay at home and record the interview over the phone. Since I didn't have to meet or be seen by anyone, I agreed. I felt safely hidden, which suited me just fine.

When the interview was over, I thought, *Wow! The Lord just used me to speak to thousands of people, and I didn't have to be seen by even one person! He understands me. How sweet for Him to spare me from my fear of real public speaking.*

The segment aired for twelve weeks. Calls came in from all over the United States asking me to do the training in person. The broadcast was obviously the *door* the Lord planned to use. I was asked to train sidewalk counselors and share my testimony regarding the Lord's incredible faithfulness.

The calls came in ever-increasing numbers. I spoke in small churches and mega-churches. I spoke at small community colleges and large universities, including Notre Dame University. I spoke to groups from thirty-five to three hundred and fifty and crowds from two thousand to over ten thousand people. Most of the time, my mouth got horribly dry. One time, I almost passed out. All of the time, I was scared.

My head was spinning as I tried to absorb all that was happening in my life. I did countless live radio and television interviews. I was written up in pro-life magazines as well as secular ones. I remember the first time I picked up a *Time* magazine on a flight to Wisconsin and read about myself. It felt so strange! I learned from another magazine that the pro-choice community was calling me the "Sweetheart of the Pro-life Movement." *What?* My heart was filled with wonder for the Lord.

I received an invitation to speak at a large cathedral in Houston during the Republican National Convention. The building was packed with people from all over the United States who had come to attend the many pro-life events scheduled that week. Two gentlemen with British accents from the BBC came up to me and introduced themselves. I learned they would be broadcasting all over Europe that night and into countries around the world. That bit of knowledge did absolutely nothing to calm my fears!

I comforted myself with the reminder there were many other people scheduled to speak that night. My part would be brief.

Jim Pinto, a priest from Birmingham, Alabama, called me to the podium with this introduction: "I would like you to help me welcome from Atlanta, Georgia, Ms. Karen Black—the 'Billy Graham of Sidewalk Counseling.'"

I stood to face the audience, completely blinded by the extremely bright lights. I don't remember what I said. Instead, the encounter I had with the pastor at Surgi flooded my mind—the man who told me I was a nobody, so I had asked the Lord to send Billy Graham to the clinics.

In that moment, the Lord had spoken to my heart. *I don't need Billy Graham. I have chosen you. I will make you a Billy Graham, and I will tell the world!*

I had never shared that word with anyone. As I made my way back to my seat, I was overwhelmed by the Lord's incredible, unfailing faithfulness to me.

From that night on, I was called the "Billy Graham of Sidewalk Counseling," as well as the "James Dobson of Pro-life."

I knew with every fiber of my being that I could not take credit for anything the Lord had done in Atlanta. It had very little to do with me. The Lord knew what a mess I would make without Him. I learned that the Lord does not call the equipped, but rather, He equips the called. And I was called. My love for the Lord made it possible for me to lay my children on the altar and follow Him in obedience.

The Word says that "obedience is better than sacrifice." I experienced that, when my obedience *also* required sacrifice, the Lord met me in supernatural ways that brought both anointing and power.

I continued to train others, greatly humbled and encouraged by those who previously had no babies saved at their clinics—or at most, only a few. Now they were seeing hundreds of children saved. These workers were male and female, young and old, from small towns and large cities. They attended different denominational churches, but all possessed the same heart's cry for the unborn and love for the Lord. As

I spent time with these like-minded workers, their love and fellowship significantly lessened my loneliness in this battle.

God's presence brought me great confidence. I thanked Him for all He had helped me to overcome. With His enabling, I did not pass out or run away when newspaper reporters came toward me with their large cameras and microphones. The Lord still had a great deal more work to do in me regarding my fears, but already He had lifted me above many of them. Every day I was reminded of His incredible transforming power, humbled by where He sent me and with whom I would speak. I prayed I would always retain a sort of wonderment that He had chosen me.

My sidewalk ministry in Atlanta continued to flourish. Living by faith, I was amazed at the timely provision of the Lord as He met all my needs.

One day before my first speaking trip, I stood outside of Surgi, reminding the Lord that I had surrendered to His will to travel and train others. I only had my faded missionary clothes to wear. If I were to represent Him properly, I needed to look my best.

Lord, will You please give me money for a new dress? And can I have a red one, please?

Within moments of breathing this prayer, a car pulled into Surgi's parking lot and parked. A woman got out, smiling as she walked up to me to introduce herself. Every morning for the past few years, she had driven by Surgi, watching me.

"I saw you standing in the awful summer heat and the winter cold. I saw you being bullied, pushed, and shoved around every day. I saw you being taken away by the police. I was amazed at how you always, always came back."

As time went on, it became a point of necessity for her to look for me every morning. Currently, she was dealing with a stressful situation at work and drew strength from seeing me before starting her day.

"I told myself, if she can do what she does every day, then I can do what I need to do every day!" she said, giving me a hug. "Thank you so much for being an inspiration and encouragement to me. I just wanted you to know." With another hug, she returned to her car.

She started to pull out of the parking lot, then stopped her car and rolled down her window. Reaching her hand out to me, she placed three twenty-dollar bills into my hand. "Honey, this is so you can buy yourself a dress. Why don't you make it a red one?"

And people wonder why I say that living by faith is so much fun!

The ministry of Women 4 Women lived entirely by faith as well. I never held a fundraiser or asked for a penny from anyone. The Lord told me not to ask anybody but Him. As more money came into the ministry, the need for accountability grew. Several elders from my church, a female attorney, and a female accountant joined our newly established board for the ministry, completing the need for both accountability and direction. Now I prayed the Lord would send me help to establish a staff. It was nearly impossible for me to deal with all the follow-up needed and carry out my speaking schedule.

I was inspired by Amy Carmichael's prayer, asking the Lord to send her women willing to work as missionaries alongside her in India. I asked the Lord to send pro-life missionary women to me as well. I wondered how the Lord would recruit them. What would their call look like?

I imagined the Lord telling them, "Come to Atlanta to work long, exhausting hours in harsh weather, caring for severely distressed women in overwhelming circumstances in which your very life may be in danger—and oh, yes, there will be absolutely no pay!"

I could not forget that *my* invitation had read, "Come to Atlanta and Die!"

Matthew 10:39 says, "He who finds his life will lose it, and he who loses his life for My sake will find it." With great certainty, I found those words to be abundantly true—for it was through the dying that I found new life.

Your hand is heavy on me, Lord. What is it You want of me? Where am I to go? What would You have me do?

I made my way down the aisle of a rustic chapel of a Methodist campground as these thoughts went running through my mind. I dropped to my knees at the altar.

The words from the Lord were precise and heavy. *Will you follow me wherever I lead? Will you be willing to walk through any door I open for you? No matter how frightening, how seemingly impossible? No matter how controversial? Will you walk through that door, even if you have to go alone?*

I recalled all the times the Lord showed Himself faithful to equip me to do what He asked me to do. These tasks would have been impossible without Him. I recalled the results achieved.

"Yes, Lord, yes," I said. "I'll go through any door You open—no matter what it looks like, no matter the price. Only please, go with me."

I didn't fully understand what He was asking of me. His hand was heavy on me, and I was afraid of what was ahead. Back in my room, I found comfort in God's Word from Joshua 1:9 and 11: "Have I not commanded you? Be strong and of good courage, do not be afraid, nor be dismayed, for the Lord your God is with you wherever you go," and "Go in to possess the land which the Lord your God is giving you to possess." I was convinced these verses were confirmation I was to go through that *door,* whatever it was. I followed the example of others who responded to Joshua's words. I prayed, *All that You command me I will do, and wherever You send me, I will go.*

Moments later, I was informed of an urgent telephone call waiting for me in the office. The caller was a pastor from another state who had tracked me down. He had befriended the owner of an abortion clinic in his city, who said she was in the abortion business because she cared about the women, not about the money. To show that she was truly pro-choice, she wanted to offer the women a choice. She was willing to open the door of her clinic to a pro-life counselor, who would be free to say whatever they wanted to say and show whatever they wanted to show. The counselor would be free to talk about Jesus, and the clinic owner specifically requested that abstinence be taught. She only asked that the pastors promise her they would meet the needs of the women choosing to have their babies.

Recalling past experiences with clinic owners and directors, my first response was, "No way! It's a trick. Those doors are not open to me. Something like that would take a move of God!" My heart skipped a beat, as I remembered what the Lord had said to me at the altar just two hours earlier: *Will you go through any door I open for you?*

My head began spinning as I considered what the outcome could be. I thought about the number of children and moms that could be spared the horrors of abortion. I was particularly excited to have my life demonstrate Christ before the clinic workers.

Lord, am I really hearing this? There is an injunction at this clinic, and pro-lifers are not allowed anywhere near. And yet—You opened the door? Is this an actual invitation?

I quickly realized this truly was an "Only if God says so!" invitation. Of course!

"Karen, are you still there?" the pastor asked, pulling me back into our conversation on the phone. "Will you do it? Will you go?"

"I think I already committed to that earlier tonight at the altar." I told him what had transpired between the Lord and me. "Yes, by God's grace and power, I will walk through that door!"

The next evening, I was scheduled to be the last speaker at the conference. All day, I couldn't get the unusual invitation out of my mind. As I made my way back to the chapel that night, my head was still spinning. I was reluctant to go through the door the Lord held open for me. I prayed, *I don't want to be inside a place that kills children all day. I don't want to hear the suction machines or feel the presence of evil. I don't want to be in that utter darkness!*

Approaching the chapel, I heard the closing words of the evangelist ring out loud and clear. "If you want to be light, you have to go where it's dark!" No longer was my comfort a consideration. I truly wanted to give Him my whole life and be used in whatever manner He saw fit.

Thank You, Lord, I prayed. *Thank You for the opportunity to go where it is the darkest. Help my light to shine brightly. Help me put aside self and remember that the babies don't want to be inside there either. Help me remember that no matter what I experience, it could never compare to what happens to them.*

Upon my return to Atlanta, I received a call from the owner herself. She had viewed my training video and believed I really did care about the women. She owned three clinics and was willing to let me train other counselors to go in there as well.

I couldn't believe what I was hearing. I told her she needed to understand I would do my best to save as many babies and women from abortion as possible, which could impact her financially. She said she understood and was still willing to keep her word. She emphasized that the only requirement was for all the ministers in town to agree to help the women, in the same way I was helping them in Atlanta.

This miraculous news spread quickly, and I was inundated with telephone calls. Most of those calling greatly encouraged me. Others called to tell me their disapproval, saying the Lord would never bless my efforts to work closely with the enemy and evil.

I'm already ten feet from the front door of all that evil every day, I thought. I was constantly frustrated I couldn't get closer to the women. So many times I had gone into clinics, only to be escorted out by a police officer. *Being in there will be horribly uncomfortable but incredibly awesome.*

With each negative phone call, I would force myself to remember the night at the altar and the Lord's encouragement to me. I was willing to go through whatever door He opened, no matter how controversial—even if I had to go against everyone and go alone.

Satan had used these same tactics in the past to discourage me from doing what the Lord called me to do. For over twenty years, I had been criticized by others who did not approve of my calling as I obeyed the Lord, not man. With each criticism that came my way—whether it was due to working politically to prevent abortion on demand in the sixties, forming crisis pregnancy centers, counseling women following their abortions, warning others about Planned Parenthood's diabolical plans, involvement in rescue, sidewalk counseling, or just praying on the sidewalk—the Lord responded and blessed each step of my obedience to Him.

The pastor who connected us scheduled a meeting with the clinic owner and many area pastors. When he called to let me know the outcome of their meeting, his voice was filled with anger and despair. It did not go well. Not one pastor offered to help the clinic owner, as she had requested. Instead, they told her how evil she was for what she was doing.

"Karen, I'm so sorry, but she has withdrawn her offer. The door has closed!"

Tears of disappointment spilled down my face. I was angered, saddened, and confused. Then I started getting mad. I yelled at the Lord, "I remember well that night at the altar, Lord! I could barely breathe. *I did not mistake one word of what You said to me!*" If I had gone through that door, He would have sent me with a supernatural covering and anointing. He had done it many times before.

I was saddened by the missed opportunities to share Christ with the clinic personnel. I began to feel a great love for the owner and wanted so much to love her to the Lord. In the weeks that followed, I tried to contact her. I left messages. I thought we might meet and discuss it further. I would find a way to help the pregnant women myself. I never received a call in return.

One night, I lay in my bed with tears running down my face, resigned that this plan would not happen. Getting up, I made my way to the bathroom to wash my tears away. It felt as if Satan was mocking and reveling in my defeat. A sudden, powerful anger welled up in me. I turned around and took a swing at an invisible evil presence I felt following behind me.

"Leave me alone, you creep! I am by no means defeated! My God still reigns!"

I started rapidly pacing around the room, swinging my arms. It reminded me of the night so long ago at Surgi Center, when someone said no one could succeed at sidewalk counseling in Atlanta.

"Lord, I told You that night You had asked a big thing of me and that I was asking a big thing in return. Remember, Lord? I asked you for a thousand babies in two years. Everyone said that couldn't be done either, but it was!"

Aggravated, I complained to the Lord that I had agreed to go through the door and was not the one who closed it. He had asked a great thing of me at the altar, and now I was asking a great thing of Him.

My heart felt like it was going to burst inside my chest. "Lord, do not let my willingness to obey You go wasted!" I yelled. "Anoint me and Women 4 Women to help these moms and babies like never before. Take my willingness to obey You in that city and do something miraculous here in Atlanta instead!"

After loudly ordering around the Great I Am, I sheepishly added, "Okay, Lord?"

Immediately the following morning, the floodgates of mercy and provision swung open. Calls came in from my church and many other churches in the Atlanta area. Both men and women had had trouble sleeping the night before as they thought of me and our Women 4 Women ministry. They all wanted to help.

And the calls kept coming, day after day. At church, envelopes with generous donations were placed in my hands. A flood of checks arrived in the Manna Mobile from all over the nation. People I had never met before stopped at the clinics expressing their appreciation, asking how they or their families could help.

Most people would never risk arrest or go to abortion clinics to sidewalk counsel, even if they were pro-life. Still, I knew they cared and wanted to do something, so I determined to give them something they could do. I developed a volunteer sheet listing all the areas of service and included categories for women, men, families, church groups, and organizations. Sue developed a database for our volunteers, and it quickly filled with the names of seven hundred and forty-two people.

Now I had a new problem. I didn't know how to put seven hundred and forty-two volunteers to work! It was overwhelming. To answer my prayer, the Lord brought us two new missionary women. Anne Franczek and Kathleen Abel were single, dedicated women willing and able to help in any way possible and quickly settled into life at their host homes. They joined Sue Yingst, our office manager, and Carol Jarvis, our communications liaison. Each one brought their gifts and talents, graciously working hard, expecting nothing in return. They sidewalk counseled, manned the phones, and spent long hours following up with our turnarounds, faithfully working with me to increase our effectiveness.

I became determined to address every excuse women in desperate situations were using to have their abortions. Many had been abandoned by their husbands and boyfriends and had other children to care for at home. Some had already missed too much work because of excessive nausea and vomiting and weren't able to pay their bills. Others were ordered to complete bed rest by their doctors, leaving them without a steady income to pay their bills or care for their children. For each of these women, we assigned volunteers to visit their homes. The volunteers cleaned their houses, washed their clothes, ran errands, and cared for their children. Some volunteers made meals while others delivered those meals. One volunteer bought an industrial-sized refrigerator to keep at her house, storing all the meals waiting for distribution.

Businessmen came forward and asked for the privilege of covering their rent, utilities, and other expenses while our moms were unable to work. Many of them paid large hospital bills. Other men came to their aid, repairing cars and fixing leaky faucets. They delivered baby and household furniture their wives collected, arriving with bags of groceries. They also ministered to the men who were involved in these women's lives.

Women who were about to be homeless could always find someone to pay for their abortion but no one willing to help them long-term to have the baby. Many families from my church took these women into their homes, some short-term, some long-term. We were quickly able to address emergency situations for those who had other children. The cost of hotels was covered until we could find apartments for them. If they had apartments but were behind on their rent, we wrote checks to their apartment complexes and covered their utility bills.

We helped women locate jobs and gave them start-up insurance for their vehicles. For those who didn't have cars, a quick call to our faithful Tom Haddock would produce one, usually within a few days, if not immediately. Volunteers took them to doctor appointments and to church. They would ask us to take them because they couldn't wait to go to the kind of church that was willing to help them in need.

Great friendships developed. So many baby showers were happening that I couldn't attend them all. Our volunteers collected mountains of maternity and baby clothes, delivering these gifts along with clothes and toys for the older children in the home. For Christmas and birthdays, the mothers and children were met with more love and gifts than they had ever received before.

Indeed, the Lord had heard my prayer to anoint Women 4 Women in Atlanta. I was overwhelmed with appreciation for all the love, help, and financial support given so freely.

I felt, however, that these were still only Band-Aid offerings we were making.

I knew we needed to do so much more!

CHAPTER 26

Farewell, Sweet Momma

My forehead pressed against the window of the airplane. My mind was fixed on the words from the Lord spoken earlier that morning, after receiving news from my sister Cindy: Mom was in the hospital, in a coma with pneumonia. Somehow, I knew she would not make it this time.

"Karen, I don't think she'll make it this time," Cindy had said, mirroring my thoughts.

As soon as I hung up the phone, I clearly heard the Lord say, *Stay by her side. Do not take your eyes off her!* I thought those words were strange. While packing for my flight to California, those words kept running through my mind.

On the plane, I thought about the tremendous influence my mother had in my life. Some might have thought my mother was of no use to society. Without physical strength, financial or social power, she still left her mark on generations to come. Others might have believed she didn't have a good quality of life. They did not understand that her life influenced everyone she met. Certainly, I would not have been where I was, doing the work God called me to do, if it were not for my mother. It was her burden for the unborn that passed on to me. I committed to being her arms and legs and standing in the gap for the moms and the babies, resulting in thousands of lives spared from the horrors of abortion and thousands of lives touched by the love of God.

Peering out the window, I smiled and whispered, "You'll finally get to see Him, Momma."

Oh, how she loved her Savior. How often she was thankful for what He did for her on the cross. The cross. I remember realizing at an early age that I was missing something regarding the cross of Jesus. It didn't mean to me what it seemed to mean to others. I was just glad He did it. After all, I sure didn't want to go to hell.

I only thought about how physically painful the cross must have been. This thought was always followed by an inward shrug as I would tell myself, "Lots of people died on crosses back then." I never could distinguish between Christ's death on the cross and anybody else dying from crucifixion.

When I was five years old, I wanted to ask my parents to help me understand, but I thought they felt I already had all the answers. After all, I was five years old, and my parents would expect me to understand all there was to know about the cross of Jesus Christ. Right? Besides, as a little introvert, I didn't ask questions. I listened, I observed, I pondered, I fretted—but I never asked questions.

Resting my head against the back of my seat, I closed my eyes and chuckled to myself. What a strange child I was—shy, quiet, reserved, polite, well mannered, and sensitive to the needs and desires of my parents. Those times when it crossed my mind to disobey them, I would feel a sharp pain piercing through my chest, spreading to my ribs and down into my abdomen. Above all else, I never wanted to disappoint them or cause them grief.

Then there was God, Who was always in my thoughts. *How could I ever disobey Him and hurt His feelings? His feelings have to be bigger than my parents' feelings. The Lord's feelings are so huge. My disobedience would probably kill Him instead of me. Then what would I do? The whole world would be mad at me for killing God!*

Looking back, I realized that my sweet temperament prevented me from understanding that I had the curse of sin passed on to me as did every other human being on the planet. It wasn't that I thought I was already saved, it was that I didn't realize how lost I was until, at nine years old, I told a malicious lie about my older sister, Donna.

On most evenings at our home, dinners produced a stack of dishes not seen by other families except on Thanksgiving and Christmas. Around our table sat Mom, Dad, their six children, two foster children, and any other kids who followed us home that day from school. Each night, Donna and I had to tackle the huge mountain of glasses, silverware, dishes, and pots and pans. One of us would wash and the other would dry, and the next night we would switch chores. Mom had secured a tremendous bargain on powdered laundry detergent that we were instructed to use for washing the dishes. She didn't know it caused a painful, red, itchy rash on my arms. I never told her because sweet little girls don't complain.

One week, Donna had made plans to go out with her teenage friends. She promised if I both washed and dried the dishes for her that entire week, she would take over the next week's chores for me. I reluctantly agreed. That long, awful week left my arms bleeding. I still didn't tell Mom.

When the first night of my reprieve finally came, Donna announced that she had plans to go somewhere that night, too, insisting she didn't have to start doing the dishes until the following night. I wanted to yell, "No way. That's not fair. You're so mean!" But sweet, well-behaved girls don't yell. Knowing from experience I could never win an argument with her, I jumped up onto the chair in front of the kitchen sink and shoved my hands into the soapy water she had prepared for me.

What neither of us knew was one of the little ones had tossed an empty chocolate syrup can into the sink. The can had been opened only halfway with the sharp lid bent up. Pain shot across my entire left hand as the lid sliced through the top of my left thumb. I ran to Mom and Dad, blood dripping.

"Donna cut me with a knife!" I yelled.

The moment the words left my mouth, I was horrified. I couldn't believe my ears! I didn't know what to do. I found it impossible to open my mouth to retract the malicious lie. With horror on their faces, Mom and Dad immediately believed me and sternly voiced their disappointment at Donna's behavior. She was sent upstairs, grounded—presumably for life!

As Donna walked by me, she did the most horrible thing ever. Nothing! She didn't say a single word! I watched her turn and look at me as she walked up the stairs. I didn't see any anger. She just looked sad. Never had she ever just quietly walked up to her room when being disciplined. She had been nicknamed "Bette Davis" because of her dramatic response to things. I wanted her to scream at me, stick her tongue out, pull my hair, something, but instead, there was only silence and a sad face. I was dying inside.

With a closer examination of my thumb, Mom saw the rash on my arms and was horrified. Now it was my turn to be scolded for not telling her.

The following week was the most awful week of my life. I couldn't look at Donna. Not when we sat at the table together. Not when we rode the bus to school together. I tossed and turned relentlessly at night, unable to sleep due to the physical, mental, and emotional pain that would not leave me.

I tried to alleviate my pain by thinking she deserved to be punished for something else she may have done. I thought about all the times she had been mean to me. Trying to make my sister out to be mean so I would feel better about her being punished unjustly for something she didn't do just didn't work. I was the one who was mean and despicable. The weight of the pain I was carrying became more than I could bear. Still, I could not bring myself to tell the truth.

I sat in silence in the car on the way to church that next Sunday. It was Easter, and my pretty flowered dress, with matching shoes, hat, and gloves, weren't able to cheer me or cover up the dreaded darkness that filled my soul. When we arrived at church, I sat by myself. I couldn't bear to be close to Donna. I refused to look up. I kept twisting the ends of the fingers of my little white gloves.

A guest missionary from Brazil was speaking. He described the agony Jesus suffered on the cross as He bore the sin of the world. The missionary explained that it wasn't just the physical pain Jesus suffered but the pain of bearing our sin on His sinless body that caused His death. This made Jesus's death on the cross different from all others who had been crucified.

Finally, I had my answer to why His cross was so special. When he mentioned how the Lord never condemned His accusers but stood silently, a searing pain went through me. I thought about how unaccusing and silent Donna had been.

The missionary asked us all to bow our heads. He asked us to think about the wrong things we had done that week, those things that brought us shame. I was horrified! I wondered how he knew what I had done!

He asked, "Do you feel the pain? Let your mind go outside to this entire town, to this state, to all of America, and to the world from the beginning of time until the end. Imagine how much pain all that sin would have caused Him."

I thought I was going to die. I couldn't breathe. It was true. I did kill God! My sin helped to kill Him that day! Sorrow and tears flowed with such force, I simply couldn't calm myself down. The burden was much too heavy to bear.

"Burdens are lifted at Calvary," the missionary said. "If you lay that pain at the foot of the cross by believing, confessing, and asking for forgiveness, you will receive the peace you need."

Inside my mind, I shouted, *Yes! Yes!*

When the invitation to go forward was given, I ran backward instead. Back to my parents and Donna to confess my horrible lie. I understood why the cross was so precious to my mother. I had found His blessed peace.

Now I, too, would forever hold dearly to the reality of the cross.

In the hospital, my sisters and I stood over Mom's bed. I remembered the Lord's instructions to stay by her side and not take my eyes off her, so I positioned myself next to her side, near her head. I stroked her forehead, and hoping she could hear me, I described everyone who came into the room to see her. Our brother Mark was the only one who had not arrived yet. His flight coming in from Oregon was delayed.

As we kept vigil, some massaged her arms and legs while others sang softly to her. Others shared memories about Mom, reflecting on the nurturing, loving things she did for us when we were growing up. They recalled how she never complained a day about the disease that ravaged her body for thirty-seven years and left her completely paralyzed. She always had a smile and a thoughtful word for everyone.

Mom had faced each day with a heart full of joy and hope. She always carried a thankful spirit. She was thankful for the little bit of health she had left, thankful for her loving, faithful husband. She was thankful for her children, who admired and appreciated the example she was living before them. She was thankful for her grandchildren, who learned how to hug a grandmother who couldn't hug back.

Mom would always remind me to give thanks in all things. How easy it was for me to thank the Lord for my beloved mother and my faithful father, who never left her side. I was so thankful for their marriage and home that brought great love and security to our family. But give thanks in *all* things? How was I to give thanks for the nights I stood in the doorway holding young siblings when our mother was taken away by ambulance again? How was I to give thanks for the pain, the walking canes, the walkers, the wheelchairs, the hospital bed, and total paralysis?

Over the years, I did learn to give thanks in *all* things regarding my mother. Without the pain and the struggles, what would she have become? Would she have learned such spiritual strength if her physical body was strong? Daily she clung to the Lord, which produced the wisdom, compassion, unfaltering faith, and peace expressed in her radiant smile and sweet spirit.

Mark arrived and joined friends of the family who had come to see Mom, including my friend Jackie. We all crowded into her small room. As the night went on, conversations turned to fond memories about the family and growing up on the farm, laughing over the fun times we had, and mischievous things done—things Mom and Dad never knew about.

Every once in a while, Dad would look at Mom and say, "I didn't know about that, honey. Did you?"

When evening came, everyone left to find something to eat. I declined the invitation for dinner, staying back to keep my eyes on Mom. I stood alone at the side of her bed, refusing to take my eyes off her as the Lord had instructed. The room was quiet. Only Jackie remained with me, sound asleep in the corner of the room. I was grateful for this quiet time alone with Mom.

Suddenly, I was gripped by fear. I would soon lose my most important and faithful prayer covering. Mom often reminded me she had nothing else to do all day but lie in bed and pray for her children. I had drawn strength from her prayers. I couldn't imagine my life without them. Instantly, I felt uncovered. I wanted to beg the Lord to keep her here, but I couldn't bring myself to ask that selfish prayer. She so wanted to be with Him.

I kept my eyes on Mom, thinking what a waste it would be when she departed this life and took that special quality with her that made her who she was. What was it? Tenacity? Persistence? Steadfastness?

With a great urgency in my soul, I begged the Lord to give it to me, whatever it was. "Don't let her take it with her. What a waste that would be. Please give it to me."

Then I saw it. Something appearing like a sheer gray baby blanket began rising off her body. I watched as it lifted, then fell ever so softly onto my face and shoulders. I was dumbfounded. I didn't know what it was. Because of the color, I thought it was something bad. I tried to jump away from it.

It's her disease! I thought. *I don't want her disease!*

I couldn't move. I couldn't speak. I looked over to see if Jackie had seen it, but she was still sleeping. I was afraid to tell anyone. They would think I was crazy.

Later, as the family returned from dinner and filed back into the room, everyone was quiet. Instead of confessing childhood sins, we confessed our love to Mom. We shared our appreciation and gratitude for all she had given to us. For the first time, I moved away from her side so others could say their goodbyes. With hugs and kisses, they whispered things to her that only they and the Lord would know.

As the night wore on, we stood around her bed holding hands, praying and singing her favorite hymns. Though each of her children knew the tenacity Mom had for holding onto life, we also knew her frail body could no longer continue. We encouraged her to go, assuring her that her job as a mother was graciously completed.

Hours later, we could barely take in what we saw. We watched as Mom's paralyzed body slowly lifted from the bed into a semi-sitting position. Her helpless arms hung limply behind her. For the first and only time, she opened her eyes and looked at the ceiling behind Daddy's head. Her face was radiant.

"George, look," she said with excitement in her voice. "Look!"

We all turned to look up behind Daddy. We could not see what she saw, but we knew it was glorious! Ever so slowly, invisible hands gently placed her helpless body back down onto the bed. We stood still, trying to absorb the fact that we had just seen a miracle. It was as if we could feel the angels approaching.

Shortly afterward, Daddy and I were alone in her room when the nurse came in to check on Mom. Somehow, I could "see" that she was leaving us.

"Daddy, she's leaving," I whispered.

Together, we watched her take her last breath.

Daddy quickly called the others back into the room. Some began sniffling, but all were smiling, glad she had gone to her rest and reward. What a sweet Momma. What a special homegoing. She'd served her family and her Savior well.

Daddy turned to me and asked me if I would be the one to speak for the family at Mom's funeral. All eyes were on me. I felt the Lord say that He would give me the words and enable me to do it. With that assurance from the Lord, I nodded a tearful yes.

In the days that followed, out-of-town family and friends began arriving at Dad's house in ever-increasing numbers, bringing delicious meals and words of comfort. My friend Joanna Luttrell stopped by as well, and I shared my experience in the hospital as I watched Mom's gray baby blanket lift off and rest on me.

"That was your mother's mantle," Joanna said.

I didn't know what she meant. She encouraged me to open my Bible and read the story of Elijah and Elisha.

"Elisha had to ask and had to see Elijah go," she explained. "You asked the Lord, and you saw her go. That's why the Lord told you not to take your eyes off her."

After reading the story again, I wished I had asked for a double portion, as Elisha did. Still, I was humbled to think that the Lord would trust me with Mom's mantle. Amazed at what I had seen and felt, I begged the Lord to help me wear it well.

The day before Mom's funeral, I still did not know what to say at her service. I excused myself to go for a walk, looking for an opportunity to be alone with the Lord. I retraced the steps I had taken just the previous month when I was home visiting. As was my custom, I had taken Mom out in her wheelchair to look at her neighbors' yards filled with bright, beautiful flowers. At one point, I realized this would be my last walk with her. Pushing her along, I kissed her on the top of her head and spoke a blessing over her. Now, standing alone in that very spot again, I hugged myself, as if holding closer the memory of our last walk together.

Help me, Lord, I prayed. *Please tell me what to say.*

Instantly, I heard this phrase in my spirit: *Rise and shine.*

I knew exactly what that meant. I quickened my steps back toward home. The Lord had given me the words!

The next day, as we were in the little chapel waiting for the service to begin, all were at peace. Sitting near the podium, I looked out at the faces of those who came to celebrate Mom's life. They all meant so much to her. I looked at the front row and the faces of my dad and siblings, more grateful than ever to be a part of a large family. The pain was not as hard to bear when there were so many to share it.

When it was my turn to speak, a supernatural peace fell on me. I shared my experiences as a young child. Each morning, I would wake up to the sounds and smells of Mom preparing breakfast for her brood while she could still walk. Lying in bed with my eyes closed, I would inhale the abundance of aromas—oatmeal, bacon and eggs, toast from homemade bread, hot chocolate, and fresh-squeezed orange juice. I listened to the dishes being moved about in the kitchen, accompanied by Mom's soft humming.

I would wait in anticipation for the sound of her footsteps approaching the bottom of the stairs, smiling at the sound of her voice echoing up the stairs, singing out, "Rise and shine! Come and get it!"

With a single bound, we were out of our beds, colliding in the hallway at the top of the stairs. We would race to see who could reach Mom first and receive their morning hugs and kisses.

"I wonder if Mom was doing the same thing while she was lying there in the hospital," I said. "Can you picture it? Was she lying there in perfect peace, eyes closed, taking in the approaching aroma of heaven? I wonder what sounds she might have heard. Did she listen to the preparations being made for her arrival? Like her children, waiting for the sound of her footsteps at the bottom of the stairs, was she, too, waiting for the sound of His footsteps? As we, her children, waited for the sound of her voice, was she lying there, waiting in expectation for the sound of His voice?

"What joy must have filled her heart when she heard His approaching footsteps, waiting to hear His longed-for voice. Can't you just hear it? I can imagine Him saying to her, 'Rise and shine, Rita. Come and get it!' How long she had waited for that invitation. Now He had come to receive her to Himself.

"As children, we had always gone downstairs, but she went up. Up to a table spread in her honor, up to white and shining garments, up to her reward, and up to her Savior, into His loving arms for all eternity. Up to things we can't even imagine, as told in I Corinthians 2:9, which says: 'Eye has not seen, nor ear heard, nor have entered into the heart of man the things which God has prepared for those who love Him.' How exciting is that!"

Looking out over the crowd, I saw the faces of other family members and friends that Mom held so dear over the years. I told them I knew Mom would want me to talk about her Savior more than her. I assured them she loved each one and would want everyone sitting there today to know her Savior as well. I encouraged them to listen intently to the words of the preacher who would speak next so they would know what they needed to do and Who they needed to trust to be sure that they, too, would someday hear the words, "Rise and shine! Come and get it!"

I believe Mom joined the angels in heaven as they rejoiced over the three souls who trusted in Christ that day.

At the close of the service, my sister Becky's voice rang out clearly, the reflection of our mother's life in the song, "Well Done, My Child." Hers was a life marked with dignity, honor, and grace.

Farewell, Momma. You remain my inspiration.

CHAPTER 27

England Bound

I marvel at how the Lord brought me out from my hiding place in the corner of my room on a small farm, in a small town, leading me across the nation and into other countries to share my story of His faithfulness. In June 1996, Dr. Frank Henderson and his wife, Carol, invited me to England. I am so grateful to them for the opportunity to share my testimony and train the "pavement" counselors there.

Before I left home, Dr. Henderson began encouraging me to attend a Christian conference that would be held in North Carolina when I returned to the States. As soon as this couple picked me up, conversation about this conference resumed. I smiled at Dr. Henderson's tenacity. During a quick tour of London, I took in the sights of Bobbies on horses, red telephone booths, double-decker buses, and yes, black taxi cabs. I looked up at Big Ben and walked by Parliament and the Queen's home, watching all the cars speeding by on the wrong side of the narrow roads. Time seemed to have stood still in London, leaving it looking the same as centuries ago.

My days in England were filled with training seminars for the pavement counselors, leading workshops for crisis pregnancy centers, giving my testimony at churches, and many radio interviews. Long hours of counseling at different abortion clinics filled my already full schedule further. Days ran into each other as I traveled from Manchester to Stoke-on-Trent and back to Birmingham. I met pro-lifers from Ireland, Australia, Yugoslavia, and Romania. My heart was greatly warmed by the faithful few in England. I was graciously welcomed by each of them and would hold tightly to the deposit of love they placed in my heart.

With one more reminder to pray about going to the conference in North Carolina, Dr. Henderson handed me ten *Morning Star Journal*s written by the people associated with the conference. I was encouraged to read them on the ten-hour bus ride to Aberdeen, Scotland, the next day.

With my sometimes insatiable need to learn, I knew I wouldn't be able to put them down.

A young man named Tim met me at the bus station and drove me the rest of the way to Braemar, a quaint little village surrounded by the Grampian Mountains. It was nearly dark by the time the car pulled through the gate at Humane Vitae House, a retreat center for pro-lifers. My spirit was immediately at peace.

The weather the next day was dreary and chilly. I spent most of the time at a small table in the kitchen, close to the crackling fire in the old stone fireplace, fellowshipping with Father Morrow as he shared his many pro-life adventures and how he had turned his home into a retreat center. I so enjoyed his accent, but I often found myself looking at others to translate something I had not understood. Father Morrow entertained us with both his humor and spiritual insight long into the night. We each retired that evening and most every evening after that filled with delicious food, hot Scottish tea, and freshly made scones.

I often walked through the lovely little village, wandering in and out of the small shops. I would always be greeted warmly by everyone, dressed in beautiful wool sweaters and plaid jumpers and kilts. As in England, it seemed like time had stood still. I enjoyed the village, but it was the mountain that seemed to call out to me. I felt the Lord say I needed to meet Him there.

The two-week-long speaking schedule in England had been quite grueling, so I was very grateful for the gift of this time in Scotland.

While making arrangements for my time in England, Dr. Henderson frequently scolded me about the insane hours that I was keeping with Women 4 Women in Atlanta. Concerned about my health, he said I needed to take a vacation. I guess he knew I wouldn't schedule it myself, so he did it for me in Scotland. *Thank You, Lord.*

It wasn't just my body that needed rest, however. Right before leaving Georgia for England, I had been under a very long and discouraging attack by Satan. The difficult situations and circumstances that he orchestrated left me feeling overwhelmed. I was overworked and greatly discouraged. I was going through a season that left me wondering where the Lord was and if He was hearing me at all. I felt that His "still, small voice" was much too still and small. I deeply needed to be reassured that He was still nearby and heard my desperate prayers. I was convinced I needed to climb the mountain to hear from Him.

Father Morrow reluctantly gave me directions to the hiking trail. He told me it was a challenging hike and that I should perhaps take someone with me. I refused his suggestion because I so needed to get away alone with the Lord.

I set out on the main street and made a right turn onto a narrow road past the butcher shop, as instructed. I continued to walk, unsure where to go next.

A young child appeared directly in front of me, standing there as if in anticipation of my arrival, her right arm stretched out to her side.

"You nearly missed it," she said.

"How did you know?"

Without answering, she immediately took me by the hand and turned me in the direction she had pointed. "It's a wee bit this way."

I was confused and surprised that she knew where I wanted to go, but grateful this child was willing to walk a stranger up the path leading to the mountain. I realized I would have passed it without her help.

She opened the gate that led to the path. "Are you prepared?" she asked. "It's a bit of a climb, you see."

Without taking my eyes off the mountain, I nodded in reply. Then, looking down to thank her for her help, I realized she was already gone.

I began to walk through the dark and foreboding forest as I made my way up the mountain. I encountered many obstacles and experienced much fear. Exhausted and out of breath, I thought I might not be able to complete the climb. Sensing a tug in my spirit for what waited for me at the top of the mountain, I pressed on.

Hours later, the path and the side of the mountain dropped behind me. I was wholly unprepared for what I saw. Catching my breath as I absorbed the beauty, words of praise rushed from my lips. *How great Thou art and greatly to be praised!*

Far below, on the valley floor, smoke from burning peat escaped the chimneys of humble cottages, filling the air with its lusty, earthy smell. The landscape, looking much like a thick green carpet, was dotted with sheep and cows feasting on its bounty. I laughed to see graceful deer dancing across the open fields. In all its splendor, creation was spread before me in glorious array. I was beholding a feast for the eyes and senses, given as a reward for conquering the formidable height of this grand mountain. I was awestruck at the sight of the magnificent, glorious handiwork of God.

I looked past the valley and saw many more mountains, most of which I could not see while I was in the valley. I took in the beauty of faraway, glistening snowcaps. I watched small butterflies as they fluttered around yellow and purple wildflowers. I looked down at the Dee River as it wound its way through the lush valley floor, relishing all the colors and various shades of green. Tall, pointed dark green and short, fluffy light green. Lavish purple heather spread as far as the eye could see.

I sat down on a large rock, barely able to breathe. Not because of the altitude but because of the overwhelming beauty I beheld. I watched in amazement as a nearby hawk lifted its graceful wings and sailed high above the valley. I marveled at the fact that I was looking down on it, higher even than this feathered friend. Looking again to the valley below, the entire village of Braemar and the nearby massive castles looked like nothing more than mere children's playthings.

My thoughts turned to the heaviness I had been carrying and how my well was so empty. My heart ached to hear the sound of His voice reassuring me He was still with me. I needed to know that His eye was still on me.

As if in response to my heart's cry, I heard a child's voice calling to her father somewhere far below me. Her words were lifted from the valley floor as the wind swept up the side of the mountain to the very place I was standing.

With fear in her voice, I heard her cry out, "Daddy, Daddy, where are you? I can't see you."

In a strong, reassuring voice, I clearly heard her father's reply. "It's okay, honey. I'm right here. I can see you."

Tears stung my eyes as I realized what a gift the Lord just gave me. I was feeling tiny and far away, just like the objects I was looking down on. He once again reassured me that my prayers to my Heavenly Father always reach His ears just as clearly as this child's cry reached her earthly father's ears. He reminded me He could always see me, even when I was unsure where He was.

With the sky darkening and clouds appearing, I stood to my feet and drew in one last breath of the cool, fresh mountain air. I turned once again to the steep trail. I had previously ignored the warning to be well prepared. The remaining hours of a very difficult descent taught me many lessons about the importance of being prepared in life and ministry and for whatever may come to me in the future.

When I returned home to Atlanta and the battle there, I would carry with me a greater realization that He understands and appreciates the sacrifices I made. He tenderly remembers and would always let me know He cares. I felt Him assure me it was my obedience that brought me to England and Scotland—and there would be more believers to meet and experiences to enjoy, in other faraway places yet to come.

CHAPTER 28

Pulling Down Strongholds

No! Not again!
A crowd of workers surrounded a man on his knees outside Midtown Hospital. He held his arms tightly around the legs of a woman whose pregnancy was well advanced. It was another situation like little Timmy's, all over again.

"I'm her husband!" he yelled. "Where are my rights? What about our baby's right to live?"

Within moments, his wife was torn from his grasp and pulled into the building.

He sat on the sidewalk, pounding the back of his head into the fence. I sat down next to him. He grabbed my hand and started twisting my fingers like they were his own. The night before, his wife had told him about her plans for the abortion. He tried to talk her out of it. When he started yelling and begging for the life of his child, their neighbors called the police. He was arrested for disturbing the peace. That morning, he bonded out of jail and rushed to Midtown Hospital, trying to save his child.

I encouraged him that the Lord would continue to persuade his wife to have their baby. However, I knew the Lord wouldn't cross her strong will. I told him if the Holy Spirit of God couldn't persuade her, then neither could he, no matter what he said or did.

His shoulders hung down, his voice filled with failure as he said goodbye. I watched as he staggered away, overwhelmed with anger and grief.

I walked to the building and pounded on the front door with both fists. "I hate you, Midtown Hospital!" I screamed.

I thought about all the horror stories women who'd had abortions there had told me—stories of dead, bloody babies on the floor and the baby-crushing machine inside. Over the years, I made multiple calls to the Health Department reporting these claims. Each time, my reports would be dismissed.

"That's not possible," they would tell me. "Those are just rumors."

Eventually, they stopped returning my calls altogether.

Overwhelmed with anger, frustration, and helplessness, I shouted out to the Lord, "Tell me what to do!"

Midtown had once been a children's hospital. No child was safe there now. I prayed that someday it could be restored to a place where children would again be safe, but others told me Midtown had been there forever and would never come down. I refused to believe it!

Clenching my fists, I yelled, "Show Yourself greater, Lord!"

Then I remembered a Bible conference in North Carolina I had been persuaded to attend. Somehow, I knew this conference held the key to bringing Midtown down.

A worker heard me shouting to God. "Shut up, Black," she yelled, "or I'll call the cops!"

"Go ahead! I just called God, and He said this place is coming down!"

She laughed, slamming the door shut.

The conference was unlike anything this little Baptist-turned-PCA-Presbyterian had ever experienced. I was a bit overwhelmed. The praise and worship music, however, caught my attention.

If only I could bring all these people to Midtown Hospital. With this incredible spiritual warfare music, that place would have to fall! I thought.

The Lord told me to take the music back with me. After the conference, I bought three tapes: *Worship*, *Warfare*, and *Vision*.

The next step was to organize a Jericho March at Midtown Hospital. After much prayer and fasting, I felt the first day of the march needed to be attended by Anne, Kathleen, Sue, and myself. We would fast breakfast and lunch, praying as we walked around Midtown seven times every morning. We started at 6:00 a.m. seven days a week, for seven full weeks.

I also felt the Lord required this be done by women, and we were to wear only skirts or dresses. I wasn't sure why. I knew we should be anointed with oil and should pray on our spiritual armor before crossing over to the clinic's side of the street.

Every day, while we waited for the light to change to cross over Ponce de Leon Avenue, we carried a large cassette player with our worship tapes. The first morning, we listened as the song "Take the Land" by Don Potter rang out clearly into the dark, highlighting those who, by faith, crossed the Jordan River, marched around Jericho's walls, and fought battles with the boldness of God.

Soon, other women joined us. Most of them had never stood in front of an abortion clinic. I made it clear they would be marching into the enemy's camp, engaging in a nature of spiritual warfare they'd probably never experienced before. These brave newcomers heeded my warning and prepared themselves spiritually. Undaunted by unseen forces, they raised their voices in songs of praise. Ponce de Leon Avenue was their Jordan River, and they walked right over!

One day, I felt the Lord say we were to ask Hebrew dancers to join us, so I invited some ladies from Beth Hallel to join us. The next day, Channel 7 News stopped to interview me and video the dancers in their beautiful, flowing white skirts. People stopped their cars, watching their graceful, synchronized dance. Those standing nearby clapped their hands in time with the dancers' timbrels.

That night, we were on the evening news.

Lord, why did You want the dancers to join us? I prayed.

He led me to the story of King Jehoshaphat, who experienced a great battle against a multitude of his enemies. When he was outnumbered, surrounded, and filled with fear, King Jehoshaphat cried out to God. He appointed those who sang to the Lord and those who praised Him in holy attire (skirts and dresses?) to go out before the army, saying, "Give thanks to the Lord, for His love endures forever" (2 Chronicles 20:21). Like those in the king's chorus, we sang this Scripture verse as we marched around Midtown.

King Jehoshaphat followed the Lord's instructions. God caused his enemies to turn against themselves, killing each other to the last man. During our Jericho March, we all told each other the Lord would close Midtown from the inside out. We believed they would cause their own demise.

We continued our Jericho March, day after day. For years we had endured pushing, shoving, harassment, and mocking by clinic escorts. Now we saw them, standing there in shock, not understanding what was happening. They only knew us as sidewalk counselors. Some attempted to scream profanities, but they were drowned out by the music. Others laughed and mocked us. The Satan worshippers, however, were not laughing.

As we marched around Midtown, we played intense, riveting music sung by powerful male voices on tape, accompanied by thousands more in the background. These songs were filled with lyrics from Scripture, such as this one from Psalm 68: "Let God arise, let His enemies be scattered."

One Satan worshipper was filled with fear and fell backward into the parking lot. For the first time, he was unable to move or come near us! I could feel the enemy's stronghold slipping. At the same time, I could almost feel Satan's anger increasing. For years, this had been his territory. The atmosphere was intense. Something powerful was happening in the heavenly realm.

During those seven weeks, I had a reoccurring dream nearly every night. In the dream, I alone was marching around Midtown, which was surrounded by demons of all shapes and sizes. Each had taken on the shape of whatever object they were on. The chain links in the fence were demons, the bricks on the building were demons, and the leaves on the trees were demons. They all hissed and snarled at me.

As I marched, a song played. It spoke of God's righteous judgments, which would break the enemy's encampments and release His power in the land, causing all to bow before Him. Quickly, the situation changed. The demons, who were shaped like chain links, began to evaporate, causing the fence to weaken and sway. The demons shaped like bricks began to crumble and fall. The demons shaped like leaves on the trees lost their grip, falling by the hundreds, screaming as they went.

High above in the clouds, there was a great heavenly host doing absolutely nothing! I yelled up to them and asked why they didn't come down or do something.

A voice responded, "Not until you have finished your part."

I realized I must be diligent and faithful to the work given to me. Perhaps the angels could do only what I could not.

Never did the dream vary the entire seven weeks.

When we began to grow physically weary, we gained spiritual strength as more truths were revealed to our hearts. Though we doubted a small band of women could ever produce a "shout" for our Jericho March, the Lord provided for our needs. One tape had a three-minute roar of thousands and thousands of people cheering, whistling and shouting. There was even the sound of a ram's horn in the background. We needed only to follow His lead.

I was convinced of the necessity and power of prayer, fasting, and spiritual warfare done through song and praise—the type of warfare needed at a place of child sacrifice, where evil is entrenched. To think any efforts or plans in the physical realm *alone* could ever make a difference is just foolishness. Week after week, we relied on the truth found in our theme verse: "Not by might, nor by power, but by My Spirit says the Lord of hosts" (Zechariah 4:6).

The weather grew cold and windy. Winter had come. Some days many women joined us; other days, I was alone. The seven weeks ended with three days of prayer and fasting and a candlelight vigil held with my staff. As we finished praying, Kathleen, Anne, Sue, and I blew out our candles and stood to our feet. We turned from Midtown Hospital, walking away in silence. I glanced at the bare trees as we walked, remembering the dream. I felt the Lord tell me our mission was accomplished.

Just then, I noticed that the fence was leaning over.

"Do you remember so many missing bricks?" I said, breaking the silence in our group.

My friends just smiled.

I never had that dream again.

On the drive home that day, the burden of sidewalk counseling lifted off me as if a tangible force left my body. I felt the Lord say that I was not to return to the clinics for a season but to focus my time and energies on the moms under our care and complete the programs to be used in our future Whole Life Center.

Naturally, I started arguing with the Lord. *Abandon the sidewalks? Who would stand in the gap for the moms and babies if no one else could do it? This has been my life for seven full years, Lord.* I was sure He was mistaken.

I am moving you on was His only reply.

Back home at my desk, I turned the page on my calendar and noticed the date: December 15, 1996, the seventh anniversary of my arrival in Atlanta. I caught my breath. I recalled the day I responded to Jack Hayford's plea and asked the Lord to give me back the years the locusts had devoured. The Lord kept His promise and had packed more life experiences and ministry opportunities into the past seven years than most people would experience in a lifetime. What an incredibly exciting, exhausting, frustrating, overwhelming, adventurous, miraculous seven years it had been.

For a moment, I was fearful my service for Him might end. Little did I know that the work, the learning, and the ministry opportunities had only just begun.

Spring arrived, bursting onto the scene with the wonder and beauty of azaleas, tulips, daffodils, and flowering dogwood trees. I basked in the sun's warmth that highlighted the Lord's creation, marveling at the great things He had done for Women 4 Women. I was grateful He'd sent so many dedicated and gifted volunteers. Anne, Kathleen, and Sue all graciously committed to serving the Lord, in agreement with the full vision of Women 4 Women. We would not settle for simply being pro-life but would strive to be *whole life*, helping to prepare mothers and children to live productive, godly lives.

Through my ministry, I taught others that to spare the life of the child from an abortion and a godless life, you must focus on the mother. Should she choose life for her child and Christ for herself, our work had only just begun. Our responsibility to both mother and child went far beyond pregnancy and the postpartum period. We asked her to agree to an eighteen-year commitment—a commitment she may not be equipped to make.

What a great mission field the Lord had given to us. We worked and prayed, believing each woman and child would become a child of God. We could not accomplish this without intense, long-term involvement in their lives by wise, caring mentors who would point each woman toward Christ, walking with her on her spiritual journey. What a joy it was to see these once floundering women become mentors themselves. We believed it was the transforming power of the Holy Spirit that changes lives and were grateful for the opportunity to be a part of His plan.

Our long-held goal was to provide these mothers with help to equip them socially, economically, and spiritually for the task of raising their children. We prayed for ways to prepare these mothers to become independent of us and, especially, of the welfare system. This would require each one to receive a higher education. To accomplish this goal, we reached out to churches and individual groups, asking them to sponsor a mother and her children, committing to meeting one of their many needs involved in completing a four-year degree—whether it was tuition and fees, daycare, or household expenses. It was impossible for a single mother to meet her many expenses while working at a low salaried job with no other means of support. She would remain trapped in poverty.

It was a great joy to assign sponsor groups for our women who desired a better life for themselves and their children. If they attended school full time, we would assist them as long as a B average was maintained. Through the generous giving of our sponsors, we could cover their rent, utilities, all childcare costs, car expenses, tuition, and textbooks.

I never tired of hearing stories from both the mothers and their sponsor groups. I wasn't sure who was most excited! I watched as mothers cried from joy at having their needs met, and I watched as sponsors cried because they were able to meet those needs.

One group leader said, "Who would have believed that so much joy could come from just being the church?"

At graduation, everyone joined in the celebrations with pride.

During this time of continuing change, many additional resources were donated to Women 4 Women, including rent-free apartments complete with dishes, bedding, and all the furnishings necessary to set up housekeeping. Our board member Randy Schlichting joined other godly men to form the Truefast Foundation. With Isaiah 58:6–12 as their inspiration, the foundation purchased houses in need of repair and renovated them, giving affordable housing to our mothers and children.

As we began to place women into their new homes, a new need was met to lift their heavy loads. Women needed not only financial support but emotional comfort and friendship. I reached out to the Encouragers Class at my church asking for help, and they graciously responded. They truly lived out the words found in Hebrews 10:24: "Let us consider how we may spur one another on to good deeds." Twenty-seven other churches joined their efforts, faithfully giving of their time and resources to help our many women and their children, born and unborn.

On September 8, 1997, I was seated at a banquet table with my sweet Kimberly in Atlanta's Swiss Hotel for a very special event. The Georgia Family Council had invited over five hundred business, church, and government leaders to attend.

Kim reached over and squeezed my hand as I was called forward as the Georgia Family Council's first female recipient of the "Power of One" award, recognizing my efforts to meet the felt needs of the women and families we served. I was humbled.

As I went forward to accept this honor, I remembered the time I carried the burden for the moms and babies alone on my own shoulders. A pastor had confronted me at Surgi, telling me I needed to stop going to the clinics. He said my efforts were useless—that I was worthless and needed to get a job to contribute to society. He mocked my ability to help women by myself.

"You're one lousy woman," he said with a sneer.

Yes, I was only one—but with the wonder-working One at my side, anything was possible.

The massive claw of the earthmover made a loud, horrific sound as it dug deep into the ground, then pulled up the last remaining fragments of Midtown Hospital's defiled foundation. The powerful claw completed its task, moved to the side, and came down hard on the Georgia clay as if it were making the statement, "There! It is finished!"

A cloud of dust blew across the property up the hill to where Steve and I stood. Over time, I had grown closer to this compassionate, gentle man. It began when I was stricken with a severe case of vertigo. On some days, it was so intense I could not drive or go to the clinics. Steve would either do my errands for me or would pick me up to take me where I needed to go. Light made my vertigo worse, causing me to stagger and fall. Everywhere we went, I closed my eyes and held tightly onto Steve's arm. He led me everywhere. I had come to trust him completely.

At one point, the vertigo was so severe, I couldn't read my Bible without the words spinning and causing nausea. Steve would call me every morning to read the Word to me and pray for me to start my day. He indeed had taken God's commissioning to be my encourager seriously. So many times, I would have quit and gone back home if it wasn't for his encouragement to stay in the battle. I loved how he called me his Gentle Warrior. Steve was my special gift from God.

Now we watched together as the impossible became possible. How long I had waited for this day. Many years had passed since the first time I stood in front of Midtown Hospital. That night I prayed the Lord would turn Midtown into a maternity home or take it apart brick by brick. Now only a pile of rubble surrounded the deep, gaping hole that was once its foundation. I had always envisioned myself on this day, shouting for joy and jumping up and down in celebration. Instead, I couldn't move or make a sound. I could barely breathe, still trying to take it all in. Tears streamed down my face.

That was when I saw her. From my vantage point, I could clearly see a woman exiting a car in what used to be the parking lot of the abortion clinic. She looked around, then down at a piece of paper in her hand. I assumed it was the address to Midtown for an abortion. Mistakenly, I had thought I would never have to counsel at this horrible place again.

I made my way across the empty lot toward her. She showed me her paper and pointed to the address written on it. She pleaded with me to help her find Midtown Hospital. She was pregnant and looked full-term.

I explained to her what had happened to Midtown and why. I talked about the possible dangers to her, regardless of which clinic she used.

She kept shaking her head. "No, no, I *have* to do it. I have to find Midtown Hospital." She wouldn't tell me why.

A man walked up to us and said he was her husband. His eyes filled with tears. "I don't know what's wrong with her. I think she's losing her mind," he said. When he learned Midtown was now the pile of bricks behind him, he let out a heavy sigh of relief. "The doctor told her she was too far along for anywhere else but Midtown Hospital."

His wife ran off, frantically trying to find someone to help her locate Midtown Hospital. She rushed up to the men operating the heavy equipment, begging for their help. She ran after people passing by, showing them her piece of paper. By the time her husband got her into their car, she was hysterical. I was incredulous. Satan was still bewitching women into taking the lives of their own children, sending them to a place that no longer existed.

I returned to my spot next to Steve, then stood there in silence, my mind speeding through multiple years of indescribable, anguished memories. I saw faces flash before me, remembering names and stories of great despair.

Knowing what I must be going through, Steve turned to me and asked, "Are you okay, honey?" He put his arm around me.

Unable to bear it any longer, I covered my face with my hands and sobbed.

We had stood by ourselves for some time when a man in a plaid shirt appeared at Steve's right side. He leaned around Steve and directed his comments toward me.

"I know what you're feeling. I was here every moment with you."

I squeezed the tears from my eyes and glanced at this stranger. I knew full well I had never seen him there before, and I wanted to tell him so—but just as suddenly as he had appeared, he was now gone.

Steve and I turned around, looking up and down the sidewalk. We never saw him come or go. It was as if he had just disappeared. My eyes grew large. I wondered if he was an angel letting me know I was never alone, even though I had felt it, day after day after lonely day.

I chose to believe he was indeed an angel.

Driving away, we recounted the events leading up to Midtown's closing. First there was Michelle, a spunky blonde with enthusiasm and drive who joined our team after our Jericho March ended. Pregnant with her fifth child, she and her husband, Mike, took over the work of sidewalk counseling.

As the weeks and months went by, Michelle refused to take the abuse of the clinic escorts—and the escorts were the ones who found themselves in court instead. Angered by the escorts' behavior, the judge went to Midtown himself to observe. Security guards who were hired to keep the peace soon found their hearts turned toward Mike and Michelle, witnessing their genuine concern for the women. Without a doubt, the Jericho March had weakened the evil stronghold there.

Twenty long months had passed since we had completed the Jericho March. As Women 4 Women continued to grow, Mike and Michelle stayed at Midtown. Michelle persisted in making calls to the Health Department. She reported obvious health violations, as well as the horror stories repeatedly told by the women when they were leaving. A new person had just come on board at the Health Department at the time Michelle began insisting on an investigation. It was no surprise. The Lord's timing was perfect. Other prayer vigils began taking place, including those organized by Father Campbell from St. John Neumann's parish. We all kept working, praying, and waiting.

We knew it was only a matter of time before we would hear the good news. And then it came, in the newspapers and on the television.

On Friday, May 22, 1998, Superior Judge William Alexander ordered Midtown Hospital closed! The *Atlanta Journal* wrote, "After five investigations, the state issued a sixty-page statement of deficiencies, revealing a startling array of severe rule violations which have a direct adverse impact on patient care."

The Department of Human Resources said, "The clinic was overcrowded, understaffed, and dirty and shows a complete disregard for the health and safety of its patients."

They caused their own demise, as they repeatedly refused to heed the warnings given by the Health Department. Midtown's administrator said they would fight the order. Instead, on June 11, the abortionist voluntarily relinquished his license.

A huge "For Sale" sign went up outside of Midtown. My heart leaped inside my chest the first time I drove by and saw it. It was a proclamation to the great and awesome work the Lord had done! The things done in secret were now being shouted from the rooftops, and we had received the answer to our prayers.

To God be all the glory!

EPILOGUE

Released and Renewed

"Finally!" This was the word shouted out as Steve and I were introduced as husband and wife at the close of our wedding ceremony. Laughter, applause, and tears of joy broke out from those who packed the beautiful little chapel in the woods. So many of our friends had shared in both the struggle and the joy our relationship had brought over the years. They had witnessed how Steve had brought blessing, encouragement, laughter, and love to me. I had consistently brought anxiety, hesitation, doubt, uncertainty, and the fear of marriage to him.

For ten years, I struggled to be restored from the effects of abandonment and abuse from my former spouses. One night, overwhelmed by my desire for the Lord's blessing and His release to marry Steve, I dropped to my knees in prayer and heard a book fall to the floor. When my prayer was finished, I went to pick it up. It was a short book written by Beth Moore which fell open to an entry titled, "Dear Bride to Be." The Lord spoke reassuringly to my heart through her beautiful words. All my doubts and reservations dissipated on the spot.

Steve's patience had finally been rewarded. On our wedding night, he took a basin of water and knelt down to wash my feet. He committed to serving me all the days of his life. Steve insisted on borrowing Mom and Dad's marriage motto: "Each for the other, and both for the Lord." Our lives and home have been filled with peace and harmony, ordered by the law of kindness—a quiet, refreshing oasis for both of us.

If it hadn't been for Dan and Melissa Duffy, I never would have met my Stevie. They were the ones who introduced us. Sometimes I wonder where I would be without their presence in my life. Not only did they provide needed office space for my Women 4 Women ministry in their home, but they also housed pregnant women and missionaries. They took me in and treated me like family. They shared everything from personal space and privacy to food and clothing. They cared for me when I was sick, which was often. They gave their time, prayers, money, and encouragement. When they visited me at Key Road Prison, they fulfilled the words of Jesus in Matthew 25:35–36: "For I was hungry and you gave Me food; I was thirsty and you gave Me drink; I was a stranger and you took Me in; I was naked and you clothed Me; I was sick and you visited Me; I was in prison and you came to Me."

Leaving the Duffys, our family, and our community of faith to move to Tennessee was one of the hardest steps of faith Steve and I ever had to take. After my sixteen years serving as a pro-life missionary in Atlanta, we had seen the faithfulness of God time after time, with nearly nine thousand babies saved during those years. Now the Lord was giving us many confirmations that He was doing a new thing in our lives, and we needed to trust Him completely again. On December 28, 2005, we slowly pulled away from our home, leaving behind everyone we knew and loved.

We brought all the experience and knowledge the Lord had imparted to continue our pro-life work in Tennessee through sidewalk counseling and helping women in need. Local churches and women's groups began collecting maternity clothes, baby clothes, and furniture for Women 4 Women to open a maternity home for expectant mothers and their children. An outpouring of love and generosity from the community provided everything we needed. After months of preparation, our Lifehouse maternity home was prayerfully dedicated to the Lord.

When state regulations forced its premature closure, the Lord opened a new opportunity for me to operate a mobile crisis pregnancy ministry from our van. But even that assignment was to be short-lived.

Before long, I sensed a change in ministry I could not accept—or even know how to accept. After three days of prayer and fasting, I knew the Lord was telling me to close down the ministry of Women 4 Women.

Days of confusion and anxiety followed.

How do I just stop doing what I am doing? How can I not be in full-time pro-life service after years of being completely consumed with serving the Lord through Women 4 Women?

I began to understand that the dreams I had held in my heart for the Whole Life Center were my dreams, not His, even if they were good and needful. If I didn't let go of my hold on Women 4 Women, I would not be able to walk through the door He had waiting for me.

After another three days of prayer and fasting, I tearfully released my hold on Women 4 Women and began the anguishing process of dismantling the office.

With all the ministry boxes tucked away in the attic, I spent every single day asking the Lord, "So what do I do now?"

One day, while kneeling under my prayer shawl, I distinctly heard Him ask, *What do you want to do?*

I was shocked. I laughed as I thought about how well He knew my heart. I still wanted to work with women, helping them to live victorious lives. I was also concerned for the men who were abusers, wondering who would help lead them out of their desperation.

He already knew *how* I wanted to serve Him. I just didn't know it myself.

That same day, the Lord connected me to a teacher who had a degree in counseling and had listened to my testimony on a CD. The following afternoon I visited her class on Christian counseling, eagerly receiving instruction as my learning genes were awakened. I yearned for more.

When the class was over, she told me she had felt impressed to pray for me. "Karen, you have spent years counseling," she said. "Not only as a sidewalk counselor but one-on-one with desperate women and everyone in their lives for every problem. I feel you should get a counseling degree. I believe the Lord wants me to tutor you all the way through to a PhD."

I immediately burst into tears. Every word she spoke resonated perfectly in my soul. I felt the Lord smiling on me. I knew it was His will.

Now in my seventies, I look back on the faithfulness of God to me throughout my years. I am a licensed clinical Christian counselor with a PhD. The Lord sends not only women but men, couples, and whole families to me.

I feel the weight of the responsibility I have to each person, yet I find counseling to be incredibly rewarding and fulfilling. My prayer for wisdom is constant. I believe the Lord had been preparing me for this for my entire life, using all my experiences to fill me with understanding and compassion for those I counsel. Graciously, He has given me the spiritual gifts of wisdom, discernment, and knowledge. Because His constant, abiding presence is with me as I counsel, I cannot accept any credit for success gained.

I yearn to press forward. My temperament requires peace, order, and predictability—but my spirit, having been trained on the streets and in the jails of Atlanta, yearns for unpredictability. My heart cries out for the excitement of living on the edge, moving with His Spirit, being sold out to Him, free-falling into His arms and purpose for my life.

Therefore, the question, "What will I do with the rest of my life?" weighs heavily on my mind. I feel like I have just begun—just begun to live, just begun to be equipped to be of some serious use to the Kingdom of God. I encourage you to ask the same question. What will *you* do with the rest of your life?

At present, many are hoping to see our nation return to our former Judeo-Christian morals. Just that possibility has been met with significant resistance. Every day, we see the consternation of those opposing righteousness on display by their violent behavior. Daily, we hear about riots erupting. We watch the news in horror as we learn of our police officers being shot and killed in ever-increasing numbers. People say they can't believe that our society has deteriorated to this horrible place, with murder abounding everywhere. I can't believe they don't consider all these years of abortion. How can we murder our innocent children by the millions and not expect the spirit of murder to spill out into our streets? When our consciences regarding the violent deaths of innocent children are seared, our minds can readily accept all other violence.

Those in opposing political views forcefully express their anger. Make no mistake, however, it is fear that is their driving force, feeling they might lose rights for many immoral practices. The reversal of *Roe v. Wade*, however, is what they fear the most. And they should. Abortion is powerfully linked to all other moral issues that plague our land. Abortion is the head of the monster, and it must be destroyed! If it is not, I believe that the strife and discord our nation is experiencing will not only continue but will grow in intensity. Some say that the battle is between political parties or liberals and conservatives, but it is simply a battle between good and evil, as it always has been since the beginning of time. It's nothing new—it's just more apparent at this moment in our history because the lines between us are no longer blurred.

I feel burdened to send out a clarion call to all who read this to consider your responsibility in this battle. Some say they are against abortion, but they feel free from responsibility regarding it because it is not their calling. Martin Luther wrote in *Martin Luther's Small and Large Catechisms*:

> If you see anyone condemned to death innocently and you do not save him, although you know ways and means to do so, *you* have killed him. It will do no good to plead that you did not contribute to his death, for you have withheld your love from him and have robbed him of the service by which his life may have been saved. (Large Catechism, Part 1, "Ten Commandments" [Concordia Publishing House, 1917], paragraph 190)

To this, I add these words from Proverbs 24:11–12:

> Deliver those who are drawn toward death, and hold back those stumbling to the slaughter. If you say, "Surely we did not know this," does not He who weighs the hearts consider it? He who keeps your soul, does He not know it? And will He not render to each man according to his deeds?

In light of the chaos that abounds in our world—and our country in particular—more than ever before, we need to take account of where we are in our relationship with the Lord and what He requires of us. Do we fully understand the call on our lives? Are we willing to answer His bidding? Will we be able to make a difference?

Please join me as we examine our lives to see if we need to readjust our priorities to align more closely with the Word of God. Hopefully then, even in consideration of our stumbling humanity, we will one day hear the words, "Well done, thou good and faithful servant."

You may now be asking yourself, "Okay, but what can I do?"

There is a lot you can *do*, but first, the *way* you will do it is far more important. Your heart's condition will determine how you move forward. If your heart is not right toward those involved with abortion or any other immoral act, then your message will not be heard and what you do will not be received.

Every January, thousands from across our nation meet at various Rallies for Life to mourn the deaths of multiplied millions of American children lost to abortion since the landmark decision of *Roe v. Wade* in 1973. As the weight of the enormity of the statistics bears down on our hearts and minds, many shake their heads in disbelief and horror, filled with anger and outrage at the evil that abounds in our nation. Thoughts go to those in authority with their ever-increasing, blatant display of immorality, dishonesty, and indifference to wrongdoing. Some respond with hearts filled with disgust and condemnation, seeking judgment to fall swiftly and surely on the unrighteousness that surrounds us.

But I say, as Christians, has it not been *my* sin and *my* unrighteousness and *your* sin and *your* unrighteousness that has grieved the very heart of God? Were Sodom and Gomorrah destroyed only because of the presence of evil, or was it ultimately because of the absence of righteousness?

It has been said that abortion is the symptom—idolatry is the crime. How dare we judge those who have abortions for selfish reasons, when we are using the same reasons to stand back and do nothing to help them or to join in the fight against abortion?

We need to ask ourselves why we so quickly seek judgment on the unjust when God's Word says He prefers mercy to judgment. Why do we not have the mind and heart of Christ for our cities and our nation? Why do our hearts not break for those held captive by darkness and sin? Should we not fall on our knees day and night in prayer for them?

Could it be that our hearts, filled to overflowing with arrogance, self-righteousness, and pride, can no longer remember our own deliverance? Could the darkness of our own hearts cause us to forget to love as He first loved us? The turning of a nation to God begins with the exposure of *our* hearts and the abhorring of *our* sin. Without the abiding fullness of Christ in our lives, we will have no more impact on the world than a political party whose strength is in numbers and not in the living God.

It is time that you and I fall on our knees in sincere repentance and return to steadfast faith in the person and power of Jesus Christ. Only then can we be the salt and light we were intended to be. We need to become holy people, carrying the vibrant, transforming power of the Holy Spirit into the lives and circumstances that we touch.

Abortion is an active evil, and we must take an active stand against it. But I assure you—abortion will not end with the passing of legislation alone. It certainly will not end through passing laws that leave room for abortions under *some* circumstances or compromises to save a *few*. Abortion will not end with rescues, sidewalk counseling, picketing, or opening more crisis pregnancy centers. And certainly, abortion will not end by bombing clinics or killing abortionists.

God's Word says we overcome evil with good. As His representatives, you and I must be without hypocrisy, full of genuine mercy and good works. John 12:32 says that when Jesus is lifted up—not our programs, not our ministries or political agendas—all men are drawn to Him. It is only with His great power that individual lives and nations will ever change.

Some say that we should have a passion for the unborn and their mothers. Yes, but if that's all we have, then neither our personal lives nor our ministries will ever meet with success or carry the mark of God. Our one and only constant, burning passion should be to become more like Christ and to possess His very likeness. As George Grant says, "It is time that you and I stop being merely conservative and become profoundly, fiercely Christian." Only then will our lives ring true and our message be received!

You may indeed have a heart that is true to your message of love, but the one thing that you lack is courage—the kind of courage needed to lay down your life for one of these children about to be murdered. The kind of courage that requires you to stand firm against all other immoral practices. This kind of courage was given to me by God, enabling me to withstand twenty-four arrests for my beliefs. This kind of courage is needed to refuse to deny Christ if it becomes illegal to be a Christian. Don't make the mistake of thinking that will never happen. We must consider these possibilities, as our world is rapidly becoming a dangerous place to be a Christian. Compared to other countries, America has been a safe place to live out our faith. That, however, could change overnight. Do you and I have what it takes to endure to the end?

Sophie Scholl was a German student who was active in the White Rose, a nonviolent resistance group against Hitler and the Nazi Party. At the age of twenty-one, she and her brother were found guilty of treason and executed by guillotine. Sophie's words still ring true today:

The real damage is done by those millions who want to "survive." The honest men who just want to be left in peace. Those who don't want their little lives disturbed by anything bigger than themselves. Those with no sides and no causes. Those who won't take measure of their own strength, for fear of antagonizing their own weakness. Those who don't like to make waves—or enemies. Those for whom freedom, honor, truth, and principles are only literature. Those who live small, mate small, die small. It's the reductionist approach to life; if you keep it small, you'll keep it under control. If you don't make any noise, the bogeyman won't find you. But it's all an illusion, because they die too, those people who roll up their spirits into tiny little balls so as to be safe. (As quoted by Richard Dahstrom in *O2: Breathing New Life into Faith* [Harvest House, 2008], 223.)

Sophie demonstrated for us what an ordinary and relatively powerless person can do, and should do, under extraordinary and difficult circumstances. Oh, that I can have that kind of courage if faced with that kind of frightening circumstance someday.

The noise of drums beating out their threatening sounds is approaching. We need to ready ourselves but fear not. We need to exercise ourselves in righteousness and be determined to take up our crosses and follow the Lord, no matter what the price.

I believe that in the years to come, many will be cast into prison after standing before unrighteous judges, guilty of righteous deeds. Others, to escape imprisonment, will refuse to take a stand. Instead, they will find themselves in prisons of their own making. Unfortunately, some are so shackled and bound, they are unable to pick up their crosses, not understanding that their crosses are the keys needed to unlock their shackles.

I believe we are about to experience a severe sifting of the church. This sifting will separate out the *believers* from the *unbelievers* and the *make-believers*. There may not be many true believers left standing, but hopefully those remaining will respond like those mentioned in Daniel 11:32: "The people who know their God will display strength and take action."

My primary goal for writing this book has been to glorify the Lord and His unfailing faithfulness to me throughout my life, even in the face of my own unfaithfulness. I want others to know that no matter their station in life, what the Lord has done for me, He can do for them. As I close out this portion of my life's story, I realize that my history is no guarantee of my future. I cannot stand on the laurels of past experiences alone. I am looking for grander vistas with a future that will require greater faith than ever before. I pray the last chapters of my life and my glorious, wondrous pilgrimage with the Great I Am will show that I finished strong and that my ending was greater than my beginning. With all that the Lord has brought me through, I have no excuse to do anything else but follow Him all the remaining days of my life.

Many years ago I changed my life verse to Philippians 1:20. May it be said that I fully lived out those words that say,

> It is my eager desire and persistent expectation and hope that I shall not disgrace myself nor be put to shame in anything, but that with the utmost freedom of speech and unfailing courage, Christ will be magnified and receive glory and praise in this body of mine and be boldly exalted in my person whether through life or through death.

I don't know what the future holds or what will be required of me, but I pray I will bring honor and glory to Him in it. I have been struggling with an unsettling urgency to pick up the pace for the Lord. I feel a pressing need to ready myself. I pray I will consider well the years left to me. To any threats to end my life, and every circumstance that comes my way, may I be quick to say, *"Only if God says so!"*

In Loving Memory

I would like to leave a tribute to my friend and fellow laborer, James Pouillon. Jim was part of the Call to Atlanta and left his imprint on my heart. The kindness shown to me with his gentle spirit in Atlanta will not be forgotten.
In Owosso, Michigan, on September 11, 2009, a gunman pulled up to where Jim was holding a pro-life sign.
The gunman then opened fire from his vehicle and shot Jim four times.
The gunman said that he did not like Jim displaying the picture in front of the students at the high school.
Those same students who lovingly called him the "Sign Man" flooded the athletic field of their school for his memorial service.
At the age of 63, Jim became the first pro-life martyr in America.
Thank you, Jim, for your unfaltering courage and great love for the Lord and His preborn children.
"Be faithful until death, and I will give you the crown of life."
Revelation 2:10
How beautiful must be your crown.

ORDER INFORMATION

To order additional copies of this book, please visit
www.redemption-press.com.
Also available at Christian bookstores and Barnes and Noble.

To connect with Karen and learn more about her journey, go
to: OnlyIfGodSaysSo.com

CPSIA information can be obtained
at www.ICGtesting.com
Printed in the USA
LVHW030138070223
738785LV00003B/130